A PAPER LIFE

Tatum O'Neal

A PAPER
LIFE

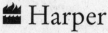 Harper
An Imprint of HarperCollins*Publishers*

A hardcover edition of this book was published in 2004 by Harper Entertainment, an imprint of HarperCollins Publishers.

First Harper paperback published 2005.

Designed by Judith Abbate and Betty Lew

The Library of Congress has catalogued the hardcover as follows:

O'Neal, Tatum.
   A paper life / Tatum O'Neal.—1st ed.
     p. cm.
   ISBN 0-06-054097-4 (alk. paper)
   1. O'Neal, Tatum, 1963– 2. Motion picture actors and actresses—United States—Biography. I. Title.

   PN2287.O545A3 2004
   791.4302'8'092—dc22
   [B]   2004059922

ISBN-10: 0-06-075102-9 (pbk.)
ISBN-13: 978-0-06-075102-9 (pbk.)

08 09 ❖/RRD 10 9 8 7 6 5

To Kevin, Sean, and Emily

My true inspirations

CONTENTS

ACKNOWLED

GMENTS

I COULD NEVER have made a new life for myself—let alone do this book—without the love and encouragement of my three children, Kevin, Sean, and Emily McEnroe. Every cell in my body comes alive when I'm around them. My kids have brought me such great joy and taught me so much about the simple yet profound healing power of love that words can't even begin to convey my gratitude. I could never have survived the battles of the past decade without them. I wouldn't know how to live. So, thank you, Kevin, Sean, and Emily from the bottom of my heart. I love you!

I might not even have the gift of a new life without the help of Dr. Richard Rosenthal. Thank you—and God love you, Dr. Rosenthal—for your expert knowledge of chemical dependency, as well as your patience, love, and belief in me. Dr. Joel Kassimir, I want to thank you too, for making me laugh. You rock!

I also want to acknowledge my brothers, Griffin, Patrick, and Redmond O'Neal.

This book would never have existed without the belief, fiery enthusiasm, and loving encouragement of Maureen O'Brien, my editor at HarperCollins. From the very beginning, she was convinced that I had a story worth telling, and she never, ever lost faith—though I sometimes did—during my struggle to get it out. She's my Irish sister and a true force of nature—a bighearted dynamo and an unfailing source of inspiration. I appreciate everything you've done to nurture this book, Mo, and I will always cherish your incredible energy and support.

Everyone at HarperCollins has been wonderful. Special thanks go out to my great publisher, Michael Morrison, and his team of top-notch pros: Libby Jordan, Debbie Stier, Sharyn Rosenblum, Lindsey Moore, Susan Sanguily, Beth Silfin, Jim Fox, Kim Lewis, Betty Lew, and everyone else at HarperCollins who helped us along the way.

The person who really brought this book to life was my loyal and courageous cowriter, Elisa Petrini. She sat with me through hours and hours of sometimes incoherent ramblings as I fought to resurrect memories that were almost too painful to recount out loud. Her loving patience is evident on every page of this book. Elisa, I love the way you captured my voice and unsnarled a lot of tangled threads to create such a rich fabric. Thank you for helping to make my life a "paper life," between book covers.

I'm very grateful to the people in my life who constantly remind me that I am an artist, watch over me, and sustain me in my work: the beautiful Allison Levy of Innovative Artists, Scott Harris of Innovative L.A. and Richie Jackson and Gary Gersh of Innovative N.Y.; the great Bryan Young of Untitled Entertainment, who stood by me and wisely guided me through so many of my ups and downs, and of course, Jason Weinberg, who *is* Untitled Entertainment and who has believed in me through all my trials and tribulations (and some triumphs too) over the past fifteen years; as well as my lawyer, George Sheanshang, who has put up with some weird calls and picked up a few pieces. A lot of what I am today, I owe to the four of you—and to Sue Mengers of ICM, my original agent, a powerhouse if there ever was one, who was such a fierce advocate for me when I was such a little girl.

I can't speak of the past without thanking the long-suffering Diane Lewis for putting up with mischief-making Tatesky through so many movies.

The people who keep my everyday life running smoothly are Arnie Herrmann, Diana Aronin, and Michael Mann of my accounting firm, Starr and Company, LLC. Thank you so much for looking out for me all these years!

I'm also grateful to my literary agent, the very handsome Dan Strone of Trident Media Group, whose calm voice always soothed me, no matter how high-strung the ins and outs of the unfamiliar world of book publishing made me. His assistant, Hilary, has been very helpful too.

My life has been enriched tremendously by my loving and devoted friends, especially my oldest ones, Andrea Feldstein, Carrie Adelson, and Esme Grey Evans. I'd like to single out a few others for special thanks because of their support during my work on this book starting with my dear, dear friend Elizabeth Clark Zoya, whose friendship I could not do without, and the fabulous and fantastic Lesley Morrison—you're the greatest! Billy Corgan's absolute belief in me as an artist, actress, friend, and mother has helped give me the courage to "live life on life's terms"—thank you, and I love you, Billy! Without Mimi Fisher's encouragement and love and support, I never could have seen this project through. Mimi, I love you and your two beautiful sons, Jack and Brendan. I also owe a debt of gratitude to Karen Curious and Andrea "A.D." DeFiore—I love you, girl. You are the best! You all know what a hard journey this book has been, and it's only with your help that I've been able to reach the final step.

Finally, to give credit where credit is due, I want to thank John McEnroe for being a great dad for my three children, and my father, Ryan O'Neal, for giving me life and turning me on—and out—to movies.

A PAPER LIFE

PROLOGUE

Ryan's Daughter

ON AUGUST 21, 2003, I pressed my palms into wet cement outside Hollywood's beloved Vista Theater to mark the thirtieth anniversary of *Paper Moon*. I was eight years old when I debuted in the movie—now considered a masterpiece—and received an Academy Award, becoming the youngest Oscar winner in history. Kneeling alongside me for handprints were Laszlo Kovacs, who shot the film in stark and lyrical black and white, and Ryan O'Neal, who was dazzling as my reluctant grifter-guardian on-screen—it was the crowning role of his career—if less brilliant as my father in real life.

Tanned and fit, my father showed no sign of his two-year struggle with leukemia. When he was diagnosed, I'd tried to mend shattered fences with heartfelt thanks for all he had given me, assuring him that he was still the love of my life. Recently he had fractured our fragile peace by announcing in print that Alicia Silverstone, his costar in a TV series, was the daughter he "should have had." To drive the insult home, he'd added, "But we can't always get what we want."

The tabloids were sniffing the air around us, eager for a scent of conflict. We foiled them by rising, with professional smiles, to perform the Hollywood Hug.

Hovering in the background was Griffin, my brother, my Irish twin, eleven months younger. Over the years, he'd gained a certain notoriety, sometimes as the victim of my father's fury—once Ryan famously knocked out his teeth—and through his own collisions with tragedy, drugs, and the law. He's fiercely funny, though, and he's my bridge to the past, to memories that lose some of their sting when he recounts them. It made me heartsick to watch him wrangle the crowd like a flak—greeting the fans, pressing us for autographs—as if he viewed himself more as an employee than as a member of the family.

Luckily, I had my own family with me. My sons Kevin and Sean, at seventeen and fifteen, already towered over me, while Emily, my youngest, was still small and sweet and girlish at age twelve. We'd spent a full day shopping for new sport coats for the boys—how handsome they were!—and cute corduroy jeans and a jacket for Emily, which she wore with my red belt. My late mother, in her southern drawl, used to call the three of them my "show kids," meaning that I should be proud to show them off. I was proud, and I felt bolstered by their loyalty and love.

The kids were protective, sensing my anxiety at seeing Ryan, always unpredictable and capable of lashing out, and wondered nervously if he'd brought Redmond, his son with Farrah Fawcett. Just a year older than Kevin, Redmond had become a somewhat forbidding figure after landing in drug rehab at age fourteen. Since then his life had been peppered with arrests and hospitalizations, and when he was sixteen, my father had kicked him out of the house. Whatever his current status—in or out of my father's favor—Redmond didn't seem to be around.

Crowded by photographers, we filed into the theater, a classic Egyptian-revival palace with pharaohs holding up the roof. There, straight ahead, lay another psychic land mine, a longtime friend of my father whom I'll call "Gavin," who had molested me when I was about the same age—and just as physically childlike—as my own daughter. He'd done it on a night when I was so embittered by adult betrayals that I'd gotten drunk and slit my wrists. When I'd complained, he was banished from the inner circle for a while, but I was punished too, for blowing the whistle on my father's lifestyle.

"Hey, Gavin," I said coolly, taking the high road. "Nice to see you. You look really good."

PUSHING PAST HIM, I reached an oasis: Peter Bogdanovich, my father-figure/friend, and the director of *Paper Moon*. He wore his signature ascot, which would have looked funny and affected on any other man. It flashed me back to the day when we first met at my father's beach house in Malibu. He'd asked me to take a walk with him on the beach.

"You don't look like you belong on the beach," I said, staring at that ascot.

He'd rolled up his pants, and we headed off for what turned out to be my audition. I was a scrawny, knock-kneed little waif at seven, with tangles in my hair and no acting training—in fact, with little formal schooling at all—but Peter took me on. He'd later say that it was my scrappy attitude that got me the job.

We exchanged warm greetings and then took our seats, with Peter as a bulwark between me and my father. As the

3

credits rolled, there was wild clapping for Madeline Kahn, also nominated for Best Supporting Actress for the film, who had recently died of cancer. Then the screen filled with my wounded, willful face as eight-year-old Addie Loggins, standing on the prairie over her mother's open grave in Depression-era Kansas.

I hadn't seen the movie in years. *Entertainment Weekly* would say that my performance "rewrote the book on movie moppets," calling me "feisty . . . a child star for a hip, cynical age." Seeing that little face again reminded me that pain was the flip side of feistiness. My own young life had eerily echoed Addie's, even though my mother was still alive. In the grip of addiction, she virtually abandoned me and Griffin, leaving us in squalor—starving, shoeless, and ragged—as well as beaten and abused by the men in her life.

Ryan finally came to my rescue, just as he was doing on-screen in a sputtering old jalopy, playing Moses (Mose) Pray, the Bible-peddling con man who is probably Addie's pa. He'd thought working together in *Paper Moon* would help us bond. "This was her first opportunity to channel her mind and energy into something constructive," he told the press. "And this movie would give her something she never had enough of— love."

I NEVER DREAMED that shooting a film would be so hard. I imagined that it would be like a play rehearsal, with everyone sitting around on stools reciting lines to one another. The reality was both far more challenging and grueling, for there was less regulation then of child actors' hours. Even the concept of acting confused me. Idolizing my father and desperate to please, I once blew a take when I panicked at his gruffness and blurted, "Daddy, are you mad at me?"

"No!" he growled, "I'm doing the scene."

There were times when my inexperience tested everybody's patience. At eight, I could barely read, so memorizing six or seven pages of solid dialogue—along with nuances and inflections, to be delivered in a moving car—was beyond me. Peter bribed and threatened me to force me to learn my lines, at one point chaining me to a tree until I nailed them. He was joking, of course, even if his exasperation was serious.

Still, when I ad-libbed, Peter trusted me. The opening sequence ends with two church ladies persuading Mose to deliver Addie to her aunt in Missouri. They're gathered near an old-fashioned pump, and a preacher says, "Let's get the child some water." As they haggle with Mose, trying to fob me off, the minister hands me a cup of water without a word of comfort. It wasn't in the script, but I knew exactly—instinctively—what Addie had to do. I turned away and dumped it on the ground.

There's such sadness and hopelessness in that gesture, coming from a character who has lost her barfly mother—the devil she knew—but there's defiance too, proof that her spirit is unbroken. It is a measure of Peter's genius as a director that he recognized how deeply I identified with Addie's bruised innocence, steely wariness, and above all, resilience. I knew firsthand what it would take for her to survive.

SETTING OFF WITH MOSE on the car trip east, Addie discovers that she can one-up him, out-con him, and even thwart her grown-up rival for his affections. It was almost spooky how much the film's scenario mimicked my own later life with my father. Now, watching Ryan objectively as a movie buff/actor, I had to acknowledge that his art was superb. Without sentimentalizing Mose, he made him human and appealing, even when preying on widows or trying to bilk Addie out of the money he had extorted in her name. That extortion yielded the famous, lisping exchange that my children used to delight in repeating:

"I want my $200. If I don't get my $200, I'll tell a p'lice-
man how you got it and he'll make you give it to me
'cause it's MINE."
    "But I don't have it."
    "Then GIT it."

At the time, Ryan was considered one of America's best and most versatile actors. In *What's Up, Doc?* he'd been laugh-out-loud funny; and in *Love Story,* he was a beautiful, crystal-clear man with blue eyes and a soft miracle voice—an irresistible heartthrob.

In *Paper Moon*, he was truly at the top of his game. He deserved an Oscar nomination at the very least, even against the tough competition that year, when Marlon Brando, Jack Nicholson, Al Pacino, and Robert Redford all lost out to Jack Lemmon for his role in *Save the Tiger*. However, as Peter Bogdanovich would say of *Paper Moon*: "Ryan's wonderful in it, and he sat there and watched the kid steal the picture."

Maybe that's what first tipped the hair-trigger scales of our relationship. Jealousy is rife in showbiz families. Legend has it—and people tell me—that when I got the Oscar nomination, Ryan slugged me. I don't remember that, but there are memories that I've blocked.

I remained Ryan's companion on the Hollywood party circuit, growing inured to sex and drugs before I was in my teens. A needy little girl, still haunted by neglect, I clung to him and even to the women in his life—Bianca Jagger, Angelica Huston, Melanie Griffith, and many more. However, the more love I craved, the more distant and abusive he grew, emotionally and physically. The role I longed to play was never written into Ryan's script: daughter.

I would go on to marry John McEnroe, another punishing man. He brought his trademark tantrums home from the tennis court and later, when I left him, to the court of law, trying to wrest my kids away. For a time, he succeeded because, after our divorce, I slipped into the darkness of depression and addiction that seems to be the family curse. To see my kids, I'd endured the humiliation of drug tests and supervision, but believing I'd failed them was my most agonizing shame. I'd told my children honestly of my struggles, and they responded with compassion greater than I'd imagined, or even thought I deserved. They forgave me at a time when I could barely forgive myself.

So, ultimately, *Paper Moon* didn't bring me love. But I did find it, with them.

Sitting with my beautiful, brilliant, healthy kids to celebrate the anniversary of the movie that saved me, changed me, and set me on my life path was the supreme joy. The film itself is a diamond, a work of art, just as beautiful and poignant and evocative today as when we made it. I felt privileged to be a facet of such a jewel in the crown of American cinema. That—besides the gift of life itself—was my father's greatest gift to me.

Watching myself play Addie from the perspective of adulthood, I can see the wise old soul behind that tiny plaintive face, and I think, *I love that little girl*. It's painful to remember the heartaches that left her so self-possessed, so tenacious and brave—and sad to know that certain struggles never end—but I'm proud of her. I'm proud of what she's accomplished and what she has overcome:

I've overcome neglect and deprivation.

I've overcome abandonment and abuse.

I've overcome physical and mental brutality—and fought back.

I've triumphed over addiction.

I've stood my ground in life, alone, even against overwhelming forces with the might and money to crush me. I've purged myself of bitterness and anger and remained open to love. I've kept my moral compass intact and aimed at true north.

I have survived—and won.

ONE

Dorothy, aka Joanna

THE STORY OF *PAPER MOON* reflects my childhood, but it also closely parallels my mother's and strangely foreshadows my daughter's. Three generations of women: we all lost our mothers early in life—the first literally, to death; the second virtually, to addiction; and the third, my daughter, temporarily, when I succumbed to familiar demons. It is a cycle that I'm determined to break.

My mother was born, like Addie, in the heart of the Great Depression, not in Kansas but in Americus, Georgia. The elder of two daughters of Henry and Dorothy English Cook, she was named for her mother but later christened herself Joanna. A letter from her cousin Libba that I discovered after her death depicts her early childhood as cozy: rocking on the old porch swing, sitting by the potbellied stove, sliding down the banister at her grandmother's.

She was the only one not in the car when her father swerved off the road because her mom fell asleep on his shoulder, plunging down a sandy embankment into a ravine. Both her mother and her baby sister, Virginia, died instantly. Libba's letter recalls, in haunting detail, how she got the news: "We were on the playground. . . . My ma had come to school. You had all visited the day before. And Momma kept saying, 'The pillow I put in my stroller for the baby to sit in had an imprint of the little body in it.'"

Henry, my mother's father, was badly hurt but lingered for a year before dying of a ruptured spleen—or, she always believed, of a broken heart. So, at age six, my mother became an orphan.

For a time she was farmed out to live with her maternal grandmother, who was confined to a wheelchair with an osteoporosis-like condition. She was also addicted to morphine, prescribed by the town doctor, making her the first known link in my family's chain of drug dependence.

Even in that environment, my mother managed to bloom. She was pretty and vivacious, with a million-dollar smile, and so talented at singing and playing the piano that she became a star at church. By the time my mother reached her early teens, however, her grandmother had grown too feeble and impoverished to raise her. She was adopted by a wealthy local family, who saw her through high school then sent her off to Agnes Scott College near Atlanta, which was one of the top women's schools in the South.

I've heard rumors that she was molested by a member of her adoptive family, but my mother never spoke of it. She rarely mentioned her teenage marriage to Willis Moore, of which her lifelong last name was the only trace. Southern women of her era were bred to smooth over unpleasantness, but denial in my mother ran as deep as her love for amphetamines. So I came to know her through a scrim of pictures and letters, lies and secrets.

SHE WAS EXTRAORDINARILY BEAUTIFUL, with blond hair, a perfect heart-shaped face, huge green eyes, and lush full lips. She had a smoky, seductive voice (which Emily and I both inherited) warmed by her southern lilt. Winning a beauty contest brought my mother to Hollywood in the mid-1950s, where she was discovered at a cocktail party and signed to Universal. A flood of contract assignments followed, in films ranging from such minor classics as *The Last Angry Man* and *Walk on the Wild Side* to teen screamers like *Monster on Campus*.

Among them was *A Touch of Evil*, the last Hollywood film directed by Orson Welles, which has been hailed as "the greatest B movie ever made." It opens with one of the most famous shots in movie history—nearly three and a half minutes long—tracking a car with a bomb in its trunk through a seedy Mexican border town. Finally the car explodes, killing the driver; and a corrupt, drunken sheriff (played by Orson Welles) tries to pin the crime on bystanders Charlton Heston and Janet Leigh. Though my mother is on screen only for a short time in the film, she is masterful as the victim's daughter. My father always said that my mother was the best actor in the family, but it was only after she died that I came to recognize her power.

In *A Touch of Evil* my mother had to darken her hair to avoid out-blonding Janet Leigh. After hours, she had to dodge Charlton Heston, who once lured her to his room, seemingly to seduce her. Later Elvis Presley hit on her with even less finesse. While making *Follow That Dream* in 1962, he actually tried to break down her door. But my mother had no use for the idol of millions of teenagers, telling an interviewer, "He's a bore."

After the mid-1960s, she worked mainly in television. She

was featured in most of the major series of the day: *Gunsmoke, The Rifleman, Bat Masterson, Wagon Train, Maverick,* and *The Virginian*—westerns dominated the top twenty—as well as *The Fugitive, Perry Mason, Route 66, 77 Sunset Strip, Bewitched,* and *The Man from U.N.C.L.E.* She became a semiregular on *Alfred Hitchcock Presents,* usually cast as a southern belle, and had a recurring role on the *Andy Griffith Show* as Peggy McMillan, the sheriff's girlfriend.

On one of those shows, she met my father, then just a struggling actor. He wasn't a dream-chasing migrant like she was but a native Angeleno, with a mother hellbent on propelling her two sons to stardom. My grandmother even pushed her youngest, my uncle Kevin, to study ballet and take growth hormones to groom him for the screen.

Patricia Callaghan, my grandmother, had sacrificed her own acting career to raise her children. She can still be seen in *Three Came Home,* the true story of a woman's survival in a Japanese prison camp, starring Claudette Colbert. Born of a Russian mother (who was named Devonovitch and rumored to be Jewish) and an Irish father, she was raised in Toronto and San Francisco and instilled with a gloves-wearing, hair-in-a-bun propriety that made her the polar—and harshly disapproving—opposite of my mother.

My dad's father, Charles O'Neal, was more accepting and shared my mother's southern roots and jolly temperament. Born in North Carolina, he attended the University of Iowa, where thanks to his accent, classmates dubbed him "Blackie," and the nickname stuck. He met my grandmother in a San Diego theater troupe but discovered a new vocation—screenwriting—after publishing a short story in *Esquire.*

My grandpa achieved modest success with screenplays for

such movies as *The Seventh Victim, Cry of the Werewolf, The Missing Juror,* and *Montana* in the 1940s and 1950s; then he moved on to writing for TV series, including *The Untouchables, The Californians,* and *Lassie.* Also the author of two novels, he developed one into the 1952 musical *Three Wishes for Jamie,* which starred John Raitt (Bonnie's father) and Anne Jeffreys and ran for several months on Broadway.

Patrick Ryan O'Neal, their oldest son, was born on April 20, 1941. He attended University High School in Venice (along with the singing duo Jan and Dean), where he was in a pretty-boy gang called the Gents. An indifferent student—his mother even claimed she did his homework—he soon dropped out to pursue acting and boxing, going on both to manage fighters and to compete in the Golden Gloves himself. But my father's quickfistedness also got him into trouble. He once served fifty-one days in jail for assault and battery after a New Year's Eve brawl.

He entered show business as a stuntman but quickly broke into acting, dropping his first name because the Screen Actors Guild (SAG) already had a member named Patrick O'Neal. Starting out in TV westerns (*Empire, The Virginian*), he appeared on *Dobie Gillis, Bachelor Father,* and *Leave It to Beaver* before making his film debut in *This Rugged Land* with Charles Bronson in 1962.

It was around this time that my parents connected in what must have been an explosive encounter. "She was pregnant within days of our meeting," my father told *Newsweek,* "and we were married within weeks."

I was born breech on Guy Fawkes Day, November 5, 1963. My mother's birthday was the tenth and, less than a year later, Griffin came along on October 28. So all three of us are Scorpios. I was not named for my maternal grandmother, as some accounts have it, but for the great jazz pianist Art Tatum.

MY PARENTS SETTLED into my mother's dreamhouse on Sabana Lane in Encino, California. It was an expansive white-pillared Georgian house, which she furnished with yellow sofas, big chandeliers, Toulouse-Lautrec prints, and porcelain dogs by the fireplace—very southern chic, which my mom loved. It also had a swimming pool in which my father taught me tricks, tossing me in and having me pop up balanced in the palm of his hand, laughing. When I was six months old, he accidentally dropped me in the garage, cracking my head on the banister and leaving me with a concussion that appears as a giant bruise in a lot of my baby pictures. In many of these photos, we look happy, with birthday cakes and Christmas trees. Across one of the pictures my father scrawled *My family is everything*.

When I was born, my father was twenty-two, and my mother was nearly seven years older. He and his parents mentioned the age gap so often—as if it were huge—that I grew up believing they were at least a decade apart. In Hollywood, where beauty equals youth and no one ages gracefully, an older wife was suspect—a cradle robber, a personal and professional liability.

My mother hit the age wall before she turned thirty. By then everything about her was glossy: her ever-present wigs, fake eyelashes and nails; her surgically taut face, and the gleaming caps on her teeth that were never tight enough. As a child, I was like the tooth fairy, ferreting out the lost caps that were always strewn around the house. I liked being helpful, and it was a comforting mother-and-daughter ritual—a way for us to bond.

The source of my mom's bright packaging was the Hollywood studio system. Though on the wane by the early 1960s, it still had a grip on actors' lives, especially women's. Like so many others, my mother was subjected to silicone injections in her face, which would shift, creating bulges; required to work in wigs that destroyed her own hair, and—worst of all—prescribed amphetamines to lose weight.

The pills agreed with her all too well. "Before I knew it, I had taken enough to eventually undermine me," my mother told *Newsweek*. Her addictions, over time, would grow unbeatable and would rob her of her natural beauty and sense of self-worth.

Despite all of her antiaging strategies, my mother's manner was straight out of the 1950s. Born on the cusp of the baby boom, my father was more of a hippie type, while my mother's sensibility was more Rat Pack than rock and roll. Cigarette and cocktails were her constant props, as if she were a stowaway from the old *Dean Martin Show.* At her memorial service, her cousin described a visit when Griffin and I were babies: "Well, Joanna had you both in her Cadillac, and she was driving with a cigarette in one hand and in the other she had a martini, straight up!"

She was a good-time gal, with a big personality—bubbly and outgoing, with a huge infectious laugh that would crack into a smoker's cough. She always mixed up expressions when she got rattled, once telling my father: "You make me so mad, I feel like I'm facing the squiring fod." The consummate entertainer, she loved gathering guests around her piano, drinking and singing till dawn. She burned with high-watt charm.

To know my mother was to love her—and I do, now that I've accepted an elemental truth: she was 100 percent crazy. Too crazy, as it turned out, to withstand the combustible mix of alcohol, pills, two babies eleven months apart, and a challenging husband.

MY MOM'S CAREER started fading when my dad's was on the rise, with his lead role as Rodney Harrington on *Peyton Place*, TV's first prime-time soap opera. The show was based on the then-shocking book by Grace Metalious, airing the dirty laundry (sex, insanity, murder) of a New England town. *Peyton Place* debuted in September 1964 and became an instant hit, airing twice—and at one point three times—a week for five straight years.

The cast's personal dramas sometimes mirrored the scripts. Rodney, my father's character, kept shifting his affections from Betty Anderson (Barbara Parkins), the rich bad girl, to Allison McKenzie, the delicate good girl (Mia Farrow). Off-screen, Mia got so disgusted with Barbara Parkins, watching her brush her long wavy hair in front of the mirror, that she chopped off all of her own, creating her famous pixie cut. Then Frank Sinatra fell for Mia after watching her on *Peyton Place*, whisking her off to get married before the show's third year.

My father's romantic life was also spilling off the TV screen. The tabloids had a field day linking him to a parade of starlets. He would describe his marriage in this period as "desolate." Very likely my mother's drinking and drug use—probably in secret—played a role. As their fighting escalated, my father grew physically violent.

But for my mom the last straw came one day in the super-market. Griffin was in the shopping cart and I was toddling alongside it. At the checkout she saw a *Photoplay* magazine with a cover story on my father's seduction of Barbara Parkins, his costar on *Peyton Place*. It was cruelly detailed, and it all rang true. My mother was devastated.

In 1966 she and my father separated, and a year later they were divorced. That same year my dad married Leigh Taylor-Young, Mia Farrow's replacement on the show, who was three months pregnant with my half-brother Patrick. Leigh claims that during her pregnancy my father made her work out every day and even timed her jogging speed. She was playing tennis on the day she went into labor. She calls this enforced regimen a "favor" from my father, and maybe it did her good. But to me it sounds like the same aggressive bullying that my father would inflict on us in years to come.

AFTER MY DAD LEFT, my mother's mania darkened, and she fell into a deeper instability and confusion. There were men around—Michael Rubini, a musician, whom I liked, but also the creepy Dr. Mel, who drove a Cadillac and had some connection to my mother's trips to the pharmacy for Darvon.

As her life grew unmanageable, ours did too. She'd adopted two huge German shepherds, Sarge and Tiara, which were ferocious former LAPD dogs. One of them bit me in the face. My mother would shut us up in our rooms for hours, leaving us no choice but to defecate on the floor. Jon Peters recalls a weekend when my mother went out, forgetting that she'd locked me and Griffin in a bathroom. When she remembered, she called Jon, who rushed over to rescue us.

Still, my mom wanted custody and imagined, in her paranoia, that my dad was scheming to take us away. She once dragged Griffin out by the pool to show him what looked like a little plastic bag, poking out from under the tile roof. "You see that?" she said. "That's where your father has been planting marijuana, so the cops will find it and arrest me."

We seemed to see so little of her that I have only one vivid memory of my mom during this time. Griffin and I woke up one morning, unsupervised as usual, and started poking around in the garage, then found that we were locked in. We cried and hammered on the door, but my mother slept on, oblivious, for the next four or five hours. When we got hungry, there was nothing to eat but dog food, and when we got bored, there was nothing to do but raise hell. We'd discovered a cache of lightbulbs and were gleefully smashing them to bits when suddenly the door flew open. There was my mother, in a white-hot fury.

"Why, why, you little . . . ," she stammered.

Slapping and grabbing at Griffin and me, she flung us into the house. There, luckily, she found an inanimate object to vent her rage on—my brother's bunk bed, which she tore apart like a woman possessed.

Frightening as my mother's temper could be—and she was freewheeling with her fists, coming from a generation that was big on beatings—beneath it, even then, we could sense her impotence. We continued to act out, unmoved by her anger. I once used her lighter to torch our plaid couch. It made a huge, thrilling blaze that the fire department had to extinguish, and I learned a useful lesson—to pin the blame on Griffin. He retaliated by setting my hair on fire.

We became neighborhood terrors by stealing whatever we could get our hands on. Griffin managed to swipe an electric garage opener and would hide in the ivy, raising and lowering the door, to torment the man who lived next to us. When Griffin discovered sharp objects, his mischief making turned serious. He slashed one of our nannies with a knife, almost severing her hand.

My mother made little effort to stop us that I recall. She seemed powerless—barely accepting responsibility for her own life, never mind for her children. She would take us with her to bars—shades of Addie's mother in *Paper Moon*—start drinking, and disappear. We'd be left clutching a slip of paper with my grandparents' phone number. The bartender would call and have them come and pick us up. "There were such emergencies for so many years," my grandmother would say. "The experience would have destroyed some children."

But it was my mother who seemed destroyed, like a passive victim waiting for rescue. It's not a choice of perspective that I respect, though I understand it now. As an adult I can see how much she really had been victimized—by her past, by Hollywood, and by men, including my father.

She wasn't always in a fog. There were times when she could pull herself together, and I remember loving her then, so much. She used to tell me a bedtime story about a beautiful white horse that would come to me—its hooves rhythmically beating *clip clop, clip clop*—and be my angel horse. As I fidgeted and twisted in the bedclothes, gnawing at my nails and sucking my thumb, she would stroke me and soothe me with the promise that the angel horse would carry me away, fly me off into the sky. I would fall asleep to the sound of her soft southern voice, intoning *clip clop, clip clop.*

THOSE MOMENTS OF ENGAGEMENT were rare. My dad's visits were infrequent, but he somehow seemed more present and involved than the parent we lived with. My happiest times were the weekends when he took me to the pony rides at La Cienega Park.

Once when we were there, he promised me a dollar if I would stop sucking my thumb. So, by sheer force of will, I did stop. In the daytime I kept my thumb clutched tightly in my fist, and at night I imprisoned it under my pillow, rubbing it on the satin trim of my blanket to fight the overpowering urge to stick it in my mouth.

I didn't do it for the dollar, though.

I did it because even at three or four years old I knew my mother was too ill to care for me and because I was miserable and frightened and lonely and longing for the comfort of a parent. I did it because I loved my big, handsome daddy and thought if I stopped sucking my thumb, that would prove it. Then, like the angel horse, he would carry me away, taking me home to live with him.

It would be another year or two before that happened.

TWO

The Ranch

WHEN I WAS FIVE my mother decided that we should change our lives by leaving the L.A. suburbs for "the country." She found a small, four-acre ranch in Reseda, then one of the poorer sections of the northern San Fernando Valley, which reminded her of her own rustic beginnings.

The ranch lay at the end of a rough dirt road and was screened by a thicket of untamed brush. To the right of the road stood a ramshackle tractor shed and to the left lay the battered white clapboard house, fronted by a fig tree and a few large oaks. In the distance were dilapidated outbuildings and ponds slimed with algae and belly-up fish, as well as a tumble-down stable with a mangy and wasted gammy horse. My grandmother, fittingly, called the place Tobacco Road.

How my mother planned to make the ranch livable, I can't imagine. She couldn't afford to fix it up. Her career was foundering, thanks to her addictions, and my father had been vindictively stingy in the divorce.

Still, for my mother the ranch seemed to hold some promise of redemption, which she never explained. Maybe she just needed to leave L.A., to get a fresh start. Maybe she wanted a clean break from my father or to escape his scrutiny. It's also possible that she saw it as a chance to re-create a new and better, idealized version of her own sad childhood. She even housed a crew of teenage runaways in the outbuildings, like ghosts of her orphaned self.

The house was cramped. My mom barely squeezed in her yellow sofas, her dining table, and her big porcelain dogs. They built me a bunk bed in the bathroom, and to this day I don't know why. Every night I'd lie awake in that bathroom, terrified of the echoey darkness and of the vivid nightmares that plagued me. But even more, I was scared of the chaos outside the door.

"I thought the ranch would be a beautiful existence," my mother later said. "But it turned into a nightmare."

MY MOM HAD a fifteen-year-old boyfriend—I'll call him "Seth"—with long, stringy hair and tattoos on the biceps bulging out of his T-shirts. Early on, Griffin and I discovered his cruel streak. We'd adopted a family of rats we'd seen running around the ranch as our pets—setting out little dishes of food and water and giving them names. We both loved animals and of course had no concept that these cuddly looking country rats were vermin.

But Seth insisted that they had rabies. Rather than get rid of them quietly, with poison or traps, he threw them in a pond and made us watch them drown. Since rats can swim, it took a very long time, and it completely freaked us out.

I grieved for days. It was one of the few times at the ranch when I remember my mother reacting to my distress, which must have been too profound to ignore. "Are you okay?" she kept asking me. All I could do was sob, "Why did he have to kill them, Mommy?" I felt that I would never stop crying.

Most of the time, my mother was either closed up in her room—sitting up for days, writing to Jesus—or else drinking and partying with Seth and his relatives or an older couple (I'll call them the "Johnsons") who sort of adopted my mom. My mother wasn't just boozing, however. Griffin recalls finding white-flecked syringes around the house, evidence that her addiction was escalating.

So were her bouts of paranoia. My mother had a fox-fur poncho, which she sometimes put on when she got high. Draped in fur, with one of her upturned wigs half-slipping off her head (her hair-loss, I believe, was the result of her long-term addiction to speed), she was a sight. One day Griffin found her wrapped up in her poncho, crouched in a large bush in front of the house, crying and rocking. She told him that she was in hiding because she was sure Seth was going to kill her. Not knowing what else to do, Griffin crawled up under her poncho and stayed there, snuggling, for three or four hours until the spell subsided.

Griffin and I were neglected on Sabana Lane, but at least there we had comfortable surroundings and babysitters. Now that we were stuck in the middle of nowhere, isolated, with no backup support for miles, we were virtually abandoned and—at just five and six years old—left to survive on our own. Our meals were erratic, basically consisting of fast food, along with whatever we could scrounge. I was so hungry that I ate raw bacon and, once, a whole tub of Cool Whip, which made me sick. Worst of all was the can of olives I started in on before I realized it was crawling with maggots. I didn't even know what they were. Griffin and I grew scrawny, and my teeth ached with cavities and from an abscess that I tried to ease by jabbing it with a fork. But my first dental appointment was still a few years off.

One night my mother, Seth, and his sister took us to a cheap restaurant, where I started drinking someone's beer. On the car ride home I was reeling. When we reached the ranch, I pushed open my door and hurtled from the moving car, hitting the ground in a rolling tumble. The adult reaction was more confusion than concern: "What's the matter with Tatum?"

Flustered, I picked myself up and ran into the house, where I continued to sneak sips from people's glasses as my mother and the runaways got progressively drunker. Evidently I passed out on the bathroom floor, for I awoke sometime later, alone and covered with vomit. But at least the floor felt cool.

Nobody took much notice of my little bender or even of such basics as whether we went to school. Griffin and I attended only intermittently, walking there alone. Even at school we were isolated, seen as odd and unkempt. My one good outfit was an orange paisley midriff top with matching hip-hugging bell-bottoms, which my father had sent from Rome. I may have looked freakish next to my classmates in their gingham dresses, but I was proud. It was my first fashion statement and, very likely, the beginning of my lifelong love of clothes.

I cherished that gift from my father and, even more, his attention on weekends when he was in town, instead of away on location. However, his visits only highlighted the bleakness of the ranch and the vast difference between his life and ours. My father had become—and was living like—a movie star.

He loved nice cars, so he would pull up in a maroon Maserati Citroën, which rose up and down, to whisk us from the dilapidated ranch to his Malibu beach house. I remember huddling with Griffin under the dashboard of the Citroën, naked, cold, sandy, and wet after one of those golden weekends, feeling sick with misery at the thought of returning to the ranch. My father was our knight in shining armor back then.

I USED TO ESCAPE the ranch through heroic fantasies, plans to help save the world. I was going to fly off to India and care for the poor and sick, like Mother Teresa. Many of my bighearted dreams, not surprisingly, featured children—distributing food to starving ones, rescuing those in danger. Closer to home, I kept an eye on Griffin, and we would bathe each other and take care of each other as well as little children could.

Sometimes we tried to escape the ranch literally, by running away. Stuffing our ragged clothes and whatever food we could find into a pillowcase, Griffin and I would make our way down the rugged dirt road, barefoot as always. Our feet would be sore and blistered by the time we reached the highway, which we would follow down to the Dairy Queen. We didn't know where else to go. There we would hide behind the Dumpster until, inevitably, some good Samaritan would call the cops to report the shoeless urchins picking through the garbage. Then the police would drive up and escort us back to the ranch—often as not, for a beating.

My mother could be a harsh disciplinarian, but it was Seth who really scared me. When Griffin and I misbehaved—or when Seth felt like it—he'd whip us with switches cut from the fig tree. Often we were beaten for stealing from the Jolly Jug, our local general store. We would take candy, because we were so hungry, and also dirty magazines, partly inspired by the weird nudist camp publications we saw at the Johnsons, but mostly because they were forbidden.

Much as I feared Seth's rage, his switches and his fists, I had enough fight in me to try to stand up to him. But my resistance only seemed to heighten his wrath, so my legs were always black and blue from his beatings, and my back was scabbed over. Once when he came after me, I ran to my mother, clutching at her, begging her to not let him beat me—if need be, to punish me herself. She did it, with her belt.

Seth was bad, but I utterly despised one of his cronies for other reasons. One night, when I was hiding out in my mother's bed during one of her drunken parties, he crawled in with me and started groping, pushing his fingers inside me. "Doesn't that feel good?" he demanded, with a boozy leer, as I entreated him to stop. I was only six. The memory of his prodding sickened me for years, and it is only in adulthood, after years of therapy, that my sense of violation has begun to ebb.

It's a measure of how out of control our lives had gotten that my mother would continually leave us alone with strange men. One of them forced me to examine his genitals, then actually tried to penetrate me—a tiny child. Mercifully, he couldn't stay hard.

But such problems were splashes of reality too cold for my mother to tolerate. Increasingly strung out, she spun herself into a la-la cocoon of denial. Everything was fine inside that protective sheath. If you tried to puncture it with the truth, she couldn't hear you.

When I grew older and knew more of the world, I came to see my mother in a different light. But back when she was my whole world, I hated her for her weakness, for making us live in squalor, and for exposing us to cruelty. There were periods when I felt completely overwhelmed—even worried about myself. Watching a TV show on which an animal died, I burst into tears, shaking and sobbing uncontrollably, consumed with grief. I adored animals but was so freaked out at one point that I actually tried to kill a cat—knowing, even in my child's mind, I was committing a terrible act as some kind of cry for help. (Luckily the cat escaped without harm.) Griffin claims that I once climbed a tree and dropped a knife down on him, slicing his face. As I recall, it was an accident, but it's anyone's guess why I had a knife in a tree. Could it be that I lacked proper supervision? Griffin still has the scar.

Even at five and six years old, I knew that my mother's view of our lives was distorted. She was so out of touch that despite the sexual abuse, we continued to socialize with Seth's pals and his extended family. One of his relatives had a house with a pool somewhere in the Valley. While the adults were indoors drinking or whatever, Griffin, who even as a child was incredibly strong, would climb up on the roof and dive into the water. So, one day, I had to try it too.

We got up on the roof together and Griffin jumped off, landing with a splash and laughing. Then it was my turn. When I looked down, the height made me woozy and I lost my nerve. Scared to jump, I toppled off the roof and, missing the pool, crashed onto the concrete. My foot, pinned beneath me, was too painful to move.

Griffin ran inside but must have been afraid to sound the alarm, for it took a while before anyone found me. My foot was badly broken, and I spent six months hobbling on crutches, in a series of plaster casts. The most emblematic photo taken during this time shows me and Griffin barefoot and dirty. Griffin's zipper is down. The strap of my sleeveless top is falling off my shoulder, and my hair is straggling out of giant rollers on top of my head. My foot is in a cast and I am precariously balanced on my crutches. Both of us are wearing phony smiles—mine tight and angry, like my face is swollen with pent-up tears.

Still, there's defiance in it too. The years of neglect and abuse on Sabana Lane and at the ranch gave me a toughness, a feisty, in-your-face bravado—"Addie attitude," as some journalist put it—that was probably my salvation.

There's a story that my mother loved to tell about my willfulness. At times of relative clarity, she would take us on road trips in her yellowish beige Datsun—long, often boring-to-us drives that gave her enormous pleasure. One day, she packed us off to the Kern River, where you could take a boat out to an island and then float on inner tubes. I don't remember the specific offense that set me off, but when it came time to go home, I refused to get back in the boat.

I was cajoled, ordered, and threatened, but I wouldn't budge. "Finally, all we could think to do was leave you," my mother would say. She would describe pulling away in the boat, watching me stand with my jaw set, my fists clenched, and my feet firmly planted. "And you were just growing smaller and smaller in the distance."

They returned an hour later, expecting to find me chastened and scared. But I wasn't. I still was rooted in the same spot. "There you stood, with your little hands on your hips, ready to spit in my eye." My mother would laugh. "And I said, 'That's my Tatum!'"

As if our lives weren't bad enough already, early in 1971, a massive earthquake struck the northern San Fernando Valley. It registered 6.7 on the Richter scale, below the most profoundly devastating level of 8.0-plus but still the strongest in terms of motion ever recorded in California. Hospitals, schools, and freeway bridges collapsed, killing sixty-five people and injuring two thousand others.

With more than 500 million dollars' worth of damage done, President Nixon declared the Valley a major disaster area. Even more frightening than the actual quake was its near destruction of the Lower San Fernando Valley Dam. We were told that only a thin dirt wall stood between us and fifteen million tons of water. An aftershock could send a gushing torrent to swallow us up at any moment.

The quake struck early in the morning, and I ran into my mother's room. She was already up, but I crawled into her empty bed, huddling under the covers. Griffin was sleeping under a pane of glass, I knew, and I was terrified at the thought that it might shatter. All the doors in the house were banging, deafeningly loud. It sounded as if burglars had broken in and were tearing the house apart.

Finally my mother came in with Griffin. "Honey, don't worry," she assured me. "We're going to build a raft, and if the dam breaks, we'll escape."

It's almost funny—and typical, if a bit chilling—that my mother's reflex reaction to the imminent disaster was denial rather than escape or action. Maybe she was trying to comfort me with her hopeful scheme, but the idea that she believed a raft could save us scared me even more. Even then I knew it wasn't possible. I felt tiny and vulnerable and sure that, with my fate in her hands—hands that had never been capable or protective—I was going to die.

Luckily, her plan was never tested. The dam didn't break. But we did escape.

After the earthquake, my grandparents and my father began to monitor conditions at the ranch more closely. Appalled at the goings-on in what my father condemned as "a poisoned environment," they began working behind the scenes to get us out.

By the time I was seven my mother had begun to acknowledge her amphetamine addiction. She checked into Camarillo State Hospital, a well-known mental institution out in "canyon country," to try to beat it. To me, though, after the tumult of our life at the ranch, her months in rehab seemed like one last, unforgivable abandonment.

When my mom was released from the hospital, I spat in her face. She called my reaction "the most painful experience of my life . . . like having a child die."

I deeply regret my behavior, but at the time she seemed so cruel to me. For the next few years, I barely saw my mother, and for much of that time, I even completely lost track of Griffin, my "Irish twin."

I have one indelible image of them from those lost years. On Thanksgiving Day, when I was about eight, my mother showed up unannounced at my dad's Malibu beach house. She had Griffin with her in the station wagon, as well as a huge roasted turkey, with all the trimmings, that she'd prepared for us.

When she got out of the car, she was weaving, obviously

drunk. My father went crazy at the sight, shouting, "What the fuck are you doing here?"

He picked up Griffin and stuffed him back in the station wagon. Then he slammed the turkey platter out of my mother's hands, grabbed her shoulders, and screaming, shoved her into the driver's seat. Her feet were still dangling out of the car, and as I looked on in horror, he slammed the door, right onto her legs.

"Now get going!" he bellowed.

She started the car and edged it back out onto the Pacific Coast Highway. It was one of the busiest roads in California, and I was terrified that she'd get sideswiped. Inside the house, my father was on the phone to the police, describing the car, telling them to pick her up for drunk driving.

My father's outburst shocked and scared me more than I dared to articulate. The force of his rage was overwhelming, yet I desperately needed to believe in him. I had already determined to move forward in life without a mother.

THREE

The Good Life

AFTER THE ISOLATION and chaos of the ranch, I felt out of step with the more civilized world—unsure how to navigate, how to talk to people, how to react. Even simple daily hygiene was confusing, for I'd rarely been bathed and had never brushed my teeth, which were full of cavities. Taken to the dentist for the first time, I went wild when he tried to give me novocaine—I'd been promised "no shots"—and kicked him in the head and the balls, trying to escape. My father had to wrestle me back into the chair.

My grandmother took on the task of taming me, transforming me from a bruised and scrappy boy-child into a girl. I still remember the way she bathed me, grooming my ragged and dirty nails, and tucked me into my first proper bed, with clean, sweet-smelling sheets. She gave me my first doll and put me in little dresses, assuring me that I was pretty—which I didn't believe. She was the first truly loving female presence in my life.

I used to stare at her, studying her makeup—pale face powder and deep red lipstick—her white outfits and gloves, and the way she wore her hair, in a sleek, elegant bun. Her favorite perfume was Rive Gauche. Her speech was measured, with a cultivated English accent. She seemed amazingly feminine compared to my mother, with those lopsided wigs and false eyelashes flapping half unstuck. I also marveled at her relationship with my grandfather, which would last for thirty-eight years. I had never known my own parents as a couple.

I loved her immaculate home in the Pacific Palisades, surrounded by the beautiful gardens she planted, and her great home cooking, a powerful antidote to fast food. I still make her tuna fish and her fried chicken, which my kids adore. In memories of that time, I associate her with a lot of laughter: zooming up to visit her on the back of my father's motorcycle, my uncle Kevin eating her flowers, pretending to be a gorilla, Kevin and my father teasing her about the touch-and-go health of Rosebud, her cat. My grandfather was big and handsome and affable, but my grandmother was definitely the matriarch of our family, the thread that bound us together. I came to think of her house at 15050 Sunset Boulevard as my home base.

IT WASN'T MY HOME base for long, though. Shortly after we left the ranch, Griffin and I were sent to Tree Haven boarding school in Tucson, Arizona. It was the first structured environment I'd ever experienced, and the culture shock was profound. Academically I lagged far behind my classmates, and socially I was totally lost, with really no idea how to communicate with the other kids. I tried to attract friends in the only way I could imagine, by reminding people repeatedly, "My father is famous. My father is a movie star."

Needless to say, that strategy didn't work. Soon I fell back on an old feel-better habit—stealing—and got caught snatching some earrings from a classmate's drawer. In the principal's office, I was spanked with a perforated wooden paddle, which was more unendurable and humiliating, coming from a stranger, than the countless beatings I'd received at the hands of Seth and my mother.

Finally, in utter misery, I chopped off all my hair. I mailed the cuttings to my grandma, along with a letter—a full page on which I'd scrawled over and over, with childlike spelling, *I hate it heer, I hate it heer.*

Griffin remembers my rescue better than I do. He was watching from the window when a big black limousine kicked up dust on the school's dirt road then circled around the fountain at the entrance. My father got out with Peter Bogdanovich and a woman, but no one summoned Griffin. The next thing he knew, the car was pulling away again, and I was in it. He had been left behind—and from that point on, his life diverged from mine.

WHERE I WOUND UP was even better than Sunset Boulevard—my father's beach house in Malibu. He was renting a place on LaCosta Beach. (A year or two later we would build a home of our own a few lots over.) It was a modern two-story house with a white-rock roof and a window wall with sliding glass doors, which opened onto a beachfront deck. My father occupied one side of the house, where he set me up with a half bed in a tiny room, and on the other side lived Greg, a tall blond artist who was his best friend.

The house had all the trappings of a swinging bachelor

pad, with a mirrored bar, a pool table, and a stereo always blaring the Allman Brothers, Led Zeppelin, Al Green, or James Brown. Greg's collages adorned the walls, along with a movie poster for *Play It As It Lays,* which starred his girlfriend Tuesday Weld. He kept a pet boa constrictor in his shower and a tarantula named Wayne in a bowl on the bar. He and my father hung out in cutoff jeans, smoking grass, which they told me was an herb, like parsley. My father grew a bushy mustache, wore an army jacket with an American flag, and carried a shoulder bag with a pot leaf appliqué. It was a classic 1970s hippie scene, on a fabulous backdrop of sunshine, sand, and surf. I loved it. I'd never been so happy.

Every day I paddled for hours in the ocean. I collected driftwood, learned to body surf, and threw Frisbees on the beach, growing tanned and strong. For the first time in my life, I made connections with other children: Monique LaBoie, who became my best friend; Michele Walker, daughter of the actor Robert Walker Jr., who always had a bunch of kids over doing tai chi; and Maria Dylan, Bob's daughter. I remember going over to her house and seeing her father, the rock icon, snoozing in his underwear.

At home, I became a little entertainer, amusing my father and his friends with my newfound skill shooting pool. Once, playing hostess, I dropped a huge tray of food in my father's room, splattering it everywhere. It got to be a running joke in our house, "Hey, who got coleslaw/Coke/ketchup in my eye? . . . Tatum?"

Not surprisingly, since I was living with two handsome bachelors, there was a steady parade of women passing through. My father was divorced from Leigh Taylor-Young soon after my brother Patrick was born, and I became the telephone screener for his girlfriends. When women called, I was instructed to say he wasn't home—that he was out running or whatever—but often I got confused. That led to some funny exchanges, for example:

"Hi, Tatum. How are you? Is your father there?"

"No, no, he, uh . . . went running."

"Ah. Well, did you get the strawberry lip gloss I sent you?"

"Oh! Hold on. Dad, did I get some strawberry lip gloss?"

Scowling—half-joking and half-serious—my father would stomp over to the phone. "Hi. I just got back. How nice of you to send Tatum a present . . ."

I developed a fondness for a few of our female visitors, all of whom were stunningly beautiful. Tuesday Weld was nice— and somehow my father's friendship with Greg endured despite his affair with her. Lauren Hutton and I sunbathed nude on the beach and went skinny-dipping in the ocean with her fishing net. Ursula Andress, who dated my father for some time, wore great short boots with her bathrobe and fascinated me by dry-washing her huge mane of hair with powder shampoo. Once I got a bad case of poison oak, and she tenderly daubed ointment all over my inflamed body, including my private areas and eyes. She took a motherly interest in my upbringing too, scolding my father in her exotic Swiss accent: "Ryan, why, why isn't your daughter in school? She needs to be in school. Ryan, why do you let her sleep in your bed? It's crazy the way you're raising her."

At that point, I often did sleep in my father's bed, even when he had women over. I clung to him, terrified of abandonment, and he did little to discourage my dependence. Emotionally I was pretty rocky—tantrum-prone, dauntingly headstrong and outspoken—and I still stole, though less often. There was some worry among the adults that I might set fires. The worst thing I did was take a collage Greg had labored over for days and cut it to shreds. What prompted that destructive impulse I couldn't have guessed. Later my father would say in print, to my chagrin, that *Paper Moon* "answered the question of what to do with this strange little girl I was living with."

ORIGINALLY PAUL NEWMAN and one of his kids were being considered for the film, which was based on a best-selling book, *Addie Pray*, by Joe David Brown. When Peter Bogdanovich was first offered the script, he wasn't all that keen on it. Polly Platt, his then wife, encouraged him to reconsider, since it was a father-and-daughter story and he had daughters himself. "I know who should play the little girl," she said.

Polly clinched the deal by reading him passages from the script, imitating what she called my "whiskey voice." "His eyes lit up," as she tells it now, "and he said, 'We'll do it, and Ryan will be the father.'"

That led to my beach-walk audition. Afterward I left the grown-ups talking and went swimming, not even realizing that I'd had a tryout and had gotten the job. When I finally learned that I'd be making a movie, all I could think was, *Now I'll never have to go back to school again.* I was ecstatic.

Then I started worrying. My legs bowed in, giving me knock-knees. What if I had to get braces on my legs? Would they still let me be in the movie? It was my grandmother who soothed my anxiety, assuring me that my legs were fine, that they'd straighten out as I grew up, and most important, that I could become a great actress.

However, disaster struck one day when I was playing with Monique. We used to do gymnastics in her bedroom, jumping off the bed to grab a chin-up bar. I bounced up, reaching out for the bar, but missed—and when I landed, I heard a sharp crack. I crumpled on the floor, filled with overwhelming dread and clutching my arm in pain. This is it, I thought. If my arm was broken, and I knew it was, I was going to wind up back in school—and my dad would be *sooo* mad.

Monique's mom, Ricky, called my dad, who ran over and carried me home. For the next week, we kept testing out my arm, trying to pick things up but failing. When I didn't seem better, my father took me to the doctor, who X-rayed my arm and stuck the image on the light box. "See that?" he said, pointing to the fracture.

My arm was broken, all right. With that I got hysterical. The months of living with my father were the happiest of my short life—with no fear, no beatings, no hunger, no neglect—just eating well, soaking up the sun, making and enjoying friends, and even feeling loved. In my mind, a broken arm meant that I was doomed to confinement, regulations, paddling, struggling to catch up, and feeling bored and dumb. Instead of getting on a plane for an adventure with my father, I'd be isolated and wretched, suffering the ridicule of classmates who despised me. I'd hated school before, but now that I'd experienced a bit of comfort, affection, and fun, I couldn't stand being miserable again. It was just too cruel and unfair to have the movie—and the ongoing happiness it promised—snatched away from me.

Luckily, that didn't happen. In what seemed like a flash, I was headed to Hays, Kansas, with my arm in a sling.

FOUR

Paper Moon

THE NOVEL *ADDIE PRAY* was set in the South, but the wide-open spaces of Kansas had impressed Polly Platt when she and Peter had driven cross-country together earlier in their marriage. Scouting for locations, she chose Hays when she discovered that many buildings and even whole streets remained virtually unchanged since the Depression.

Meanwhile, Peter began listening to the music of the time and came across "Paper Moon," which struck him as the perfect theme song and title for the movie. Paramount balked, refusing to accept it unless he could work a paper moon—literally—into the story. Finally he came up with a carnival scene, in which Addie poses sitting in a paper moon at a photo booth.

A year or two before, Peter had made an atmospheric black-and-white film, *The Last Picture Show*. He decided that *Paper Moon* should be black and white too, to give it a similar intensity and a period feel. He also feared that, in color, my father and I would come off as too blond and attractive to seem convincing as Depression-era con artists.

I thought there was nothing attractive—or even nice—about my costumes. My hair was cut very short, like a boy's, and they put me in overalls and orthopedic-looking, 1930s-style shoes. "You can't make me wear these," I protested, horrified by the way I looked. Peter had to make a personal plea to convince me. "Come on, Tatesky," he coaxed, using his pet name for me, which I kept for years. "Baby, you look beautiful, it's just for a short time, I love you, and you're gonna be great."

He may have had his doubts during the early read-throughs, with the whole cast—my father, me, Madeline Kahn, John Hillerman, and all the others—gathered in the Holiday Inn conference room. When it was my turn, my dad would prod me—"Tatum!"—and then I'd always ask, "What page is it?" Meaningful glances would shoot around the table, as if to say: *Oh, my God. What have we gotten ourselves into?*

In fact, I could barely read, and I was totally bored. Rote memorization was very hard work for an eight-year-old. I still have a script covered with doodles, my make-believe notes.

At one point, my father, who rehearsed with me, said, "Let's run lines," and I said no.

"Why not?" he asked.

"I don't want to get stale."

"Stale?" He was amazed. "Who taught you that word?"

I said, "I don't know," but I knew instinctively that it was true—and that I'd have to trust my instincts in order to play Addie. Later in life, my instincts would benefit me even more.

When I got outside in the field, under the big arc lights, for the opening scene, I didn't feel scared at all. Even at that age, I felt very connected and perfectly calm, like I knew what I was doing. I understood this little girl.

Sometimes Peter and my father would fool me, to use my natural reactions. At one point, Mose grabs at the door of a truck, which falls off. I jumped backward in genuine shock. I wasn't warned ahead of time. Later in the movie, gangsters beat up Mose, and I was truly upset, having been told that something bad had happened to my father. One of the most intense exchanges in the movie—when Madeline Kahn as Trixie has to persuade me as Addie to give up the front seat, so she can sit with Mose—was totally in tune with my own psyche. When it came to my father, I wasn't about to take a backseat to anyone.

That scene was a lot harder for Madeline Kahn, whom I never befriended—not because I didn't like her but because I had no ability to relate to women. I did come to admire her sense of humor and her big personality. In the movie she had to wear a special "jiggle" bra, and Peter insisted in one scene that she call herself "Trixie, with her big tits." Madeline hated the word *tits* and refused to say it through all our script readings. Finally, Peter tricked her into saying it once, with the cameras rolling—and it worked.

Peter wanted me to smoke in the movie, but the cigarettes were filled with lettuce, not tobacco. They glued sandpaper to my fingers so I could strike a match one-handed. Before each take, I got to smack shut the clacker, which I loved. The minute Peter yelled "Cut," I would jump out of my mikes—we were all wired up while we were shooting—and climb up to be with my pals on the crew on their flatbed truck. That drove my father crazy, because he'd have to wait for me to be remiked before every shot. For the most part, he stayed patient.

Even more maddening, certain scenes kept tripping me up. At one point Addie tells a hotel clerk, "I'd like a piece of Juicy Fruit gum."

I'd mastered the line, but they'd switched the brand from Dentyne when someone discovered that Dentyne didn't exist back in the 1930s. We were shooting late at night, and I was tired, so I kept saying, "Can I have a piece of Den-Ju?" "Can I have a piece of Juicy Den . . . ?" to the poor actor who kept cueing me over and over, "What would you like, little lady?"

I could feel the exhaustion and irritability mounting, with a whole fifty-member crew—the sound guy, the cameraman and the camera lighter and the wardrobe people, the set designer, the gaffers, the electricians, the grip, the people on the dolly truck, and all the rest—hanging on my little-girl ability to nail a line. We redid the scene a couple dozen times, and it must have been 4 A.M. by the time I got it right. I never froze up or cried in frustration, but I was painfully aware that I was keeping people awake. It was a lot of pressure.

Peter envisioned the movie in long single shots, keeping the camera trained on the actors for up to five or six minutes. It's hard to stay perfectly in character that long, with every movement, expression, and word of dialogue impeccable— and it was supertough for an eight-year-old. As Frank Marshall, our associate producer, recalls, "Quite often these long takes led to great laughter."

In one scene Addie comes downstairs at the hotel to find Mose eating breakfast and asks, "Whatcha having?"

"Waffles," says Mose, sticking a big bite in his mouth.

For some reason, the way he did it kept cracking me up. I'd start giggling and forget my lines, someone would yell "Cut!" and my father would drop his fork in exasperation, pretending to break down in tears, pleading, "Tatum!"

"Ryan must have eaten fifty waffles," Frank Marshall says.

Our most challenging long shot took place in a car traveling (actually, being towed) down the one stretch of road, about a mile and a half long, that had no visible anachronisms. The whole shot rested on me—not only did I have pages of dialogue to deliver, but I also had a lot of stage business, fiddling with the map and other things while my father pretended to drive. If either of us blew a word or gesture, the car couldn't back up. They'd have to haul it all the way to the end, where there was room to turn around, then head back to the starting point to try again.

The first day we did a grueling twenty-five takes, partly because of my clowning around. "Ryan was freaking out," Peter recalled. "Screaming, 'Tatum, goddamn it.' At the end of the first day, he came over, put his arms around me, and said, 'I can't, I can't, I'm gonna kill her.'"

We finally got it right a few days later, after another fifteen takes. Peter would later surmise that the scene in the car ultimately won me the Oscar, because the Academy judges recognized how difficult it was for someone so young.

There were also some dicey moments, like being yanked into a moving truck by a stuntman and nearly toppling off a stack of shifting boxes in the back as the truck sped away. The physical risks didn't really scare me, though I panicked briefly in one of the closing scenes, when I was supposed to chase after Mose, who was leaving, and I felt something buzzing in my sweater. No one believed me. "Come on, Tatum," I was urged. "Just run down the hill and catch him."

So I swallowed hard and took off running. When I got to the bottom of the hill, I shook my sleeve and two wasps fell out. "See?" I said, pointing to the big swollen stings on my arm.

The hardest part of the work for me was the loneliness and boredom. Child actors were pretty unregulated then, so no one monitored my time on the set, which could stretch into the wee hours. During the carnival scene, which was an all-night shoot, I was so bored that I pigged out on candy and spun on the rides until I got so sick I threw up all over my costume. Maybe it would have been different if I'd had a mom watching over me.

When I wasn't working, I was stuck in a hotel in Hays with the rest of the cast. I shared a pair of connecting rooms with my hired chaperone, Diane, the soon-to-be wife of Hedgeman Lewis, a famous boxer from Detroit whom my father managed. My uncle Kevin later made a documentary called *The Contender* about Hedge's struggle to capture the welterweight title. Ultimately, Hedge lost out to the Cuban boxer Jose Napoles, so the film was never released.

I was crazy about Diane. She was black and six feet tall, with long legs and a good sense of humor, so I had no end of fun with her Afro. Diane even let me poke through all her fascinating girly creams and makeup. She did the best she could to entertain me, but twelve weeks is a long time to keep a pent-up child amused.

I was never the kind of child you could plunk down in front of the TV. But I did love movies and watched them compulsively from the time I started living with my father. He never tried to restrict the movies I saw, whatever their ratings. It was his way of educating me, and it's left me with a pretty comprehensive knowledge of film. Though the other grown-ups thought it was weird, he let me watch *In Cold Blood,* which scared me to death, during the making of *Paper Moon.*

For a while, I had a playmate, sixteen-year-old P. J. Johnson, who came from Texas for the role of Imogene, Trixie's maid. I loved her, and she taught me some cool *Soul Train* dance moves. But when I was on my own, which was most of the time, I got into mischief. I'd wake up early in the morning and start knocking on people's doors, looking for companionship. "Go away!" they'd yell. "I'm sleeping. Leave me alone." I'd make my way dejectedly down to the lobby, where there was a big telephone switchboard. I messed with it all the time, wreaking havoc on the phone system.

One day I found a little cat by the railroad tracks and brought him back to the hotel. Because he was an alley cat, I named him Alio. Though we set him up with a cat box, I didn't really know how to take care of it, so my room—and my poor chaperone Diane's, right next door—began to reek of cat urine and feces. I would bring the cat to the set with me, and on one long ride to a location, he took a dump in the car. All the adults rode with their heads hanging out the windows the rest of the way. I thought that was pretty funny.

The worst time for me was the evening, when the other actors would watch "dailies"—that is, study the film that had been shot that day. I wasn't allowed to see dailies because Peter worried that I'd pay attention to how I looked on-screen and start self-consciously "acting." That made me mad. I felt terribly left out.

Since I was so bored and lonely, I began to wonder how my mother was doing. I hadn't spoken to her in ages. I knew Griffin had left boarding school and gone to live with her, but I was still angry and a little afraid of her. I'd heard plenty of negative talk to the effect that she was a drug addict and a bad mother. But then I came across a *Photoplay* magazine with a headline like "Ryan O'Neal Steals Daughter from Joanna," over a story on how losing me was the greatest indignity of my mother's life. At one point during the shoot, when I wasn't getting along with my father, I screamed at him: "It's true—you stole me! You stole me from my mother!"

He drew back, cocking his fist, and for the first time, I believed he was actually going to hit me. Peter held him back, and the moment passed. Still, his show of temper shook me up. I loved my father so much. It was the first crack in our golden relationship.

Despite all the hard work and the boredom, I loved the communal feeling of making a movie. I never felt more secure than when I was with my father in a roomful of people, with everyone laughing. There were a lot of funny people involved with *Paper Moon*. Madeline Kahn, of course, was a major comic talent, but Frank Marshall, our associate producer, was hilarious too. He always made me laugh when he came out to my little room in the cast trailer, which was called a "honey wagon." Joe Amsler, my father's stand-in (who'd done three years in the penitentiary for his role in kidnapping Frank Sinatra Jr.), also loved to joke. He once fed me Rocky Mountain oysters—bull's testicles—claiming they were fried chicken. Peter and my father could both be funny, Polly Platt was loving and motherly to me, and I adored Laszlo Kovacs. It was a warm, close-knit group.

I turned nine while we were making *Paper Moon,* and the cast and crew threw me a party on the set. They even had a cake set up on a prop table. I'd never in my life felt so warmly embraced, that I was part of something and truly belonged.

———

PAPER MOON HAD its premiere in New York City. My father and I stayed at the Pierre Hotel, where we'd race in the halls. We had so much fun. Sometimes he'd count off, "On your mark, get set, GO!" and then stick out his foot and trip me. One day when we were running up Fifth Avenue to the hotel, he slipped and fell, sliding along a sidewalk grate on his butt. "Hahaha, you big handsome actor," I screamed. "You always trip me, and now look at you, sliding!"

My father started laughing wildly, right along with me. We were both so exuberant then that it was okay—even fun—to goof on stardom. Later my father took me to Bloomingdale's and bought me some red high-heeled platform shoes that I'd seen somewhere and set my heart on. I was too little to wear even the smallest adult size, so we had to get a sample pair. However I must have looked, with my skinny little knock-kneed legs, I felt very grown-up teetering around in them.

The premiere itself was more of a blur. I remember that I got a big ovation, which was thrilling. Then the press was all over us, and I didn't know how to cope. I tried to stockpile canned answers to reporters' questions like "Who's your favorite actor?" "Laurence Olivier," I'd say, though I didn't know who he was. "Your favorite actress?" "Uh, Katharine Hepburn—I mean, Audrey Hepburn . . ."

I was bored right away by the media blitz and baffled by all the attention I was getting. Coming from an acting family, I didn't see filmmaking as unusual, and no one gave me the sense that I'd accomplished anything special. Even my own mother didn't make a fuss over me. In our first phone conversation since our estrangement, she praised my father's performance but said that mine seemed "cold." "Mother," I told her, with an exasperation that covered my hurt, "I was playing a role."

But I soon picked up on the fact that I was the focus of every interview, at my father's expense. The recognition made me very uneasy. He was all I had, and the thought of losing his affection—of facing another abandonment—was more than I could bear. He began to make snide little jokes, to belittle me and undermine me in ways I couldn't quite grasp. In the press, he played the doting father, but in his eyes I read the truth: deep resentment that his own brilliant performance was being dismissed. I soon started getting such bad stomachaches that the doctors thought I had ulcers. And I started to wish that I could grow up really fast.

FIVE

The Oscar

MY STRETCH OF FREEDOM and happiness couldn't last. As soon as *Paper Moon* wrapped, my father left for Ireland to make *Barry Lyndon* with Stanley Kubrick. He was to live abroad for the next two years.

I was devastated. For my father—my lifeline, my rescuer, the one I looked to for stability and love—to simply pick up and move thousands of miles away, across the ocean, was an unthinkable betrayal. Not only did I feel profoundly abandoned, but on a practical level, I had nowhere to go. I was only nine, I was estranged from my mother, and for some reason couldn't live with my grandmother, whom I loved. The most convenient option was the one I dreaded most: sticking me back in boarding school.

This time, it was a different place, the Ojai Valley School, about an hour's drive from Los Angeles. But the psychic atmosphere for me was much the same. Thin and gawky, with my hair still boy-short from the movie, I was an ugly duckling, which made me fair game for teasing. My childhood was so different from my classmates'—little formal schooling, an unconventional family, plus the fact that I'd just made a movie—

that I felt like an alien. I was much more comfortable with adults than with other children.

I tried to ingratiate myself by telling outrageous tales. One great one was the claim that, while I was swimming, a shark had bitten off my ear; I even showed off my fake "replacement." I also said I had a horse ranch, which was a powerful fantasy of mine. When no one believed me, I called my father and put one of the doubters on the phone. "Oh yes," he confirmed, at my insistence. "Yes, she does."

These lies did nothing to enhance my popularity. Instead I was scorned and picked on, ganged up on, even despised. Kids can be terribly cruel. I did make one friend, Carrie Earle, but much of the time, I stayed holed up in the quarters of the dorm mother, Mrs. Quill, crying and playing with her dog Mouton.

Then came the opening of *Paper Moon*. Suddenly I was a bona fide movie star, and everyone wanted to be my friend. I'd never experienced such hypocrisy before, and it shook me up. Being hated was miserable, but my newfound popularity was worse because I knew better than to believe in it. It left me feeling that there was no one I could trust.

I looked forward to the Christmas break, when I would visit my father in Ireland, hoping more than ever that I could beg him to pull me out of school.

MY FRIEND CARRIE came with me to Ireland, each of us armed with a huge Sugar Daddy on a stick for the twelve-hour flight. We spent the whole time gnawing on those toffee suckers and running up and down the stairs to the jet's first-class lounge. It was thrilling, and so was the manor house where my father was staying, which looked like a castle. We were sure the place was haunted.

To welcome me and Carrie, my dad had a room all decorated with posters of Rod Stewart and Marc Bolan. However, it soon became clear that something had changed in the father I'd missed so badly. He was always cranky and preoccupied, and he seemed determined to pit me against Carrie. He'd stage footraces between the two of us and then cheer her on. "Wow, look at those legs. Carrie, you're so fast! You're such a good runner—so much better than Tatum!"

Jealous and confused because she'd somehow gained my father's favor, I took out my frustrations on Carrie. "My dad paid for you to come here," I'd tell her. "And I'm bigger than you, so I'm the boss."

So we fought a lot during that trip. I did succeed in one thing, however. I managed to persuade my father to let me stay on with him after Carrie returned to the States.

However, any hopes I had of recovering his affection were quickly dashed. As usual, an entourage surrounded my father, including my uncle Kevin, his artist friend Greg, and a glamorous Belgian blonde named Caroline. Caroline had originally dated Greg but, like Tuesday Weld, wound up with my father instead, after considerable drama. In what would become a lifelong pattern, my father maneuvered Caroline and me into an even more lopsided and painful triangle than the one he'd set up with Carrie.

It was lopsided because in this case I was seriously overmatched. Caroline was an icy beauty, always perfectly turned out in gleaming silk blouses and gabardine slacks—very intimidating to a gawky, self-conscious preadolescent. She had something powerful to offer my father that I didn't even understand yet: sex. As if to drive that point home, my father locked me out of his bedroom, once actually shutting the door in my face and shouting, "You don't get to come in here. Only Caroline can."

I cried outside his door for what seemed like hours.

After my love-deprived childhood, what I craved—intensely—was the assurance that I had an unshakable place in my father's heart. My faith in him had been rocked when he left for Ireland and then again during the *Paper Moon* publicity and Carrie's visit. I badly wanted him to love me again. But rather than honor my need for fatherly affection, he seemed to lump me in with his other "demanding" women, making me feel like the lightweight in a tug-of-war for his love. Of course, the harder I had to tug, the more needy and possessive I got.

BARRY LYNDON, DIRECTED by the great Stanley Kubrick, was based on the Thackeray novel about an eighteenth-century Irishman who fights for England in the Seven Years War, travels the Continent, and then reinvents himself as a member of the British aristocracy. My father starred and was also going to do the voice of the offscreen narrator. Striving for strict historical accuracy, Stanley even shot scenes by candlelight and modeled other scenes on famous paintings of the era.

One of the film's locations was Dublin Castle, which caught the attention of the Irish Republican Army. Outraged to see even a fictional representation of English troops on

Irish soil, they sent death threats to my father and Stanley. As a result, the whole production had to pick up and move to England. My father rented a house in London and sent me to live with the Kubricks, whose youngest daughter, Vivian, was just a few years older than me.

They lived outside the city in a big old Gothic house on the moors. The place was a little eerie but also wonderful because they had lots of dogs and books. I started reading for pleasure, for the first time, while I was there. The walls were lined with the beautiful artwork of Stanley's wife, Christiane, who encouraged my efforts to paint and draw. At dinner I copied the way they used their knives and forks, and at night I found it curious to sleep European style, as the Kubricks did, under down comforters with no sheets.

Stanley impressed me tremendously. My dad had all his movies screened for me alone, in one sitting, when I first got to Ireland. I loved Stanley because he always spoke to me like an adult, discussing things like the reason he always drove a Mercedes—"It's the safest car in the world"—as if they were perfectly natural concerns for a nine-year-old. He'd ask me questions and listen intently to my answers. Now and then, though, I'd catch him looking at me a bit askance, as if I were an odd little thing. Often, around that time, without understanding why, I got the sense that people were starting to feel sorry for me.

Stanley and Vivian were very close, which I envied, given my shifting relationship with my father. I had first met her in Ireland, where we would take long walks on the beach, laughing and playing and talking. Vivian seemed so exotic, with her dark Russian looks, her poise, her humor, and her obvious brilliance. She was musical, she wrote and spoke beautifully—in short, she was everything that I was not: gorgeous, amusing, and educated. Yet I felt an identification with her because we both came from offbeat, bohemian families. She was a person I could aspire to be. I totally idolized her.

Unfortunately, my adoration didn't endear me to Vivian for long. She was nearly a teenager and I was too much younger to hold her interest. Once I moved in with her family, the tension between us increased. Vivian seemed to find me wild and rough around the edges, and she made no secret of her annoyance. "Tatum," she'd scold, "that's not how you say it. You've got to say it like this. . . ." She constantly put me in my place with "Tatum, what rubbish!" Even years later, when I'd write her heartfelt, loving letters, her replies would always be full of corrections: "Tatum, that's not how you spell it!"

Her criticism always embarrassed me, making me feel stupid. We squabbled a lot, and I once stuck gum in her hair. She got her revenge by offering to trim mine and then practically scalping me.

But there was more going on between us than childish fussing. Vivian's charms weren't lost on my father, who had started to set us at odds. "Vivian's so talented," he'd say. "Tatum can hardly read and write." Or "Vivian, you're so beautiful, so graceful, so funny, so smart. Tatum, you're just a silly little girl."

My father mesmerized full-grown women, so it was no wonder that twelve-year-old Vivian fell for him. He was so handsome, funny, and seductive that she developed a deep and desperate crush on him. I began to worry that she tolerated me only as a conduit to my father. Worse yet, her crush didn't seem entirely unrequited. While I'm sure they never had any sexual contact—my father never had a thing for young girls—he evidently relished her affection enough to keep pouring on the charm.

When Vivian told Stanley about my father's flirtation, he was outraged. I never heard what he said to my father about it, but they had some kind of falling out. Stanley later dropped my father as the narrator of *Barry Lyndon*.

IN LONDON MY FATHER had become part of a glittering social circle—rock stars, actors, the rich and famous of his generation. One night while I was visiting, I fell asleep at Mick Jagger's, and he carried me out to my father's car. That was thrilling, but even more than Mick, I loved Bianca. Slim and dark, she was strikingly beautiful, with an incredible, individualistic sense of style.

Up to that point, my primary female role models had been my grandmother, my mom, and Diane Lewis. Bianca's brand of femininity was much more inspiring—more sophisticated, glamorous, and even playful. At an age when I was struggling to figure out my own identity, flying blind without benefit of a mother, I found myself almost magnetically drawn to such strong, stylish, self-possessed women.

Bianca intuitively grasped what I needed and indulged me. She let me paw through her closets, admiring her fabulous vintage dresses, and encouraged me to buy a Victorian frock just like one of hers. She also had a collection of men's antique suits and tuxedos, which she wore with a cane, a bowler hat, and tremendous élan. I copied that look too, getting myself a little cane and a hat to wear out and about in London, feeling utterly smashing.

At some point my father began an affair with Bianca Jagger. Once, when she was visiting us in L.A., I picked up the phone and heard Mick yell, "Put on your knickers and get out of there!" Then they started speaking French, so I had to hang up. I thought it was interesting that Mick was so demanding, considering how unfaithful he was to Bianca.

During that time in London, my father took me to my first concert. The Faces—Ron Wood, Kenney Jones, and the others—were performing with Rod Stewart. I loved them. I started a little collection of my favorite artists—everything from Carlos Santana and Buddy Miles on eight-track to the Allman Brothers, the Beatles, Leon Russell, and Creedence Clearwater Revival. That was the beginning of my lifelong passion for music, for which I will always be grateful to my father.

While I was in London, I stayed on a cot in my father's dining room. As soon as I arrived, I'd line up my toys and trinkets on the edge of the table, to feel at home. All the adults slept late, so I would wake up alone, with nothing to do. One bored morning, I started rooting through some cabinets and discovered what looked like a tin of peanut brittle. I was dragging it out when Greg came into the room. "Look, it's candy!" I told him, all excited.

I pried off the lid. A huge snake shot out—a fake one, like a jack-in-the-box—as I jumped back screaming. Greg burst out laughing. Inevitably, riffs on "Tatum and the peanut brittle" became a running joke in my family for years.

In London, I soon discovered, there were new limits on humor. Once, during a party, I poked fun at my dad for getting his teeth capped. "Don't look too close, or you'll see they're all different colors," I teased. "And some of those teeth are fake."

He didn't like that. Just months before, when we were together in New York, it was okay—and even fun—to joke about his stardom. Now there were things I wasn't allowed to say, especially in front of women. The easy intimacy I used to have with my father was gone.

Walking on eggshells, I felt increasingly shaken by the precariousness of my position, trying to clutch at a father who was doing his best to drive me away. He had belittled me, shamed me with Carrie and Vivian, and now sometimes would simply declare, flat out, "I just don't like you, Tatum."

I'd started noticing that there were drugs around, which seemed to make my father mean. Once so loving and funny, he was growing crazily moody. At the airport one day, my dad flared up and punched my uncle Kevin in the face. His emotional swings scared me so much that I started writing him little pleading notes: "Please, Daddy, don't be mad at me. Please, I'll be a big girl, I'll be a better girl, I'll try. Daddy, I love you. Please don't hate me!"

I WAS IN ENGLAND when we got the call. *Paper Moon* had garnered four Oscar nominations: Best Sound, Best Screenplay Adapted from Another Medium, and two shots at Best Supporting Actress, for me and for Madeline Kahn. Peter was passed over for Best Director, and Laszlo's brilliant cinematography went unacknowledged. Worst of all, for the Best Actor nomination, my father didn't make the cut.

You'd think an Oscar nomination would be an indelible

moment, a victory to cherish and savor for a lifetime. But for me it must have been a trauma instead of a triumph. I can't remember it at all. Where I was, who told me, whether anyone gave me a hug, shook my hand, showered me with praise, or glossed it over, I couldn't say. The memory is totally lost to me.

It was Vivian who first revealed how my father reacted to the news. He socked me. For a child already obsessed with losing her father, who was living in terror, believing that his love was ebbing away, that would have been way too painful to process. If I've blocked it out, it's no wonder.

I do know that my dad let his bitterness leak to the British press, saying, "She's lazy by nature . . . but she took over the picture. To start with it was known as Ryan's Daughter and then after a while it was called Tatum's Dad. . . . No, she's not going to make another picture. I'm not going to work with her again, nor is Peter."

I guess his jealousy was out of control.

Returning to the States for the ceremony—alone, shaky, and sad—I felt like Little Orphan Annie. My father stayed behind in England, ostensibly because he was too busy with *Barry Lyndon,* and there was no word from my mother or Griffin. I was still too cut off from them. It was as if I had committed some unmentionable, possibly unpardonable sin by winning the nomination.

Once again, my grandmother stepped into the breach. We went to Jon Peters's beauty salon for the same pixie haircut I'd had (and hated) in *Paper Moon.* I loved high heels, and she helped me find a small enough pair, so I could wear them for the awards, then took me to Nolan Miller to have an outfit made. I asked for a little tuxedo, just like Bianca Jagger's Yves Saint Laurent model.

On Oscar night, she and my grandfather were my escorts. I was up against Linda Blair (*The Exorcist*), Candy Clark (*American Graffiti*), Sylvia Sidney (*Summer Wishes, Winter Dreams*), and of course, Madeline Kahn. No one else from the movie attended—not even Peter—so there was no celebratory air, no sense that anyone was cheering me on. As the ceremony dragged on, I got tired and bored. The biggest highlight of the evening was a streaker, who prompted a funny ad-lib by the host, David Niven, that he was "showing off his shortcomings."

Then my name was called. I headed to the stage in a blur of confusion. I must have looked very vulnerable and small, standing there in my tux, all by myself, until, like an afterthought, my grandfather ran up to join me. I didn't even have a speech ready, so all I said was, "I want to thank my director and my father."

That's how I became the youngest Academy Award winner in history.

Afterward, my grandparents took me back to their Pacific Palisades home. We didn't have a party or do anything special to celebrate. Peter called to say, "Good job, Tatee," and later sent me flowers. I phoned my father to tell him I'd won, and he said, "I knew it, kid. I knew you could do it."

Talking to the press, he would add drama to our exchange, claiming he told me that the Oscar was pure gold but that I corrected him, saying, "I think it's bronze."

It was as if he suddenly saw that there was cachet in having an Academy Award–winning daughter. He put my Oscar on display on top of his TV. In years to come, he would publicly play up my achievement, as well as his own role in it. Often, I would buy into and contribute to the mythology that sprung up around us as an inseparable father-and-daughter team.

At the time, however, I had little sense of accomplishment. There was no fanfare from anyone who mattered to me, so the pride and self-worth I might have gained from what most people would consider a life-defining honor was leached away. The feeling I associate most with winning the Oscar is an overwhelming sadness at being abandoned by my parents—both of them, for my mother remained silent—one more time.

My only defense against that terrible sadness was forgetting. But forgiving was harder.

SIX

The Bet

THE ACADEMY AWARD did make an impression at the Ojai Valley School, where I wound up once again. Although I continued to endure my old nickname "Mutat"—*Tatum* backward—I now had a new one: "Oscar." The popularity I'd gained after the release of *Paper Moon* skyrocketed for a while. On a little-girl level, the lesson was clear: to make friends you didn't have to be empathetic or even charming and fun. All it took was fame.

The realization made me a little cynical and even more mistrustful than before. My experience in England had also taken a heavy toll. Without understanding how, I believed that I'd turned my father against me. Winning the award seemed to cost me whatever was left of his goodwill. My image of myself as a "great little girl"—a spunky, talented, at least somewhat lovable child—had started to shatter. I now felt flawed, essentially unlikable, unable to trust myself—and much more tentative and uneasy in the world. Even my posture changed. I started walking sort of stoop shouldered, hunched over protectively.

I did have a few things going for me, though: enough intelligence to find my way in the world, even without the comfort and guidance of parents; an innate honesty, giving me a pretty infallible bullshit detector; the nerve to fight; and a compulsive urge to question, to find out exactly where I stood. "What do you mean by that? Explain it. Tell me what you mean," I was always demanding. It was the only way I could learn. I think I picked that trait up from Sue Mengers, my agent—a heavy-duty woman, if there ever was one—who was always fierce enough to pin people down.

These were the skills that enabled me to survive.

I WOULD ATTEND Ojai Valley School, on and off, for the next few years. Eventually I settled in and even enjoyed it a little, though I was never keen on the constraints. But when my Oscar glow wore off, I became an outcast again. I was too insecure—and too much of a loner—ever to feel completely comfortable around other children.

I always envied the kids whose parents sent them care packages of candy and cookies. One day, a bunch of girls lured me to a dorm room to share their loot and began viciously bad-mouthing Carrie. Still stung by the way my father had favored her in England, I started bashing her too—only to have her jump out of the closet, furious, to confront me. It was a setup. I was mortified.

When the school staged *The Wizard of Oz,* I was embarrassed even more publicly. I had only one line: "She'll be black when she's white and white when she's black"—something to do with the witch. As an Oscar winner, I felt saddled with a huge burden of expectations, and I got so flustered that I could barely speak. Everyone laughed mercilessly.

Always a mischief maker, I used to chew huge wads of gum and stick them under the desks. For some infraction like that, a teacher slapped me in the face, a punishment I could never tolerate. I ran away from school, only to be picked up a few hours later in Ojai Village. I became desperate to escape for good.

Then one day in 1975, I got a welcome call from Sue Mengers. She was a force of nature, with a booming voice and a powerful delivery. "Hello, hello, hello," she began, as usual. "Got a picture for you, kid. You're coming back."

IT WAS *The Bad News Bears,* the story of a painfully inept Little League team coached by an alcoholic former Major Leaguer, Morris Buttermaker (Walter Matthau) who now made his living cleaning swimming pools. Every man of a certain age I meet tells me how much he loved that movie—that it was a major milestone of his youth. Quentin Tarantino owns a film print of it (as well as one of *Paper Moon*) and claims that he can recite every line. He has called it his favorite movie of all time.

In it, I play Amanda Whurlitzer, the pitching-ace daughter of Buttermaker's ex-girlfriend, whom he recruits to save the team. It's a motley crew of foul-mouthed kids described by one of them as "a buncha Jews, spics, niggers, pansies, and a booger-eatin' moron!" The only other decent player around is Kelly Leak (Jackie Earle Haley), a juvenile delinquent type who smokes and rides a Harley and helps out in a crunch.

On *Paper Moon,* I made $16,000 (Paramount grossed close to $50 million), but now the stakes were different. My fee was $350,000, plus a percentage of the profits, the highest ever paid to a child actor at the time. I would have to earn it.

To begin with, I had to learn how to pitch. Every day for three months, I'd be driven out to a field in Chadwick, where I would train with a major-league pitcher whose name escapes me. I have a pretty high degree of natural athletic ability, and eventually I got quite good. Most of the pitching in the film is actually mine. But training was easy compared to the challenge of throwing pitches over and over, in the sweltering summer heat, while wearing an itchy, tight woolen uniform during the shoot.

In between takes, there was no slacking off because now there were new laws governing the treatment of child actors. On the set I had to have a tutor to school me daily for three hours. My teacher was a short, stocky blonde who had bad breath and wore skin-tight jeans, cowboy boots, and frosted lipstick on chapped lips. I'd sit with her in my trailer struggling to concentrate. I hated her even more than I hated math.

The shoot itself was very different from what I'd experienced on *Paper Moon*. Peter Bogdanovich was a strong, hands-on, instinctual director who worked with actors like a collaborator. A former actor himself, he knew how to use gestures and expressions to convey emotion and would sometimes play them out, to demonstrate. Through a series of little actions, he could help you build a character, drawing on your own expressive powers. But Michael Ritchie, the director of *The Bad News Bears*, was much more focused on the broad strokes—the story line, the scene mechanics—than the specifics of a performance. Most of the time, I felt left to my own devices to figure out where to stand, how to carry myself, and how to interact with the other characters.

At that point, I had no formal training as an actor—not even a class in basic technique. I had a certain smart-alecky feistiness in common with Amanda, but nothing like the emotional resonance I'd felt with Addie. The role didn't come as naturally, and with Michael's sketchier direction, I had a tough time puzzling it out.

To make matters worse, there were studio executives on the set. Stanley Jaffe, the producer, often came to observe. He once told me that, to relax, he would sit in a full bathtub and then watch the water run out. I tried it, but it didn't work for me. I was feeling the pressure.

All the other kids in the cast were professionals, many trained by top acting coaches in New York. It was obvious that they knew what they were doing, which made me feel my inexperience more acutely. And most of them had another big advantage I lacked: a parent hovering around to give them moral support.

One day I did get a visit from Griffin and my mother. She had remarried and was living on Bolas Street in the Chatsworth section of L.A., and we were back in touch. When they arrived on the set, I was eating an ice-cream cone. I offered it to Griffin. "Do you want a lick?"

"Yeah," he said.

I shoved it in his face. I'll never forgive myself for that. It's a measure of how off balance I was—so impatient with myself about the acting, so frustrated by Michael's directing style, so eaten up with anxiety because so much was riding on my success, and so isolated, with nowhere to turn for nurturing and help. I'm told that, around this time, the press nicknamed me "Tantrum." I did act out—I was ten-going-on-eleven, I was overwhelmed, and recent events in my life had left me angry and belligerent.

But the movie wound up being fun. I enjoyed hanging out with some of the guys who played my teammates, and I totally adored Walter Matthau. His character in the movie was a big, lumbering bear, and Walter was like that too, only warmer, in real life. In our scenes together, he really boosted my confidence, and he wound up being a wonderful father figure/friend.

I also loved his wife, Carol, who was my favorite kind of woman—ultrafeminine, with pale, perfect makeup, pink lipstick, and a lyrical voice. She'd been the original inspiration for Holly Golightly in *Breakfast at Tiffany's*. She gave me a copy of her book, *The Secret in the Daisy,* which was a fictionalized account of her rags-to-riches childhood. I also grew quite close to Lucy, Carol's daughter with William Saroyan, an actress who was dating her actual godfather, Marlon Brando.

When we finished shooting *The Bad News Bears,* I felt a huge sense of accomplishment. It was my movie, made by me alone, not in my father's shadow but under my own steam. It had been hard, but I could see that the final product was great. That made me proud.

AROUND THE TIME I was making *The Bad News Bears,* I was invited to appear on a new comedy show hosted by Cher. My whole life, I've had huge adoration for very stylish, divalike women—hold that sad little photo of me as a child on crutches up to an image of one of my silky-haired, elegantly turned-out idols, and you can see why. Still, Cher was in a class apart. She was probably the ultimate high-powered, high-fashion diva of the time.

In one sketch on the show, I got the thrill of playing Cher herself, decked out in a flowing wig, platform sandals, and a sequined gown. I fell totally in love with Cher—not in a sexual way, of course, but with a desperate hunger for her attention, as in "Please take over my life. Let me be like you."

As soon I finished with *The Bad News Bears*, I embarked on an intense campaign to win her over. I called all the time and literally camped on the doorstep of her mansion right off Carrollwood Drive, next door to Jayne Mansfield's former home. I implied that I had nowhere else to go, which wasn't quite true. My father had bought a house in Beverly Hills, where I was staying with a babysitter. Once I even conspired with my half-brother Patrick to pretend that I'd fainted and there was no one he could call but Cher.

Cher took it all with remarkable good humor. She even let me live at her house for a few weeks. It was heaven! Her daughter, Chastity Bono, was around sometimes, but she was so much younger that I never really played with her. All I wanted to do was to hang out with Cher.

Cher got her nails done every other day. We went shopping at Theodore on Rodeo Drive, where she bought one of everything. All her clothes were brand-new, with the tags still on them. She had the same shirt in every color. I was blown away.

My room was way down the hall from the master suite,

where Cher slept in a huge grand bed. Hating as usual to be shut out, I once knocked on her door, insisting that I had to see her. She came out stark naked. "What are you doing here?" she said, angrily enough that I never did it again.

Instead, I started to create havoc with other people, out of jealousy. Cher was close to Raquel Welch, who was appearing on the show. I told Cher that I'd overheard Raquel complaining that she hated her segment and that Cher was terrible in it. That caused a big rift between them for a while. Raquel wound up hating me, and so did David Geffen, who at the time was Cher's lover.

I was with Cher the night that she met Gregg Allman. I have a picture of us at the Troubadour, the club where he was playing. I'm wearing a little satin jacket, and she's all Cher'd out, looking spectacular, in a hat. When I realized she was falling in love with him, I took the drastic step of confiding that I'd seen him shooting heroin—having no idea what *that* was—in her house.

"Oh, he's a big drug addict," I told Cher.

He wasn't, but Cher believed me for a while—I was that good a liar. They wound up getting married, and needless to say, Gregg joined the long list of people in Cher's life who disliked me for years.

But Cher forgave my troublemaking. After dislodging me from her house, she would still take me on outings, picking me up in her fabulous light blue Ferrari. I started to obsess about cars after that, picturing myself in all the fastest, latest-model Jaguars, though it would be years before I could legally drive. I wanted a fur coat too—and all the other trappings of glamorous, powerful womanhood. Of Cher-hood. Through it all, Cher was very kind to me.

———

BARRY LYNDON WAS SLATED for release at Christmas 1975, and *The Bad News Bears* would follow a few months later, in April 1976. One hot summer day my father and I were speeding down the Pacific Coast Highway in his beige Rolls-Royce, with the top down and the radio blaring something like the Allman Brothers or Ry Cooder. The conversation turned to our soon-to be-released movies, and he brought up the hit comedy he'd made with Barbra Streisand in the early 1970s.

"Do you think *The Bad News Bears* will be as big as *What's Up, Doc?*" he asked.

"Definitely," I told him.

"Well, then, which picture is going to do better—*The Bad News Bears* or *Barry Lyndon*?"

"*The Bad News Bears* is going to make a ton of money," I insisted.

"I'll bet you a lot of money that *Barry Lyndon* beats it."

I took the bet.

Barry Lyndon was released that December. Its three-hour running time and low-key emotion discouraged a lot of moviegoers and even some major critics (like Pauline Kael of *The New Yorker,* who called it "an ice-pack of a movie"). When *The Bad News Bears* came out in the spring, it struck such a chord with young male baby boomers that it far outstripped *Barry Lyndon* at the box office. So I won hands down.

This time I didn't need Vivian to remind me of my father's reaction. He punched me. It didn't look like our relationship, which began to erode so badly in England, was due to get better anytime soon.

SEVEN

Dear Fanny

FANNY, THIS IS MY first day writing, so I'm going to say a lot. First of all, I am doing a movie. It is called Nicelodian. *I think that's how you spell it. . . .*

Yesterday they chopped all my hair off. It looks awful. But I guess if Peter wants it for the movie, I had better do it. . . .

My dad is in a great mood. I hope he stays that way. . . .

Almost as soon as I could write I started keeping a journal, which I named Fanny, inspired by *The Diary of Anne Frank*. I wrote to Fanny nearly every day, sometimes adding little sketches and, after my kids were born, pasting in cute or funny pictures of them. By now my diary is dozens of note-books long. Some of them are sad to leaf through, especially the ones from the chaotic years after my father's return from England.

Apart from a few stretches at boarding school, I was living with him, both in Malibu and at our Beverly Hills home at 9897 Beverly Grove Drive. It was a Spanish-style mansion, with a sundial on the patio, that had once belonged to John Barrymore.

After *The Bad News Bears*, my dad hired a babysitter to look after me, Sabrina Guinness, of the Guinness beer family. She was in her early twenties, and I liked her because she wasn't big on rules. She once crashed my father's Rolls-Royce with me in it. I was okay, but as I noted in my diary, she had "semi-whiplash."

Sabrina's favorite thing to do was take me to rock stars' houses, where she liked to hang out. I'd get tired of sitting around and do crazy things. One day, when we were over at Rod Stewart's house, I recorded, *This really weird thing happened. A fire started. It was really strange because it wasn't from electricity. . . .*

In fact, I knew exactly how the fire had started. I had set it, out of boredom. Since my father read my diary—despite my note on the opening page, demanding that he stop—I couldn't be entirely candid with Fanny.

Another time, Britt Ekland was with Rod when we were visiting, and when she wanted to go home, I stole her shoe so she couldn't leave. I guess I needed attention. It was a weird period and I was feeling very lost.

THOSE YEARS WERE a blur of crazy Hollywood parties. My agent Sue Mengers's were legendary, and all the top actors would come: Clint Eastwood, Michael Caine, Jack Nicholson, and Robert De Niro. I remember sitting on the floor one night and noticing that Robert De Niro's wife wasn't wearing any underwear. Sue would be working the room, puffing a joint like it was a cigarette, and breaking in on people's conversations: "Hello! I'm talking here!"

I was always amazed at how aggressive she was.

At one dinner, I was seated next to Woody Allen, and he scolded me. "You have to stop doing that!"

"Doing what?"

"You're scratching it. You're making this noise. You're scratching the fork!"

All I could say was, "Oops—sorry!" I was so embarrassed.

Most of the time, though, I'm sure people saw me as a crazy little thing who was too young to be so up front and challenging. God forbid you had a funny expression on your face, because I'd say, "What's that look for?" I had no edit button.

I was always watching the adults around me and judging them, wondering how I was going to be, what I would turn into. My diary is filled with critical observations: *A lot of the people were drunk—it wasn't the greatest party. . . . My dad and I went to Goldie Hawn's—it was so boring I could not believe it. . . . This party we went to last night—about 3 million stars were there: John Denver sang. Frank Sinatra sang. Diana Ross sang about fourteen songs, but after the third one she put me to sleep. Barbra and Jon were there. Barbra has got this new haircut. It looks awful. She is with such a putz it's unbelievable but if he makes her happy, I guess that's all that counts . . .*

It was at a party for the American Film Institute tribute to John Ford that I met Dustin Hoffman for the first time. I fell madly in love with him. He had a ballet-dancer wife and a child, but I felt sure that someday we were destined to be together. I even wrote him a song, which Griffin makes fun of to this day:

Dusty, where's your heart?
Do you know that mine's right with you?
Can't you see how I'm mesmerized by your smile?
I look through eyes, which think you're mighty wise.
Doesn't that mean anything to you?
Oh, why do I dig you? . . .

Inevitably, my partygoing drew a lot of attention from the press, which began to characterize me as a wild child who was growing up too fast. The stories picked up momentum after my appearance at the *Tommy* premiere, wearing my sequined gown from the Cher show and glitter on my eyes, with my short hair. Around the time of *Nickelodeon,* I got a cover story in *Newsweek,* headlined "Tatum! The Hollywood Kid." By then I knew what publicity could cost me, and I wrote: *It's a great article. I'm just a little worried. The whole thing is about me, and I think my dad might be a little jealous. I feel sad about that . . . my dad is in a bad mood tonight.*

MY WHOLE WORLD REVOLVED around my father's volatile moods. He was doing a lot of drugs and was arrested for possession of marijuana after a police raid on the Barrymore house. He would sleep away half the day while I tiptoed around, scared to wake him and rouse his temper. When we were making *Nickelodeon,* he stayed holed up in the hotel or his trailer. It was a very difficult shoot.

Nickelodeon was Peter's tribute to the early movie business, with some echoes of the career of D.W. Griffith. My father played a lawyer-turned-writer-turned-director, shooting a series of silent films in a tiny desert town. His leading man was Burt Reynolds, Jane Hitchcock was the love interest, and I played a crew member/odd job helper/bit actor in the movies-within-the-movie. I even learned to sing and tap-dance for the picture.

The movie was a comedy, but there was little humor on the set. I remember that Burt and my father once raced their cars to Vasquez Rock, with my father driving 150 miles an hour.

But that was a bright spot. A lot of the time, the members of the cast weren't talking to one another.

We were shooting near Modesto, which was hot and desolate and poor. I was reading *Of Mice and Men,* and being in a setting so similar to Steinbeck's just broke my heart. I remember crying a lot. I was also upset by the way we were treating animals on the set of *Nickelodeon.* There was ostrich riding and trip wires for horses—things that are no longer allowed. It was as if my heart was really open, and I was very strongly affected by anything sad or disturbing.

I was forced to study for three hours each day with a tutor and—just my luck—got the little blond lady again from *The Bad News Bears.* I'd sit there in my trailer, staring at her teeth, waiting miserably for the door to open, hoping to be called back to the set. Though I read books constantly throughout my entire life, no one had ever encouraged me to go to school. I didn't understand the value of it. I just had to endure it, supposedly for my own good.

Once again, Diane Lewis was my guardian on the set. She wore hard contact lenses, which made me curious. I tried them on and got one stuck in the back of my eye. So, for one night, my father was forced out of his seclusion in the hotel while I was rushed to the hospital to have it taken out. I had scratched my cornea.

The only other time I remember seeing him was when we were working. Then he was always angry and belittling, and I was really defenseless. I wrote in my diary:

My dad makes fun of me the whole day. Then every time my dad yells at me, Peter puts in his two cents. That adds up to be about twelve dollars. They don't think I have any feelings.

Another time I confided to Fanny that I cried on the set

because Peter scolded me in front of everyone for being fat, telling me not to finish the sandwich I was eating. I was so unhappy that I started acting out, arguing and fighting all the time. Peter finally took me aside to warn me that I was getting too difficult to work with, that people disliked me on the set. I listened and, for the most part, started behaving myself.

Recently Peter reminded me of a time when I was helpful. There was a lot of slapstick in the movie—rolling around, jumping, doing pratfalls—and Burt Reynolds was always getting hurt. He kept messing up a scene with me sitting on his shoulders until he finally told Peter, "No more takes. This is killing me. I hate Modesto, and I've had it with this movie."

Peter asked me to do him a favor—if the take didn't work, to claim that I had screwed it up. So when Burt messed up again, I insisted that I had blown it. Burt accepted that and kept going till we got it right. So I saved the day.

Burt was usually wonderful, and I developed a little crush on him, but I really loved John Ritter. *Nickelodeon* was his movie debut. He used to zip me around in his little Karmann Ghia and taught me to drive a stick shift on the lot. He would do impressions of lots of funny, made-up characters, like the Mad Humper, a guy standing near the side of a building, looking furtively around as he humps the wall with these little, subtle thrusts. It was hilarious. John was one of the most brilliant and generous young actors I have ever met—a really magical human being.

NICKELODEON, THOUGH A very good movie, was a flop, which made life with my father even tougher. He smoked

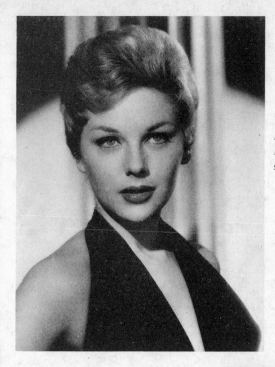

My beautiful mom's
Hollywood studio head
shot, circa 1950s.

My mom, Dorothy Cook
(aka Joanna Moore),
around age eleven in
Americus, Georgia.

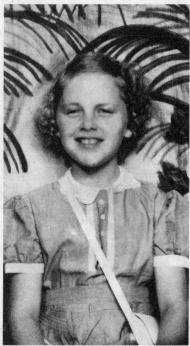

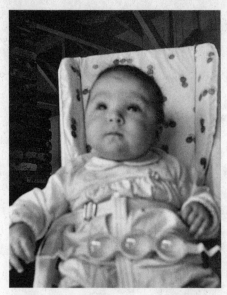

Baby Tatum, 1963. Encino, California.

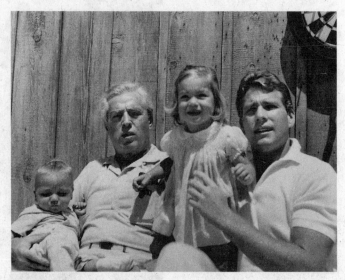

The O'Neals in 1964 (left to right): baby Griffin; Grandpa
(Charles "Blackie" O'Neal); me; my dad, Ryan. *On Sabana
Lane, Encino, California.*

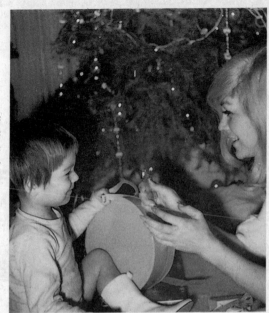

Me and mom on Christmas morning, 1964. Check out my groovy white patent leather go-go boots and my mom's ever-present wig and false eyelashes.

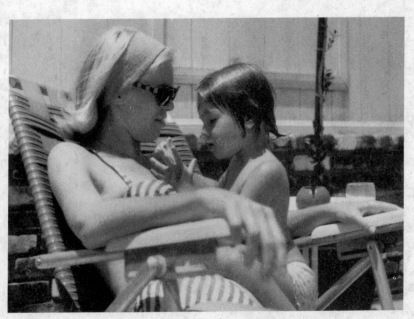

Mom and me in better times.

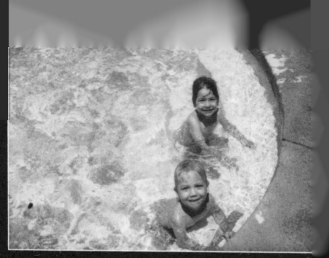

My brother Griffin and me in our pool on Sabana Lane, 196

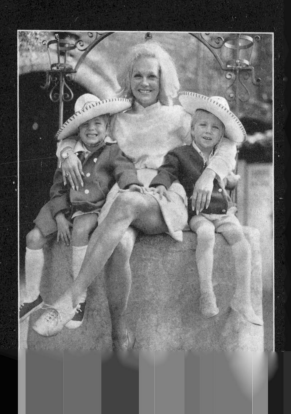

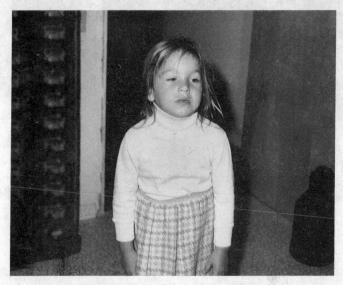

Shortly after my parents' separation,
here I am at home looking somewhat forlorn.

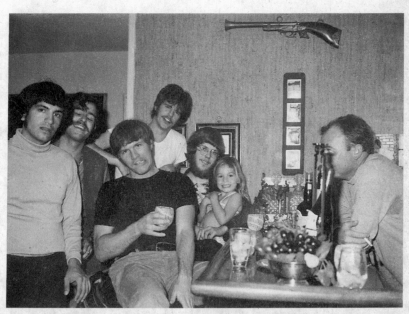

Where is my mom? That's me in the middle in our living room in 1967.
Check out the gun on the wall.

A letter that I wrote to my mother after one of her drinking binges.
The words speak for themselves. I was probably six years old. So sad.

From Tatum

I hope you get Beter
mommy I Dont kere
if yoy Spak me From tatur
to mommy

Love

YOU

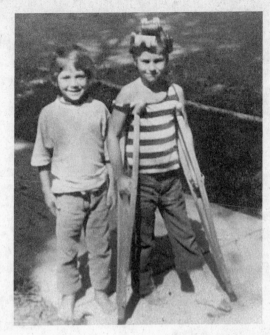

What a pair we make: Griffin's zipper is down, my hair is in rollers, and I'm on crutches after having fallen off the roof at a neighbor's house in Reseda.

Look how little Griffin is. Here we are in 1972 at the ticket counter at the go-cart park in Reseda. I'm mad.

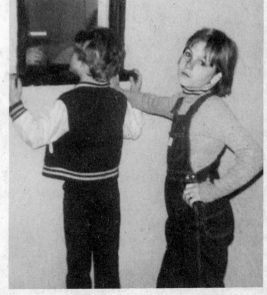

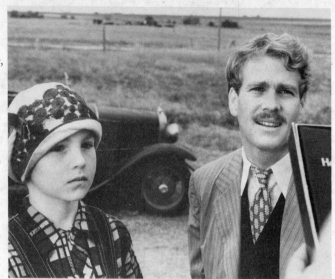

Selling bibles, 1973, on location in Kansas for Paper Moon. *People have always said I had a pretty mean stare.*
PHOTOGRAPH BY STEVE SHAPIRO

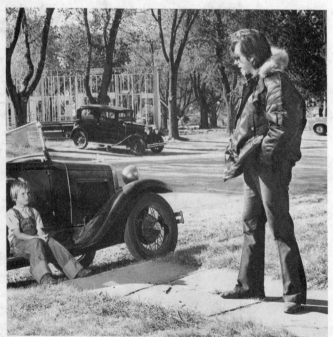

On location for Paper Moon *with director Peter Bogdanovich, who is trying to get me to do something it looks like I don't want to do.*
PHOTOGRAPH BY STEVE SCHAPIRO

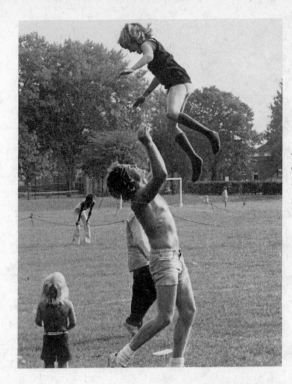

Age inappropriate. Me and dad in Hyde Park, London, England.

PHOTOGRAPH BY STEVE SCHAPIRO

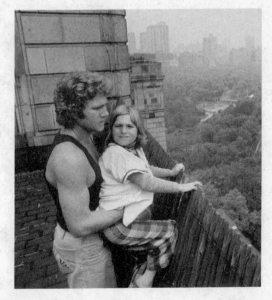

A happy time with my dad. Here we are looking out over Central Park in New York City, 1974.

© CORBIS

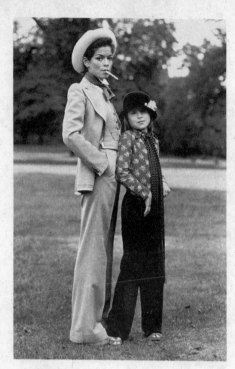

My absolute "style guru,"
Bianca Jagger, back in the
day wearing her suit by
Yves Saint Laurent.
Her look inspired me to
wear a tiny tuxedo to the
Academy Awards.

There I am winning
the Academy Award.
I never told anyone
that neither of my
parents attended.

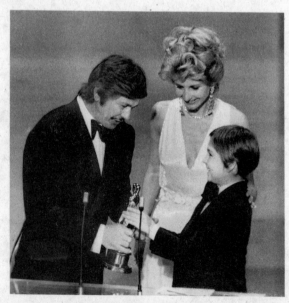

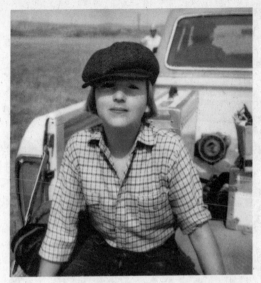

On the set of Nickelodeon, a really great movie that no one saw. 1977. I was twelve years old.

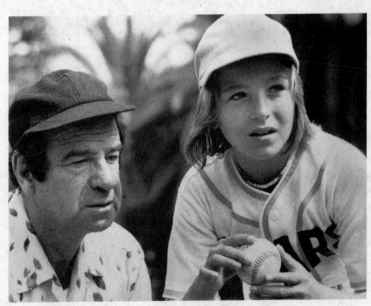

Could I have loved working with an actor any more than this guy, Walter Matthau? One of the greatest. (Check out the puka shells.)

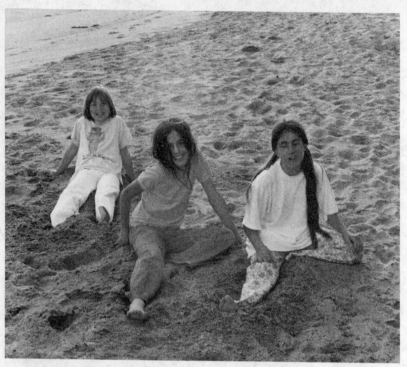

*Happy times. Me and my best friends on the beach in Malibu.
That's me on the left, Maria Dylan is in the middle,
and Monique Lavoie is on the right.*

PHOTOGRAPH BY STEPHEN JAFFE

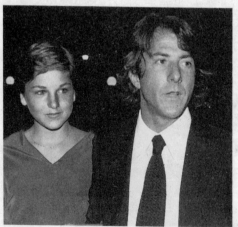

*My big first crush: Me
and Dustin Hoffman
at an awards show in
Hollywood.*

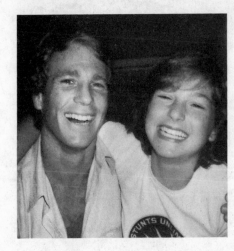

Proof! Yes, there were some really good times.

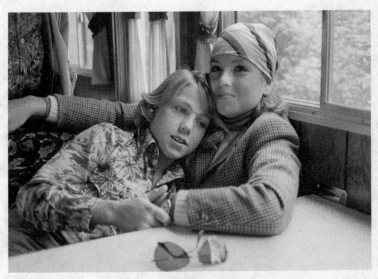

Griffin and I consoling each other during a break on the set of International Velvet *in England.*

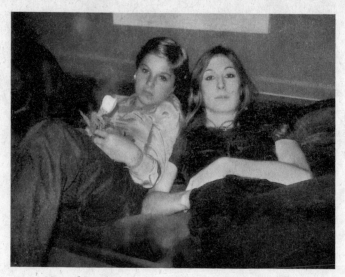

*Me and Anjelica Huston at Blake's Hotel in London.
I was twelve years old.*

Right: *At a photo
booth in England:
me and my new
best friend, Vivien
Kubrick, daughter
of Stanley, my
alltime favorite
director.*

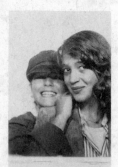

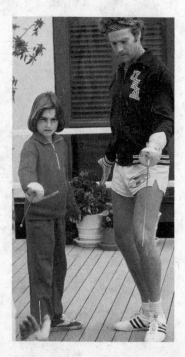

Far right: *Helping
my dad learn to
fence during the
making of* Barry
Lyndon. *Not happy.*
PHOTOGRAPH BY STEVE
SCHAPIRO

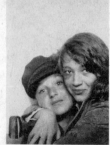

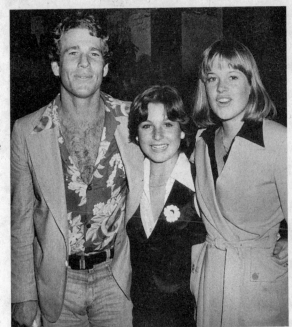

My father, me, and Melanie Griffith at the Palm Restaurant in Los Angeles, February 20, 1977.

PHOTOGRAPH BY RON GALLELA

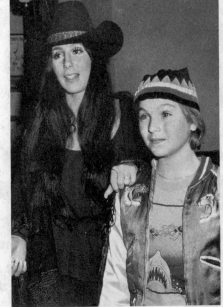

So desperate for a mother figure. My hero, Cher.

PHOTOGRAPH BY RON GALELLA

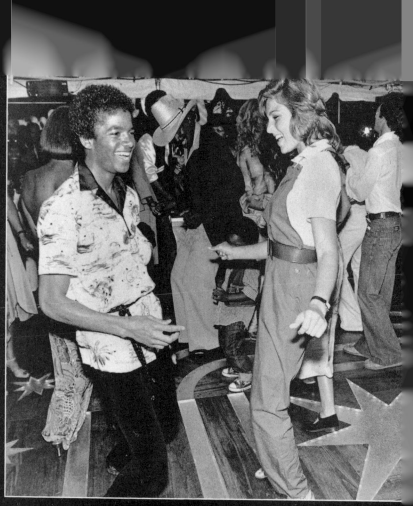

Dancing with Michael Jackson in 1979. I would say he was the better dancer.

grass all day long and was constantly belittling me. "Look at your hair," he'd say. He'd always make me cut it short, though I hated looking like a boy. I could never figure that out. It was as if he wanted me to be androgynous. He would tell me that when I smiled I looked like I smelled something funny. Unnerved, I grew increasingly self-conscious.

Yet we continued to appear as a unit on the Hollywood social scene. I needed him and hung on his erratic spurts of affection. If he resented my natural, preadolescent need for his love—which he called my "very strong jealousy syndrome"—he reinforced it and seemed to thrive on it.

At the same time, his womanizing became even more compulsive. Women were always coming through our houses, where the very air grew erotically charged. I'd see my father and his dates French-kissing and hear them have sex—both riveting and repellent for a prepubescent child. Afterward, he'd often be cruel to the women, kicking them out, putting them in cabs in the middle of the night—and sometimes literally kicking them. I remember shaking with fear hearing my father scream at Anouk Aimée while hitting her over the head with a pillow.

Sometimes I felt sorry for my father's women, but it was hard not to feel contempt for the one-night stands who kept calling and trying to see him again. I was his daughter, so it was impossible for me to escape being emotionally entangled with him. But these were free agents, adult women, actively chasing a man who was obviously using them—who didn't even like them, never mind love them—and who had a mile-wide abusive streak. "Don't you get it?" I'd want to scream. "Tomorrow he'll just send you home with the maid."

A few of these women had staying power. I was drawn to

one of them for my usual reasons, her glamour and sophistication and my yearning for a surrogate mother. She would let me experiment with her makeup and try on her beautiful clothes. One night she got really high—everyone in my father's circle did drugs—and we started playing dress up, trying on little nighties together. Then, as we kissed and held each other, she started fondling me.

I didn't know how to react or feel, especially when she murmured, "I wish I had a penis." Maybe I was caught up in that classic abuse syndrome of pleasure, guilt, and fear, compounded by living in such a highly sexualized environment. For the most part, though, I saw the experience as a kind of feminine involvement—the motherly glow I was always looking for. If the woman hadn't been stoned, I doubt that our encounter would have turned sexual, and I'm sure that she deeply regrets it today. But now—and even back then—it was just one more sign of how wildly out of control my life with my father was spinning.

The whirlwind picked up speed when my father hooked up with Anjelica Huston, who was living with Jack Nicholson, another famous ladies' man. Though Jack was cheating on her, it was still a major Hollywood drama when she left him for my father. Then, after Anjelica moved in with us, there was an even bigger crisis when Roman Polanksi allegedly drugged and raped a thirteen-year-old girl at Jack's house while he was out of town. Polanski was arrested and, faced with jail time or deportation, fled to Paris. So we were at the center of that storm too.

Anjelica became another one of my role model/idols. She was the daughter of John Huston, one of Hollywood's greatest directors, and an Italian ballerina, Enrica Soma, who died in a car accident when Anjelica was in her teens. Anjelica was ultrathin, with dramatic smoky eyes, and, like all my idols, stylish in a maverick way—what I thought of as a European look. She had in fact gone to a French school in London and spoke several languages. She was also a talented artist and poet.

So, of course, I didn't want to be my little, scrappy, San Fernando Valley limited self anymore. I wanted to be Anjelica—someone who'd lived in castles in Ireland and could draw perfectly and had rings on her fingers and bracelets up her arms and great shoes and all sorts of perfumes; and who'd lived with Jack, who had a romantic tragedy in her past, who was nicknamed Toots, and had a whole grown-up, sophisticated existence.

Drugs were definitely an element of that existence. Anjelica became the official joint roller in our household because she was the best at it. Conflict was also an element. There were a lot of screaming matches between Anjelica and my father. I would hear him harassing her, tearing up her diaries, as I cried myself to sleep.

YET, AS TURBULENT and frightening as life with my father could be, he was the devil I knew. My mother was more of a mystery. I visited her occasionally on Bolas Street in West L.A.—not a very good neighborhood—and observed what she'd do and wear and even eat, weird country combinations like apples with salt and cheese or salted grapefruit and watermelon. She and Gary, her husband, who was a roofing contractor, were members of an evangelistic religious sect. Griffin had to go to Bible study classes at Pat Boone's house. Once, around the time of *Paper Moon,* I got a serious blast of her religion when she started speaking in tongues and beating the hell out of me.

So my mother was nothing like the fashionable, worldly, and independent women I found so inspiring. Today I respect and deeply love her, though I'm saddened by what she made of her life. But back then, I was very confused, writing a bit melodramatically in my diary, *God, how I love her!* while wishing for a mother who was more like the Bianca-Cher-Anjelica kind of woman I hoped to be.

I was also a little afraid of her. I heard about her mainly when there was some new crisis involving her or Griffin—and there were plenty. One day Griffin fell off his bike on Gary's job site, landing in the hospital because a stake went straight up his rectum. That was terrible. However, the main problem was my mother's alcoholism. She was constantly drunk—Gary left her because of it—and poor Griffin was losing his mind.

He would tape-record her when she was drunk. Once she caught him at it and chased him all over the house till he jumped out the window to escape. She climbed out after him, knocking her wig half off, and went lunging down the street, shouting, "Goddamnit, I'm gonna kill you, Griffin."

Griffin was becoming the neighborhood menace, spray painting obscene words on the sidewalk and running hoses into people's mail slots, flooding their houses while they were out of town. He once threw an ax over a fence, narrowly missing someone in a yard. He'd steal my mother's car when he was still so small that he had to sit on phone books to drive it. I hated hearing those stories. I was already living in a madhouse with my father.

THE LAST PIECE in the crazy collage of my life was school, which I couldn't avoid forever. I'd switched to yet another place, New Dimensions, which a lot of Beverly Hills kids attended. Carrie was there, and I made some new lifelong friends, Esme Gray (named for the character in J. D. Salinger's short story "For Esmé—With Love and Squalor") and Andrea Feldstein, who lived in Jack Benny's old house, which we all thought was really cool. I started reading a lot, but my main association with that phase of my education is drugs. Everyone—all my fellow students and their parents—seemed to be getting high.

I'd grown up around drugs, of course, and always hated seeing my parents impaired. Now, though, I wanted to experiment myself. So one day when I had a girlfriend over, I turned to the most obvious source of drugs—my father—and asked, "Can we try some grass?"

He gave us a joint, and we lit it up sitting on my bed. After a couple of tokes, we were hysterical with laughter. So that was why people liked smoking marijuana—it was fun. Before too long I had my own little stash and was smoking every day. And becoming a pretty bad student—what a shock!

Then there was a tragedy at school. A kid named Brent Weinberg, whose father had dated Elizabeth Taylor at one time, died in a Jeep accident on Laurel Canyon that was drug-related. That sort of put a damper on things for me. So I asked my father if I could drop out of school.

Partly I just wanted out, but I could also very easily see myself sliding in the same direction. To my relief, he said yes.

EIGHT

A Bridge Too Far

I MET MELANIE GRIFFITH at Hugh Hefner's house, which wasn't exactly a place where teenagers hung out. The only reason I was there at age twelve was that my father had dragged me along. The scene bored me, and I used to watch movies, eat candy, and play video games while he and his pals chatted up the ladies.

So it was great to encounter someone at least close to my own age—Melanie was eighteen—who was also an actress, with several movies to her credit. She, like me, came from a Hollywood family, and was named for Melanie Daniels, the character her mother, Tippi Hedren, played in the Alfred Hitchcock classic *The Birds*. For a young girl always on the lookout for mentors, she was magnetic. Yes, I dreamed of becoming Cher, Bianca, or Anjelica, but they were adults and more exotic than I could imagine myself getting to be anytime soon. Melanie belonged to my own generation and had a girl-next-door, incredibly sweet, and feminine brand of glamour. So she became an ideal role model—and better yet, a friend.

I never had a lot of friends my own age, and the few I did have inhabited a different universe. They were kids, consumed with school and boys, not with making movies, doing publicity, and earning a living. Finding a semipeer like Melanie, who walked my walk and spoke my language, was like stumbling on an oasis in the desert. She wrote me lovely, little friendly notes and was tremendously loving and kind—which was rare for me, so I ate it up. And she could drive. I wound up going with her to her auditions, growing close, and also becoming extremely clingy.

Young as she was, Melanie had established an independent life, having moved in with her rising-star boyfriend, Don Johnson (then in his twenties), at the age of fourteen. With that relationship in eclipse, she'd been linked to Hollywood's most eligible bachelors, including Warren Beatty, Jack Nicholson, and Harrison Ford. It bothered me that Melanie was involved with so many men, but at the same time I admired it. She seemed like such a free spirit. So far my own crushes played out only in my mind and in my diary, but I looked forward to the day when I'd have my own passionate romances with a string of brilliantly talented lovers.

I should have guessed that Melanie's string would include my father.

I DIDN'T QUITE CATCH on until we all went to Europe together, during what must have been some school vacation. My father was making *A Bridge Too Far,* a World War II epic set in Holland, with Richard Attenborough. We set off in a group that included my father, Melanie, me, the ever-present Joe Amsler, his old friend Greg, and "Gavin," a drug dealer who seemed to be around a lot. Before going through customs, my father shoved a packet at me. "Here, Tatum, stick this in your boot."

In Amsterdam, we toured the famous red-light district, where prostitutes posed half naked in the windows, showing off their wares. One night we took in a sex show. No one seemed to question whether this was an inappropriate—possibly even upsetting—spectacle for a young adolescent. But then, no one seemed to be thinking of me at all. Something about the movie was making my father miserable, and he was self-absorbed and angry.

However, what disturbed me even more was Melanie. She seemed distant, not interested in being with me, though I believed she was traveling with us as my companion. She started to disappear for long stretches, which left me feeling painfully rejected. Desperate to know what was going on—and dreading the truth—I did something intrusive. I got a key to my father's room. When I unlocked the door, I found exactly what I feared—Melanie was in bed, having sex, with my father.

It was a huge betrayal. Nothing hurt me more than being shut out by my father with his she-can-come-in-but-you-can't game. I always felt I was being taunted. Abandonment wasn't something I could cope with either, having been left to fend for myself so much of my life. That someone I trusted so much—and I wasn't big on trust—whom I considered my best friend, would choose my father over me just freaked me out. I loved Melanie, absolutely adored her, even idolized her. Now, this seemed like proof that she'd never really cared about me and that my famous father—one more Hollywood-heavyweight lover—had been her target all along.

I was so devastated that I felt ready to die, literally. I couldn't see a thing to live for at all. I went back to my room and stood by the window, imagining what it would be like to jump. The ground below looked very far away. Grabbing a pillow, I threw it out the window as sort of a trial run. As I watched it fall, though, I knew I couldn't jump. I was too afraid.

Then I broke a glass and started slicing at my arms, having heard that you could die by slitting your wrists. I made big gory slashes, but I didn't bleed to death.

That failure left me even more depressed, and I decided that pills might be the answer. Since I didn't have any, I went to see Joe. "Give me your drugs," I demanded.

He refused. I kept begging to no avail, growing almost hysterical. Finally I had to rifle his minibar and steal some little bottles of liquor. I didn't feel too good after downing them, but I wasn't dead yet.

So I headed to Gavin's room. In retrospect, my actions seem almost farcical, except for the fact that I was truly determined to die. There was still no sign of Melanie or my father, and no one put much effort into stopping my self-destructive spree. I suppose they thought I was trying to get attention— and I probably was—but I was serious too. My arms were clotted with blood, and I was out of my mind with misery.

When I asked Gavin for drugs, he said okay and gave me some cocaine and a handful of pills, which I washed down with booze from his minibar. I must have passed out then. When I came to, I was in bed—not in my own, but in Gavin's. I was naked, and he was touching me.

It was like something inside me just shriveled up in horror. I can't even remember how I got away from Gavin, dressed myself, and made it back to my own room—physically sick from the pills and booze but suffering more with the psychic hangover. When my father saw the condition I was in, he went crazy. "You fucking idiot," he shouted. "You're an embarrass-ment. You're a fucking disgrace, Tatum."

"I hate you," I screamed back, crying as I accused him of selfishly co-opting Melanie, my friend. I was still too raw to tell him what had happened with Gavin. His response to my jealousy was to let me sleep in his bed that night, along with Melanie. Boundaries were never the strong suit in my family. Then he got rid of us both. He gave Melanie a few thousand dollars in cash and told her to take me to Paris.

WE CHECKED INTO the Plaza Athenee. Maria Schneider, who had made *Last Tango in Paris* with Marlon Brando, was staying with a male hairdresser in the room next door. They had some drugs and were into wild partying, so we wound up hooking up with them.

One night we all smoked opium and hash. I sank into the bed, dizzy from the drugs, getting so nauseated from the opium that I leaned over the edge and threw up. When I raised my head, a very confusing scene was taking place before my eyes. Melanie, Maria, and the guy were tangled up together. As an added sordid touch, one of the women was apparently menstruating—something I was too young to have experi-enced myself—and there was a lot of blood. It was surreal, be-ing so high and embroiled in such a strange, blurry scenario, yet I had a cool, objective voice running through my head, like a tape loop, saying "Tatum, where are you? What are these people doing?"

Then one of them reached out for me, drawing me into yet

another confusing erotic experience. Overwhelmed with conflicting emotions, I didn't resist.

The next day, Melanie and I went to visit Roman Polanski at the Paris home he'd established after jumping bail in the United States. Neither of us acknowledged how crazy the night had been. This was mid-1970s, the height of the sexual revolution, and everyone was into feverish experimentation. I might have been too had I been nineteen or twenty, but I was barely in my teens. I felt hollowed out.

Polanski tried to entertain us by screening *In the Realm of the Senses*, an X-rated Japanese film about erotic obsession, ending in castration—not the movie I'd have picked to show two young girls. As vulnerable as I was, that freaked me out.

Then we were off to London for a few days. At Blake's Hotel, we bumped into Melanie's archrival, Anjelica Huston, who was still seriously involved, on and off, with my father. She gave me a once-over. My arms were bandaged, and I must have looked as shell-shocked as I felt. "Tatum, what the hell is happening to you?" she asked.

"I don't know. I think I'm dying . . ." was all I could say.

It turned out that, after London, Melanie was leaving for Israel to appear in a film called *The Garden*. Why I tagged along I can't remember; Melanie probably didn't know where else to dump me. We toured the Dead Sea and a few other sights, then Melanie went off to her shoot, leaving me alone in the hotel. Not being old enough to navigate in a strange country, I got increasingly miserable and bored with each passing day.

Finally I decided to try to make my way back to the States. Somehow I got a ticket, but the flight wasn't direct, and I couldn't figure out what to do. In a fog of panic, I wound up transferring from plane to plane and, in between, sleeping on benches in foreign airports. Imagining my daughter, Emily, in that position makes my blood run cold. It took me several days to get home.

That was one of the rockiest experiences of my life—which is saying a lot, considering what I've faced—being lost and totally alone in strange countries, where I couldn't speak the language, as a terrified little girl. The helpless abandonment I felt has stuck with me to this day. If I'm lost somewhere, I go into post-traumatic stress syndrome—I get literally locked in fear.

Finally I reached Los Angeles, ready to collapse, and called the person whose love and comfort I always craved and looked for in so many substitutes: my mom.

MY MOTHER'S WEIGHT was always a barometer of her addictions. On speed she stayed thin; on booze she got heavy. Now, picking me up in her old station wagon, with her wig on her head and her constant cup of coffee in her hand, she looked heavy. I was glad she was off speed and back on Jesus again.

My whole sad story started spilling out: my heartbreak over Melanie and outrage at my father, the shock of being molested by Gavin, my suicide attempt, the weird scene in Paris, and my miserable solitary trek back from Israel. I wanted my mom to be strong, to be my advocate and protect me—I didn't want the abuse and neglect hushed up. But my mother was too scattered and hysterical to stand up for me. Instead she freaked out and called my grandmother.

I could have predicted what happened. With typical

loyalty to my dad, my grandmother turned on me. "Your father didn't do anything wrong," she said. "It was you who created this whole scene. You're in love with Ryan. Did you sleep with him?"

Of course I hadn't—my father was not a pedophile—but it shocked me to think that if he had been, my grandmother would have blamed me, the child. That realization showed me once and for all that there was no one I could count on—not my mother or my grandmother—not then and not ever.

Denial didn't stop my grandmother from reporting what I'd said to my father. When he got back, he wouldn't even speak to me. Gavin was exiled, though only temporarily, because my father believed that the abuse was at least partly my fault. But I had to go on living with my father while being treated like a whistleblower for telling the truth—for exposing the crazy, drug-fueled, out-of-control decadence of our lives. To him, that was the ultimate transgression.

I DID SEE Melanie again after that trip. My father and I were out at a Moroccan restaurant, Dar Maghreb, on Sunset Boulevard. We were with a bunch of people, all sitting on pillows on the floor.

Melanie was in the group. She made some remark to my father—I don't know what she said—and he pushed her hard enough to send her flying.

There was a moment of stunned silence. I went numb with horror, as I always did when my father suddenly lashed out in rage. As much as Melanie had hurt me, I felt sick at seeing her humiliated—and, because I missed her sweet friendship so much, very sad.

I still can't entirely forgive her for not really loving me. She took advantage of my tremendous affection and admiration, which could have been a youthful mistake, but I felt that she never properly apologized.

Yet I do believe she loved my father. I think she even got a shamrock tattooed on her ankle in his honor. It must be an uncomfortable reminder of crazy times that she was glad to put behind her.

NINE

9897 Beverly Grove Drive

AROUND THE TIME I connected with Melanie, I also made another Hollywood friend, Michael Jackson. I met him at On the Rox, the club Lou Adler and Jack Nicholson opened upstairs from the Roxy on the Sunset Strip. Michael was around seventeen at the time, about five years older than me, and he seemed very sheltered and fearful and lonely—not at all what you would expect a world-renowned performer to be. As I recall, he didn't even know how to drive a car.

He gave me his number, and we started talking every day—long drawn-out phone conversations that sometimes got so boring that I would hand over the receiver to my friend Esme Gray. Michael would just keep on, thinking he was talking to me. His usual subject was sex. Of course, at twelve I didn't have much to say about sex—all I knew was that it went on, pretty steadily, in my father's room, which was next to mine. But Michael was intensely curious about anything and everything sexual—he was, after all, a teenage guy—though in an incredibly sweet and innocent way.

He was a huge star, but it seemed that he'd barely even dated and knew little about life. He once came to my house and asked to come upstairs because he'd never been in a girl's bedroom before. He sat on my bed, and we kissed very briefly, but it was terribly awkward. For all my passionate crushes on people like Dustin Hoffman, I was just twelve and not at all ready for a real-life encounter. So I said, "I can't."

Michael, who was sweating profusely, seemed as intimidated as I was. He jumped up nervously and said, "Uh . . . gotta go."

That's the closest I ever got to Michael—which is why I was amazed by his recent claim, on national television, that I'd seduced him but he was too shy to carry it through. I absolutely adored Michael—as a friend—and I admire him to this day. I believe that he fell in love with me. I'm told that he wrote the song "She's Out of My Life," on his album *Off the Wall,* for me.

What an honor.

At the time of my supposed seduction, however, I was barely pubescent, and what I'd seen of sex so far was unappealing and gross. It may have been Michael's fantasy that I'd seduce him—and it's a little sad that he cast himself as failing, even in his dream—but it just didn't happen.

What we did do together was go to concerts. I remember seeing Queen with Michael at the Forum in L.A., which is interesting, considering his androgyny now. He came with me and my father to Hugh Hefner's mansion, where I think Hefner's menagerie—monkeys and peacocks and other exotic birds—gave him the idea for Neverland. Michael would hang out and jam sometimes with my brother Griffin, who was now living with us and had set up his drum kit in the guest room at the Barrymore house. Griffin was like a musical savant; he played the piano, guitar, and drums beautifully. Michael would play drums, and outside on the deck, my father would be boxing to the rhythm.

Unfortunately, my friendship with Michael came to an abrupt ending. He'd played the Scarecrow in *The Wiz*, the urban remake of *The Wizard of Oz*, which starred Diana Ross as Dorothy. For the film's New York premiere, Michael invited me to be his date. I asked my dad, who didn't care one way or another if I went, but my talent agency was dead set against it. I was told, in exactly these words: "You can't go to a premiere with a nigger."

Hollywood!

That upset me tremendously. Had I been old enough—or had I the parental support—I could have stood my ground and insisted "Oh yes, I can." But my father was too disengaged to help me think it through. So, without telling Michael the reason, I turned him down.

He was devastated. After that Michael didn't speak to me for years, until I ran into him at the Helmsley Palace in New York. For old times' sake, we caught a concert together, Kool and the Gang at Madison Square Garden. Michael dressed in full costume for the event—coming in blackface, with a pasted-on beard—the whole nine yards. But things were never the same between us.

GRIFFIN HAD MOVED into the Barrymore house because life with my mother had gotten unbearable. His acting out had escalated to the point of arrests for possession of stolen goods and replica guns. One day he just lost it, kicking his bunk bed in total rage, and called to tell my father he couldn't take it anymore. Little did he know that he was jumping out of the frying pan into the fire.

Griffin always believed that I was the lucky one—the one with a career and money, the one with a glamorous Hollywood life, the one my father preferred. Once he came to live with us, my father played on that simmering resentment by constantly pitting us against each other, just as he had with me and Carrie and so many others. He was like a mad jock, always making us run with him—or worse, box. He'd go *ding, ding,* and then we were supposed to box each other until one of us won the "match."

Since Griffin stayed small into his early teens, he often came out on the losing end of our competitions. His slight frame also made him an easy target for my father's bullying. Sometimes my father would get so angry that he would just pick Griffin up and toss him into the pool. That always struck me as terribly degrading and almost as bad as hitting, which my dad did plenty of too.

I think he must have hated being a parent. One child was bad enough, but the two of us were just too much, strangling him, cutting off his freedom. He felt put upon, like it wasn't his job to take care of us. It made him angry and he let us know it.

He'd storm around, with spit collecting at the edges of his mouth as he fumed at us. Griffin started mocking him (only when we were alone, of course) by squirting toothpaste into his mouth so it would foam out the sides as he growled, in a angry-dad-like voice, "Where's my paper?" It was hilarious, but also sad.

At one point my dad hired a weird babysitter to look after us. She used to take us on crazy drives in the Malibu mountains. One day she came up with a more creative way to entertain Griffin and one of his friends. She shaved off her pubic hair, while Griffin and his friend watched, and then attempted to have sex with them.

The friend went home totally traumatized and told his parents, who called the police. The babysitter went to prison. Even so, my dad laughed off the whole ordeal and, taking his cue, so did Griffin. There was no room for my brother to acknowledge his feelings about this experience or any other—not even to himself.

HOWEVER, THE REAL nightmare for Griffin centered on drugs. My whole family seems predisposed to addiction, and Griffin started smoking pot furiously from the moment he moved into the Barrymore house. My father would get high with us, and then there'd be ugly scenes.

For example, we'd set out in the car, and my father would say, "Where the hell are we going?" as if two stoned teenagers could keep anything straight. When we couldn't remember the directions, he'd shout, "I'm fucking turning this car around. You better figure it out!" or else he'd haul off and hit us. Our lives took on an increasingly frenzied anything-can-happen quality.

It made me wildly anxious when my father started dispatching Griffin to buy his drugs. Though we were underage we both drove, and I even owned a car. It was my little BMW that Griffin would use for his drug missions. One night the police caught him and escorted him back to the house. He was only around thirteen. My outraged father demanded, "How dare you bring the cops home?"

Charges were filed, but somehow my father managed to wriggle Griffin out of them. This was Hollywood in the 1970s, a time when stardom really counted. There was a huge sense of entitlement among people like my father, a conviction that they were above the law—and it was true. At times I almost wished that Griffin would get busted, not so that he'd get in trouble but so that some responsible party would investigate the way we were living and intervene. There was no parental perimeter, no one who seemed to be watching us, and my father seemed to be losing his sense of reality. It was really overwhelming for me.

So it was a relief when I was cast in a new movie, *International Velvet,* which would be shot in England, a continent and an ocean away from my father.

The movie was the sequel to *National Velvet,* the 1944 classic that made Elizabeth Taylor a star at the age of twelve. I played Sarah, grown-up Velvet's niece, an orphan determined to win an Olympic gold medal for horseback riding. So I had to learn how to ride, which was exciting. Anjelica, who was back together with my father, would drive me out to the Valley every day for my lessons. We got lost quite often, since she usually smoked pot on the way.

I hadn't ridden much before, but as it turned out, I was a natural. I loved animals and was athletic enough that it came easily to me. And at the time it was a godsend, a great healthy outlet and reason to get out of the house—both of which I needed—as well as being satisfying and fun.

Then I was off to Pinewood Studios in England for four months, again with Diane Lewis, whom I loved, as my guardian. I'd begged to bring my friend Esme as my stand-in, and her mother agreed, as long as she went to school. The movie had a great director, Bryan Forbes, whose wife, Nanette

Newman, would play Sarah's Aunt Velvet, and a fine cast including Anthony Hopkins as her riding trainer and Christopher Plummer as Velvet's boyfriend.

I'd never had so much fun making a movie. The crew was like a big, loving, playful Cockney family. I adored Christopher Plummer, who was really funny and used to take Esme and me to the pub with him all the time. Anthony couldn't drink because he had just gotten sober. Sober? What did that mean?

I continued my riding lessons in England with some famous trainers, including Richard Mead, who rode with the queen and Princess Anne, and Bill Steinkraus, one of the foremost equestrians in the world. They were extremely encouraging and urged me to take up riding seriously after the movie was over. Sometimes I wish I had, instead of slipping into less wholesome grown-up indulgences. They thought I could have a major equestrian career.

We got to travel all over Britain—to Leicestershire, Lancashire, and Devon, as well as London. Esme and I had a blast driving Mini-Coopers, and I got some stylish new clothes, including a pair of thigh-high boots that I believed made me look fantastically mature. We went to sophisticated parties. At one of them given by the Ronsons, who were a great couple in 1970s London, I was turned on to "mandrax," a kind of downer. Keith Moon, who was also at the party, asked me for my phone number, which was a thrill, but we never connected.

It was during *International Velvet* that I lost my virginity to a much older man. He was one of the stuntmen on *Superman,* which was being shot on a different lot at Pinewood Studios. I'd recently gotten my first period and felt that I was finally a woman, so with a combination of curiosity and longing for intimacy, I seduced him. It shocks me to look at my daughter and remember that at the time I was still as small as she is now—and that my world was so "adultized" that I could possibly imagine that I was ready to have a lover.

The stuntman and I had sex in one of the changing rooms on the lot. It wasn't very romantic and it hurt. After that, I tried to get him to come to my hotel, but when he didn't, I was relieved.

I FELT THAT I was blooming while making *International Velvet,* learning to feel liked and even liking myself a little bit. It was one of the brightest spots of my adolescence. As comfortable as I felt on the movie, though, I always knew that I had to go home. That shook me.

What had gotten me through life up to that point was a bravado shield. Attitude—even the bratty behavior I was sometimes accused of in the press—was my protection against the chaos I lived with every day. However, by my early teens, I'd been through so much that my shield was full of cracks and broken places, and I had started to lose my sense of who I was and what I was doing in the world.

My faith in myself had been so badly damaged that it impaired my acting in *International Velvet.* Instead of relying on my innate abilities and playing Sarah as Tatum, the raw girl-woman I was, I tried to become a different person. I adopted a self-conscious "Hello, Mummy, hello, Father" English-y sort of voice that makes me squirm when I try to watch the movie today. The critics didn't really pick up on it—the *New York Times* called me "a unique, superlative actress"—but I think my unnatural performance is part of the reason the movie wasn't all that successful. It didn't have enough heart.

The whole time we were shooting it, I felt acutely aware that my essence, my life force, was dissipating. That frustrated me, and I'm afraid that I took out my discomfort on Esme. I would fly into rages and yell at her or mock her, just as my father did to me. Like him, I could zero in on someone's most sensitive, sorest points and deliver a soul-killing shot. I wasn't proud of my behavior, and I feel lucky that Esme and I managed to get past it and remain friends to this day.

So, as positive an experience as the movie was, I was already a little rocky when my father showed up with Griffin for a visit.

"Where the fuck are my flowers?"

My father was livid because I'd neglected to welcome him with flowers in his hotel room. I had no idea that he'd be expecting some or that I was supposed to have arranged it. The tirade went on and on.

"I made you, Tatum, and look at what you are. You're nothing but a fucking piece of shit, the way you treat me . . ."

For the entire duration of his visit, my father kept attacking me, creating one drama after another. It was as if he sensed that I was being nurtured on this movie, watered like a parched plant. As I got greener and healthier and started stretching new tendrils toward an independent life and career, I would grow away from him—maybe even grow more successful than he was—and he couldn't stand it. So he had to savage me, shear away any delicate new shoots, and even rip me out by the roots if necessary to keep me in his sway.

INTERNATIONAL VELVET WAS released in June 1978 with tremendous fanfare—a Kennedy Center gala and also a royal premiere, where I met Queen Elizabeth, Princess Margaret, and Prince Andrew. From the outside, it looked like I was leading a charmed life, but behind the glittering facade lay crazy darkness. My father came to the London premiere, bringing, among other people, Gavin—the man who molested me, who after just a brief banishment was now back in the picture. It seemed to me that my father had simply dismissed the abuse because I wasn't worth defending. I was not really surprised.

Afterward, the three of us took a trip to the South of France. It was my idea—a bad one, as it turned out—that we should go by car and see the countryside. Gavin and my father had a big stash of marijuana and were so stoned that I had to do all the driving. It was pretty hair-raising—I was only fourteen, and the road ran along the edge of a steep cliff. The air in the car was so thick with pot smoke I could hardly see. But we made it.

In France my father hooked up with a French perfume spokesmodel—his primary reason for the trip—leaving me to hang out with Gavin. That was creepy, even though Gavin seemed sheepish and tried to ingratiate himself with me again. Not knowing how else to play it, I went along. Clearly my father didn't care about my feelings, and I was too beaten down to protest. At that point, I was more afraid of my father, with his casual brutality, than I was of Gavin.

I have a photo series from that trip, five linked images, which encapsulates our relationship. I'm on the beach in my little sarong, looking gawky and sad and broken. Then there's an encounter with my father, all menacing and big, who cocks back his fist to slug me. I shrink away before he throws the punch. In the final frames, he's leaning back, with his arms folded across his chest and his whole demeanor radiating smugness and contempt. He's obviously pleased with himself for his intimidating show of force, for asserting his power over me. He's the king of the castle and proud of it.

As devastated and diminished as I felt, I kept up a professional front for the press. It amazes me to see that, looking over old clips. The *Washington Post* called me "the picture of sophistication," claiming, "You'd think you were talking to a thirty-four-year-old." Always, in those interviews, I defended my father—the classic abuse syndrome—even saying, "My father is actually very mature. I know he acts like he isn't. . . . He feels like he missed out on all of his young years, so he's trying to relive them now. . . . We're like equals—like the same person. I feel like I'm his support. I know he needs me.

"Being who I am, I've had to take on a lot of responsibilities. I've had to be older."

It's bizarre that no one ever stepped back and said, "This is a kid talking. What's wrong with this picture?"

BACK IN L.A., the responsibilities I'd hinted at in the interview were overwhelming. I was more or less running the house; taking care of my grandma, who was ill (and addicted to Percodan); worrying about Griff, who was getting more deeply involved with drugs; and financially supporting my mother. I'd bought her a car, a Chevy Blazer, and later a house. I was Nurse Tatum, the caretaker.

Angelica seemed to be out of the picture now, and my father was seriously womanizing. He and Diana Ross were slated to do a movie together called *The Bodyguard* (which was canceled and later made with Kevin Costner and Whitney Houston as the stars). They began having an affair, and once again, I found myself in the role of my father's call screener. "Tatum, hi," Diana would say, in a very sweet voice. "Is your daddy home?"

Whenever she called—which was often—I was supposed to lie and say that he was out. That made me feel terrible because she seemed so nice. She wasn't hanging around the house, so I didn't actually meet her until the late 1970s, when she came with my father to the set of my next movie, *Little Darlings*.

The film was a forerunner of what would become an entire genre of teenage losing-your-virginity comedies. But unlike most of those, which were male-oriented, *Little Darlings* centered on girls. Kristy McNichol (as Angel Bright) and I (Ferris Whitney) played two fifteen-year-olds from opposite sides of the tracks who meet at summer camp and stage a contest to see who can lose her virginity first. Ferris, the child of privilege, goes after an older counselor (Armand Assante) and Angel, the tough street-wise girl, sets her sights on the young Matt Dillon. Though the movie had all the screwball antics you might expect, like food fights, it also was a poignant coming-of-age story about falling in love and being true to yourself.

As on *The Bad News Bears*, most of the other kids in the cast were trained actors from the East Coast (including Cynthia Nixon, with whom I reconnected years later when I guest-starred on *Sex and the City*). Though the shoot itself was fun, I didn't especially click with anyone. Kristy McNichol and I never had any real chemistry, and while Matt Dillon was nice, he seemed young, though he was born just a few months after me. Since we were all teenagers, there were a lot of social undercurrents—cliques and jealousies rippling through the cast—that I found stressful. So I kept to myself, holing up in my room and smoking a lot of marijuana.

We were shooting in Madison, Georgia, a lovely southern

town where there wasn't much to do. So Diana Ross's visits to the set were a highlight. She was like a queen—and very much in love with my father. She even wanted to marry him. He claimed that he didn't like her because she would never let him see her without makeup. He cruelly mistreated her, and eventually they split up.

At one point, my dad brought Griffin to Georgia for a visit. I met up with them in Atlanta, where I developed a big crush on Eric Clapton, who was also in town. Griffin shot pool with Eric, with cocaine as the prize. By then Griffin had started stealing coke from my dad, and he stole some drugs from Clapton too. Eric was too decent a guy to say anything, but the theft fired up my anxieties about my little brother. I started to lose myself in fantasies that my love, Eric Clapton, would rescue me, spiriting me away from my crazy self-destructive, ready-to-implode family.

It wasn't long before I was stealing drugs from my dad too—mostly Quaaludes and Valium, which I would share with my friends. Back in L.A., late one night, a friend and I got so high that she drove the wrong way on Sunset Boulevard to my house, where I stopped in to get my overcoat. My father was partying and didn't even question my going back out, despite the hour and my obviously impaired state.

Then we stopped to pick up two other pals. I can't even remember how it happened, but one girl slashed her hand badly on some glass. We had to take her to the emergency room at the crack of dawn—four young girls, with no adults around, stoned out of our minds on our parents' drugs.

That scared me. It was like an omen. We were living so close to the knife's edge of danger that something had to give. And pretty soon, it did.

TEN

Circle of One

"COME ON UP to Big Sur."

My father had gone with Griffin to his vacation house, a place where he was always planning to cultivate marijuana. Joe Amsler was living there as a caretaker. I didn't feel like going, but saying no was never an option when my father summoned.

Alone in L.A., I'd been running with an older, somewhat rowdier crowd, including Mackenzie Phillips. Mackenzie was a regular on the sitcom *One Day at a Time* and at that point in her life was also heavily into coke. I had been up all night, hanging out with Carrie at my dad's house, and then spent the day visiting a drug dealer in Malibu with Mackenzie. So I was a wreck. I hadn't slept. And then there was the matter of how I'd get to Big Sur, since I wasn't old enough to drive.

"Just take your mother's car," my father said.

She let me have it, never questioning whether Carrie, who I brought with me, had her driver's license yet. It was the red Chevy Blazer I had bought her. Since California didn't have seat belt laws then, neither of us put them on.

We got as far as the Ventura Freeway, then suddenly Carrie lost control of the car. We crashed into the guardrail, the seats behind us flipped, and both of us flew out, into the middle of speeding traffic. It was a miracle that we didn't get hit.

Carrie's clothes were ripped away as she skidded on the pavement. I was wearing shorts, and as I slid, the asphalt tore up my bare legs. I blacked out, and the next thing I knew, someone was standing over me. Barely conscious, I begged to know, "Is my friend okay?"

I passed out again and was roused by a cop, asking, "Miss, can you hear me? Can you see?"

My face was so nicked up that I'm sure he was convinced that I had a head injury. The cops rushed us to the hospital, where it was determined that I didn't, amazingly, and that neither Carrie nor I had broken bones. Another miracle.

Carrie was scraped and red all over, but I had serious third- and fourth-degree roadburns, embedded with gravel. The emergency room staff called my father about admitting us to the hospital. If my children had a car accident—God forbid!—nothing could keep me away. But my father didn't come. Instead he made the weird choice of calling a limo service to continue our trip to Big Sur.

It was a three-hour drive. On the way we both went into shock and our hair started falling out. When we arrived, my father set up Carrie on the floor in a pile of blankets and insisted that I come and sleep in his bed. When I refused, it made him furious. I didn't care. My life was already shattered. I slept on the floor with Carrie.

My dad grew even madder as I got sicker. My legs were getting septic and I couldn't walk. Unable to ignore such living proof of his bad judgment, he had to fly with us back to L.A., punishing me all the way with icy silence. He dropped off Carrie at her mom's, but he had no intention of getting stuck with me. He didn't want to take me to the hospital—acknowledging that he'd been wrong to dismiss my injuries—and he obviously couldn't leave me alone at home. So he drove me to the home of my agent, Sue Mengers.

That was one of the bleakest moments of my short life. I had never felt so worthless, so unloved, even hated. That I could be badly hurt and in terrible pain and have my own father deny me the care and compassion that any human being would instinctively grant to another was simply beyond my understanding. All I could think was that I deserved his cruelty—that I was a disposable human being.

Sue Mengers wasn't exactly the mothering type either. She wasn't inhumane, but she was a tough battle-ax who lived and breathed deal making. The only reaction I could imagine her having to my surprise arrival was: "Hello! What's this? What am I, a nanny? A babysitter? I can't put this in a movie!"

But Sue was kind to me, and she had the decency to take me to the hospital. One of my legs was completely black with ground-in asphalt, and I was feverish and shivering, turning weird colors. They instantly admitted me, and for the next six weeks, my legs were treated with hot salves to draw out the gravel and cement and to debride the destroyed tissue. When they finally got down deep enough, they did skin grafts on my legs, using tissue from my butt. It was a miserably painful experience.

CARRIE WAS BRIEFLY HOSPITALIZED too, right down the hall from me. Though her injuries were less severe than mine, she was screaming and carrying on. I couldn't take it because

I was trying really hard to be stoic, though I felt maimed and was facing skin grafts. We fought bitterly about what I perceived as her self-indulgence—I'm sure she had a lot of guilt too—and it shattered our friendship.

Another reason I resented Carrie was that she had a caring mother by her side, while I was completely alone. My mother showed up once, carrying a bowl of gardenias. She wasn't capable of comfort or support. My grandmother took the position that I'd gotten what I deserved for calling attention to my lack of parental supervision and embarrassing my family. As for my father, he too came just once, with his latest female conquest in tow. I passed the time smoking pot that had been prescribed for Larry Flynt, wondering whether my parents were coming back. They weren't.

My only loving visitor in those terrible weeks was my dear friend from *The Bad News Bears,* Walter Matthau. When he came shambling in, with that kooky expression on his face, an armful of flowers, and a mouthful of wisecracks, I think I cried.

As I sank deeper into depression, though, I stopped wishing that people would visit me. I was ashamed of the accident, internalizing the notion that I'd brought it on myself and deserved what happened. I felt like the bad seed. Voices kept nagging in my head, mixing my father's words—"You suck, Tatum!"—with my own: "You're not worth coming to the hospital to visit. You weren't even worth picking off the highway. . . ."

By then I'd already attempted suicide more than once—the night when I was molested by Gavin and another time when I'd slit my wrists with a razor, only to have my father tell me: "You cut them the wrong way, Tatum."

The accident convinced me that my dad wanted me to die,

if only so he could play the grieving martyr father. I was so filled with self-loathing that I kept trying, going on to take pills and to cut myself with knives.

Yet as I lay in the hospital, consumed with despair, a tiny spark began glowing inside of me—a spiritual spark, like a pinpoint of light from God. I began to question why I was alive. How could anyone survive being thrown from a car on a major thoroughfare, like a California freeway? Didn't 99 percent of the people that happened to die? Why didn't I? And how could my brain and even my face be intact?

Did I have some kind of guardian angel? Was there a reason I was still on earth? Did I have some task to fulfill, some purpose? Over the years, I've kept asking why because I've had extra chances—not just second or third but tenth, even twentieth chances—to survive. Despair has extinguished my internal, divine spark, but it's flared up again—at times, more faintly than I've wished. It's taken me decades to fan it into a steady flame.

ONE IMMEDIATE POSITIVE RESULT of that moment of spiritual awakening was that I vowed to stay off alcohol and drugs, including pot, and I stuck to that promise for the next few years.

Adjusting to my injuries would prove harder, however. When I finally left the hospital, I was temporarily reliefed out to my grandmother, whose attitude toward me unfortunately hadn't softened. They took the bandages off my legs, exposing huge, raw-looking scars, and she coldly dismissed my alarm at being so damaged. Most teenagers are painfully self-conscious about their bodies, but for a fifteen-year-old girl in Hollywood—where nothing matters as much as beauty—being disfigured was traumatic. I felt monstrous, and I blamed myself.

Even when I was well enough to move back home, I still had to endure the ritual of bathing my legs in saline solution and changing the dressings, with the help of a nurse. For some reason, having a nurse come in for a few hours seemed to annoy my father, and before I knew it, there was no more nurse. So I had to change the dressings myself and constantly confront the ugly consequences of the accident. Needless to say, this did not improve my morale.

It was at this point that my father threw a script at me and said, "You could do this piece of shit movie."

The director was Jules Dassin, famous for *Night and the City* and *Never on Sunday* (starring his wife, Melina Mercouri), who had been forced to move abroad by the McCarthy blacklist. *Circle of Two* was the story of an artist in his sixties (Richard Burton), who is blocked but starts to paint again after becoming involved with a teenage girl (me). She falls in love with him and tries to seduce him, but he heroically resists. Even so, her parents forbid him to see her, leaving her devastated.

The premise of the movie was a little pedophilic and creepy, but the worst part for me was having to do a seminude scene. It's agonizing to watch—this awkward young girl disrobing for the artist in his studio. Even from the back, my body language shows that they'd forced me to take my shirt off—at least it's obvious to me—and that I'm standing there miserably aware of my half-developed breasts and my scarred legs (I appear only from the hips up). I got through the scene, but it's a measure of how unprotected I was that no one—not a parent, not even my agents—objected to my being so frankly exploited.

Even when I had my clothes on, I felt ill at ease making the movie. I was still limping from the accident. I'd gained some weight, so I look different, and my voice sounds a bit artificial because I'm just not present—my essence as an actress is missing. The feeling of emptiness that had plagued me on *International Velvet* grew far more acute after the accident, as if my psyche had been as shredded as my legs. I was in my midteens but I felt weary, as if I were a hundred years old.

Still, I did enjoy working with the legendary Richard Burton. He used to say that he was Dante and call me his Beatrice—which is my middle name—and a "divine enchanting creature." He was a lot of fun.

Richard was under doctor's orders not to drink, but evidently the rule didn't apply to beer and wine, which he drank freely. On the side, we later discovered, he was sneaking shots of hard liquor, which often made him a bit lecherous. When he was drunk, I was no longer just a "divine enchanting creature" but "the most divine enchanting fucking little cunt I have ever seen." He'd beg, "Oh Tatum, come sit on my lap, you divine enchanting little creature."

I didn't, of course, but I loved him and learned a lot from working with him.

WE WERE FILMING in Toronto. My father came to visit (and did a tiny cameo in the movie as a theater patron), along with his entourage. One day when I was in the hotel lobby with my uncle Kevin, I had a celebrity sighting that would change our lives. "Hey, isn't that Lee Majors?" I asked my uncle.

It was indeed Lee Majors, TV's *Six Million Dollar Man,* who was there with his *Charlie's Angels* wife, Farrah Fawcett. We started chatting, and they wound up hanging out with my father, who knew Lee from the TV world of the early 1960s. At one point Lee, who wasn't going back to L.A. for a while, asked my father to take care of Farrah.

Bad move! He asked the wrong person. When I flew home after finishing *Circle of Two,* my father picked me up at the airport. Farrah was in the car.

ELEVEN

A Certain Fury

THEN IN HER EARLY thirties, Farrah was at the height of her beauty—an all-American, white-bread, unsmoldering kind of beauty that I could admire but didn't relate to at all. She was the opposite of the exotic sophisticates—the Ursulas, Biancas, and Anjelicas—whom my father usually fell for and who so impressed me.

She and my father had quickly become inseparable. He was always going "up the hill" to the mansion overlooking the Valley that she would wrest from Lee Majors in her divorce. When you entered, you'd have to pass through what we called the Hall of Farrah, where she had hung literally every single magazine cover featuring her. It was profoundly intimidating, like running a Farrah gauntlet. The two of them spent whole days up at the house exercising and sauna-ing, drinking their superdiet tea—the perfect cliché of the movie-star life.

Griffin and I were used to playing second fiddle to my father's girlfriends, but now it seemed that we were running a distant third—behind a woman and a house. Then my father picked up and moved in with Farrah, leaving Griffin and me—at fifteen and sixteen, respectively—living on our own.

It wasn't long before he put the Barrymore house up for

sale. Stuck at the beach, Griffin and I contemplated moving to Big Sur. It was like our days at the ranch, scheming about running away from home, with our little bags of food and clothes. Instead I found an apartment not far from my mother so we could enroll at Hollywood Professional for our last attempt at getting high school diplomas.

Eventually Farrah colonized the beach house too, moving the pool table, so Griffin no longer had a bedroom. Of course, there was never any question of making space for us in the vast expanse of Farrah's mansion. I could never figure that out.

My father tried to justify his abandonment by pinning the blame on me. "I had to make a choice between Tatum and this girl, and I chose Farrah," he later told *Vanity Fair*. "Tatum made me choose. I said that's a bad idea. I sleep with this girl, Tatum, I don't sleep with you."

Farrah backed him up, shrugging off my resentment in the press. "We excluded her," she said. "When you're in love, that happens."

When love comes in, does parental responsibility fly out the window? My father and Farrah seemed to think so. But we were underage, just fifteen and sixteen, too young to fend for ourselves. Whatever jealousy and exclusion I may have felt were eclipsed by the huge burden of caring for myself, managing a household on my own, and looking after my brother—oh, and his increasing drug problems—while trying to work and finish high school. It was preposterous to expect a teenager to rise to those challenges—and to believe that forcing them on her could be anything but negligent.

WE MAINLY SAW my father in command performances at Farrah's—usually competitions on her racquetball court. He'd become fanatical about the game and would viciously trounce us or—better yet—play us off against each other or Farrah, while barking from the balcony: "No, no, no! Get in front of her!"

It was like a weird, almost sexualized fantasy scene for him—his daughter and his lover scratching and biting like a couple of angry cats on the racquetball court. All the while he'd be goading me: "Come on, Tatum, she's beating the pants off you. Come on, you little coward!"

I could never understand what made him choose that put-down, which became his favorite epithet for me. It was such a harsh word for such a young girl—and for one whose life up to that point would seem to prove that she was anything but a coward.

RACQUETBALL BECAME JUST ANOTHER excuse for my father to bully us. Griff and I were always covered with racquet-ball bruises. Once my father pushed me to play so hard against Farrah that I tore some ligaments in my ankle—as if I wasn't scarred up enough. It swelled up like a tree trunk, and I had to be taken to the hospital.

I started to have panic attacks when the phone rang and I heard my father's thundering voice, summoning me "up the hill." But if I didn't show up, he'd come to the apartment look-ing for me, screaming my name and banging on the door with his fists while I cowered in the closet.

During all the screaming and hitting and terror competi-tions, Farrah did not utter a word in our defense.

It didn't make her any more endearing when, one day, my father, with an almost calculated cruelty, said, "Farrah, show Tatum your scar."

She lifted her skirt to reveal a perfect, impossibly thin body, with a superflat tanned stomach and on it a tiny and faultlessly precise white incision. It was a far cry from the ropey keloid scars my body had produced after the accident, and seeing it, I felt even more damaged.

Yet Farrah seemed oblivious to my father's game and to my distress. She seemed to have no interest whatsoever in the effect her relationship with my father—our only functional parent—would inevitably have on me and Griffin. It was as if Farrah didn't want to feel old enough to play the role of stepmother to two young teenagers.

I WAS SEEING A psychiatrist during the racquetball era, Dr. Beatrice Foster, who had been recommended by Sue Mengers. She was the first one to hammer it into my head that I didn't deserve the abuse I was getting. At her request, my father came to a session with me, though he made it clear that he considered the process a big joke.

"I made her," he told my therapist, reciting his usual litany. "If it wasn't for me, she would never have traveled, never made movies, never met anyone in Hollywood. . . . She would have nothing! And be nothing! Just like her mother!"

Having spoken his mind, my father went storming out of the office. Dr. Foster said, "You need to get away from him, Tatum."

I knew it was true. "But how?" I said.

As it was, I was terrified to leave when my session ended. I was sure my father was still outside, pacing and flexing his fists, waiting to torment me for telling our secrets. I've experienced the same emotion while writing this book.

Eventually racquetball would create an unhealable breach between me and my father. I showed up late for a game one day and found him waiting for me, his face twisted with anger. "Where've you been?" he said—and I knew I was going to get it.

I started to apologize, but before I could get the words out, he raised his fist and coldcocked me, right in the head. I collapsed, then picked myself up, ran off the court, and drove away. I vowed that I'd never, ever see him again, and for a few years, I didn't—but I had to endure plenty of punishment before then.

MY FATHER TERRORIZED ME, but Griffin was his real whipping boy. Everything Griff did seemed to provoke my dad, especially winning at pool. Being an excellent pool player, my father insisted on worthy opposition, but he was also too competitive to tolerate losing. Then he'd often let loose with fists and sometimes even with pool cues.

I remember once coming out of my room at the beach house because my father was getting beaten and shouting, "Fuck you, Griffin!"—clearly gearing up to start swinging.

I just stood by the pool table and glared at my dad. "*What are you doing,*" I thought. "*Griff is so little . . .*" My dad turned away from Griffin and said to me, with perfect comedic timing—though not meaning to be funny—"Who the hell do you think you are, Joan Crawford?"

Then he threw a pool cue at my head, hitting the door frame just above me.

Most of the time, I couldn't protect Griffin from my father. He was always covered with bruises, which he'd account for with crazy stories about falling downstairs with his hands in his pockets. Griffin had been through so much: the ranch, the hard days of living with my mother, buying my dad drugs, and flirting with his own addictions, as well as being a lightning rod for my father's anger. I knew my own road to a positive adulthood would be rough, but I worried that Griffin wouldn't have a chance even to make it to adulthood.

Still, Griffin wouldn't allow his big sister to take care of him at all. He resisted my efforts to get him into high school. Early on he'd been placed in "alternative" classes because he couldn't concentrate, despite his high intelligence. Since I'd hated school myself, I wasn't strongly motivated to go either, so we ditched the Hollywood Professional plan. Neither of my parents cared whether or not we got an education.

It made me hopeful when Griffin got the chance to appear in a couple of movies, *The Escape Artist* and *Hadley's Rebellion*—and he did well. Vincent Canby of the *New York Times* praised his "natural screen presence," which he "shares with his sister."

However, Griffin's drug use was spiraling out of control. My brother's story in the early 1980s is a tale of woe: crashing his Mini-Cooper into Sylvester Stallone's car; getting arrested for having a parking meter in his apartment, then ripping the police station pay phone out of the wall; and most notoriously, losing his front teeth after a headline-making, face-smashing beating by my father. After punching Griffin, my father held him, in a weird display of narcissistic guilt.

At one point, my mother made a stab at an intervention. As Griffin tells it, she showed up one day and asked for cocaine. He got out his stash, and my mother snorted all of it, right there in front of him, and then said, "Let's go shopping."

When they stepped outside, a nurse grabbed and restrained Griffin, hauling him off to rehab and leaving my mother behind, rocketing to the moon on his coke.

"Needless to say," Griffin's punch line goes, "I did not get sober that time."

Then came the day when I got back to the beach house and found my brother frothing at the mouth, in the middle of what looked like an overdose. He refused to go to the hospital and, luckily, came through it okay. That freaked me out—I loved my brother—so I called my therapist, who offered to help get him into treatment. I made the trip "up the hill" to talk to Farrah and my father about putting Griffin into rehab.

Finally they agreed, and Griffin went away to the Habilitat center in Hawaii, where, for a while at least, his self-destructive cycle could be broken.

I'D MANAGED TO GET help for Griffin, but I wasn't doing all that well myself. I didn't crash and burn as visibly as he had—not then, anyway—but I was definitely on a mission of quiet self-destruction for the rest of my teens. I was a time bomb.

On a positive note, I had a semi-boyfriend for a while, An-thony Shriver, the son of Sargent Shriver and Eunice Kennedy and brother of Maria, whom I'd met in Aspen. He was a little younger than me. Anthony lived in Washington and I was in L.A., so our contact was largely confined to calls and letters, with periodic visits. I always felt self-conscious and unpar-ented around the Shrivers, who were very kind to me. Anthony and I managed to sustain a pretty nice relationship for nearly a year. It couldn't last, of course, but it was a wholesome con-nection at a time when I didn't have many.

Even by late in my teens, though I'd had dozens of crushes, I'd had virtually no boyfriends. I just wasn't sure how to read the signals I got from guys. For example, not long after my father moved in with Farrah, I met Tom Cruise at a party at Timothy Hutton's. I had just seen him in *Taps*.

I spent most of the night dancing with Tom—he was a great dancer—and the next day, he called me at the beach house. I was a pretty messed-up young woman at that point, trying to cope with my father's leaving and my responsibility for Griffin, so I was too disoriented to respond like a normal person. All I could think of to say was, "Did Tim Hutton give you this number?"

I think Tom felt very rejected by that, and he never called me or talked to me again. I've always felt deeply regretful for hurting his feelings—and foolish too, because he was so cute, and I really would have loved to go out with him. But at the time I couldn't quite process the idea that he might be interested.

What a shame!

I WAS VERY LONELY during those years, which is what drove me to try to reconnect with my mother. I wanted her advice on dealing with my father—his rages and those horrendous racquetball sessions—but she always got too caught up in the he said/she said aspects of any incident. I'd be looking for answers, but she'd be gathering intelligence on the man I believe she never stopped loving, cruel as he had been to her. So we were at cross-purposes.

Then at one point, I even moved in with my mother for a few months. I had a powerful fantasy that we could expand the house I'd bought her or build a little guest cottage in the back. Then the three of us could live together again—me, my mother, and Griffin.

In the beginning, I felt very happy just being with my mother. I told my diary: *She's a great lady. . . . What more could I ask for—a great mom, a great dog, a great house. . . .*

Too many years of loneliness—they're over now.

I was staying with my mother when I ran into Warren Beatty, who asked for my phone number. He was one of the most notorious ladykillers in Hollywood, but my mother gave me some surprising advice. She said, "Go for it. You might get hurt, but if you're willing to take that chance, you could probably learn a lot from him."

Pretty interesting, huh? I confided to my diary. *Sometimes she's the coolest person I know.* Luckily for me, nothing ever happened with Warren Beatty—much as I wished it would. I was already involved in too many complex and heartbreaking grown-up dramas.

And nothing came, ultimately, of my fantasy of living with my mother. She was always loaded, unfortunately, and so was no more capable then of sustained mothering than she was before. I still had a lot of anger, and within a few months we were clashing enough that I had to leave. Even so, we'd recovered a bond that we would maintain for the rest of her life.

WHAT FOLLOWED FOR ME was a period of drifting and—finally abandoning my vow to stay clean—losing myself in drugs. It started when I got a bit chubby, by Hollywood and Farrah-comparison standards. My dad had encouraged me to diet for years, and now I learned that cocaine was good for weight loss. The person who tipped me off was a new friend, Victoria Sellers, the daughter of Peter Sellers and Britt Ekland. She also shared another powerful dieting strategy: vomiting.

Between doing coke and throwing up, the pounds started melting off me effortlessly. It didn't take me long to get down to about ninety pounds.

I found that coke made me feel so much better. It was like the panacea I'd always needed to ease my tormented thoughts. I had a great capacity for it too, which let me keep going for hours—sometimes all night long—after other people had to stop. Though I'd grown up surrounded by addicts, I didn't know enough about the actual mechanics of addiction to know that this was a danger sign. Even if I had, it wouldn't have slowed me down.

Victoria was totally wacky but so much fun that I invited her to share my apartment on Keith Street, off Doheny, in West L.A. We took a trip together to New York, where we stayed at the Helmsley Palace. There, I got to meet her boyfriend—a Colombian drug dealer. That was just too heavy for me, and I had to get out. Survival instincts . . .

However, the clincher was the other guys Victoria was bringing home—among them Charles Bronson's son Jason, a heroin addict who would wind up dead of an overdose. I had to ask her to move out. Victoria would go on to make a sex-tips video with the notorious Hollywood madam Heidi Fleiss.

Antics like Victoria's were way beyond me, even when I was at my most dismally unhappy. I was a lone druggie, who never wanted to be around too much riffraff—who never became a crazy party girl, was never promiscuous, and never got arrested.

I always had more of an earnest quality, a sense of purpose and a determination to work, whatever else was going on. In the mid-1980s my most notable movie gig was *A Certain Fury,* directed by Stephen Gyllenhaal, the father of Maggie and Jake and a really nice guy.

It was a female buddy/action movie, with lots of shoot-'em-up violence. Irene Cara (the black Hispanic star of *Fame*) and I (the tough girl, Scarlet, with dyed red hair) were two young women waiting to be indicted on separate charges— murder for her, car theft for me—when the courtroom erupts in a gun battle. We flee together and wind up having to escape both the cops and plenty of scary situations, including an exploding sewer (where I had real rats on me), a yacht (where Peter Fonda slashes my face), a dope den (where Irene's character is shot up with heroin, plus there's another explosion)— and more! It was a real slugfest, with a major body count, totally over the top—and a lot of fun to make.

Of course, my father showed up on the set and tried to play director. He had been doing that on Farrah's movies, but it was awful for me. I got so frustrated with him standing behind the camera, telling me to look this way or move to the right or left. It was so demeaning—though this was my eighth movie, my father couldn't stand to acknowledge that I had my own, independent career. It was embarrassing too. I was twenty years old, and no one else in the cast had a bossy parent trying to override the director. Finally I had to demand that he leave the set.

Apart from smoking pot after hours on *Little Darlings,* I never did drugs while I was working. However, when *A Certain Fury* was over, I resumed my self-destructive ways. Up all night, high on coke, I took to driving around L.A. alone, feeling that there was nowhere that I belonged.

Sometimes I'd drop in at parties or places where friends might be hanging out. For the first time in my life, I had some one-night stands, with guys who turned out to be scary. I was trying to die again. The time bomb was ticking loudly.

It wasn't necessarily any safer back at the beach house, where I was staying. One night when I returned, strung out, from one of my excursions and crashed in my bed, I awoke to find Gavin lying there next to me. I hadn't even heard him sneak in, and I was horrified. All I could do was scream, "Get out, just fucking get out, you crazy pig."

Another time, when I was sleeping late, my father exploded into the beach house. Normally I was pretty good about keeping the place tidy, but I'd been up for a few days, all by myself, doing drugs, and I'd let things go. He yanked me up, shaking me over the mess, as if he were rubbing an animal's nose on a carpet, and then dragged me outside to where my car, a Porsche, was parked. Snatching open the door, he shoved me in the car, bellowing, "Get the fuck out of here! Go to the rehab with your brother!"

Then, with all his might, he slammed the car door on my legs.

I flashed back years to that awful Thanksgiving when my father slammed my mother's car door on her legs and sent her out, drunk, on the Pacific Coast Highway to be arrested. All she had wanted was to share a turkey with her family, and she'd wound up sadistically abused for being weak. Now the same thing was happening to me.

So I knew I had to get out—out of L.A., out of harm's way, out of my father's reach. The time bomb was perilously close to detonation. Then—just seconds, it seemed—before the bomb went off, I met John McEnroe.

TWELVE

Johnny Mac

VICTORIA SELLERS AND I were at a party at the Beverly Hills home of the record producer Richard Perry. It was one of those scenes full of people who do drugs but are also fanatical vegans—no meat, no dairy—which, to me, is L.A. in a nutshell. I walked into the living room, and there was John with his friend and fellow tennis champion Vitas Gerulaitis. They had been at a Romeo Void concert and just arrived.

It was October 1984, and John was at his hottest, the number one tennis player in the world. He'd just made history by winning eighty-two of his eighty-five matches that year, including every major tournament except the French Open—a record that's still unsurpassed. He was also notorious as the bad boy of tennis, wired and aggressive, known for his screaming tantrums.

So when he came and sat down next to me, I was surprised at how sweet and normal he seemed. He was even a little silly, laughing a lot, which made me think he'd been smoking grass. We hung out together for the rest of the night and then exchanged a nice kiss before I hopped into my black Porsche and headed home.

Later I heard that John was shocked that I left instead of

going home with him. But since we'd just met, that didn't even occur to me. I was never one for jumping into strange men's beds, and besides, I was pretty heavily into coke at the time, which wasn't the greatest aphrodisiac.

I saw John again a few weeks later, when Alana Stewart had a party. What he was wearing was really odd—an almost-knee-length leather jacket and midheel black boots, with chains on the back. I thought he looked so funny and cute. We had a good time talking and finally wound up at the end of the night in a guest room, in bed together.

That was a letdown, to say the least. We both were so high that sex—or even just touching and talking—seemed impossible and weird. We were lying there uncomfortably awake at dawn, when someone started knocking a tennis ball around at a neighboring house. It was surreal to hear that sound while shifting awkwardly in bed next to the world's best tennis player.

Still, I really, really liked John. I hoped we could find our way back to the easy connection of the night before. But then he slid out of bed and vanished—into Alana's closet, she later told me—where he wound up sleeping on the floor. It must have been the drugs. So I got up too and left, thinking, *Case closed.* Whatever budding romance we'd had was over. Too bad!

AT TWENTY, I'D KEPT my vow to leave L.A. and was living in a horrible, dreary, little sublet on West Sixtieth Street in Manhattan. I headed back there, still thinking about John, and with the encouragement of Victoria Sellers, decided to call him. We met at the apartment where John still lives today. The place was like a castle in the sky: a four-story penthouse over-looking Central Park with three terraces and views of both the Hudson and East rivers. I'd never met anyone as young as John, then only twenty-six, who lived that way.

We drank ginger ale, ate pretzels, talked, and laughed over *Honeymooners* reruns on TV. Then I left. It was a perfectly innocent evening—hardly even a date—but it rekindled the spark between us.

John had mentioned that he owned another apartment on East End Avenue, right on the river, for which he needed a tenant. I accepted his offer to have his mother show it to me. It looked like a real bachelor pad, with worn carpeting marked here and there with beer stains in the living room and the two bedrooms, some beat-up, left-behind furniture, and an old TV.

Still, I could see that it had possibilities. I told Kay, John's mother, who seemed very competent and nice, that I'd think it over.

That was my introduction to John's family and my first clue that it was very different from mine. Kay handled all of John's financial affairs, right down to paying his bills; and his father, John Sr., a partner in the high-powered law firm Paul, Weiss, Rifkind, Wharton and Garrison, managed the business and legal sides of his career. It was as if John's family was a pyramid, with him standing at the pinnacle and a broad, solid structure supporting him from beneath; while my family was the upside-down version, with so much of the responsibility for myself, my mother, and my brother—financial, emotional, and physical—bearing down heavily on its fragile tip. Me.

Cozy as John's arrangement seemed, however, I would come to see that there was a downside to being the "product" at the heart of a family's cottage industry.

BEFORE I COULD DECIDE whether to rent John's apartment, I had some business to deal with back in Los Angeles.
Since work was being done on the beach house and they'd be
out of town, my father told me that I could stay at Farrah's.
Talking to John from there, I learned that he'd been suspended from tennis for three weeks for calling the queen of
Sweden "the pits of the world"—his classic put-down—and
spraying soda all over the king, among other infractions. Oh,
and one more thing—he was on his way to California.

I was thrilled!

Finally, I thought, John and I would go out on a real,
bona fide date, which was exciting. But when the day came
he insisted on staying in. Maybe that should have told me
something, because if you don't get wooed on your first date,
you never will. What I wanted more than anything, though,
was to see him and be with him, so I invited him to come to
Farrah's.

He showed up with drugs. I wished that he hadn't because
of our previous bad experience and because I knew I was already way too susceptible to the allure of drugs. Still, I couldn't
say no.

We did the drugs and took a grand tour of the mansion—
the Hall of Farrah, with all those eyes staring off the magazine
covers; the infamous racquetball court, the site of so much
abuse; and the incredibly romantic view "down the hill" from
Farrah's windows of illuminated ribbons of highways and brilliant dots of light against the pitch-dark city.

It was freezing cold in the house. We clung to each other,

and I guess the intensity of our desire overpowered the chilling effects of the drugs. That night we consummated our relationship, not with full thunder-and-lightning special effects, I must say, but we did it. After that, for the next ten years, I could barely tear myself away from him—or he from me. I knew he was the man of my dreams.

I COULD SEE THE toll that John's intense, record-breaking year had taken on him. When we went to get his luggage from the Beverly Hills cabana house where he was staying, we found flames still burning in the gas fireplace. John had forgotten to turn it off. Luckily, in the two days we were at Farrah's, it didn't explode or set the place on fire.

When we resettled at my father's beach house, John seemed so happy just to swim and lie in the sun, smoke a little grass, and play his light blue electric guitar, which had been made "lefty" just for him. He clearly needed to relax.

He knew he was burned out. He was slated to play the Davis Cup final in December but decided to withdraw from the Australian Open, which followed it. That prompted an arm-twisting phone call from his dad, John Sr. (or J.P., as I came to refer to him), who was totally focused on achievement and winning—no excuses. Though John really was exhausted and needed a rest, in his father's view, he was slacking off right at the peak of his momentum, when he seemed unstoppable, at the end of an astounding year.

They had a huge argument, with J.P. insisting that the Australian Open was critical and John saying "no way"—he wasn't going. Of course, John won.

In retrospect, I think John needed me to help him separate from his family and finally develop an independent identity. I, in turn, unconsciously may have been counting on him to help me throw off the emotional shackles of my own crazy family—and to escape from Hollyweirdness.

Yet in those idyllic days between Thanksgiving 1984 and the New Year, our only focus was each other. I turned twenty-one on November 5, and it was as if my coming-of-age had been blessed with a magnificent gift. I truly loved this curly-haired genius boy-man, who was so secure and together and strong—and he seemed to love me back.

I COULD ALMOST HAVE predicted what happened when John first met my father. We were invited up to Farrah's, where my dad performed a whole macho circling-and-sniffing ritual, grabbing and squeezing John's biceps, then delivering his verdict: "Not very big. You're so skinny."

I was terribly embarrassed, but John wasn't the least bit fazed. He was too confident about who he was and what he was doing in the world to care about being appraised that way. He didn't find my father and Farrah intimidating or even all that impressive.

Then, inevitably, my father challenged John to a game of racquetball. Though my dad was very good, the idea of it was ludicrous—imagining that he could beat the number one tennis player in the world at any racquet sport, or even at Ping-Pong. But John graciously indulged him and handicapped himself by playing right-handed and in his jeans. I couldn't bear to watch—not because I was worried about the outcome but because it was such a blatant display, on my father's part, of jock competitiveness.

John later claimed my dad kept aggressively hemming him in and that he held back, letting my father beat him to avoid a fight. As I recall, my dad's unsportsmanlike tactics failed and so John wound up the winner. But the truth is, neither of us cared, either way. To John, it was just meaningless backyard play; and for me, it was yet another charade highlighting the reasons I needed to escape my family.

It made me feel lonely to realize that I respected my father so little that it was a chore, not an honor, to introduce him to the man I loved. I didn't even value his opinion, never mind seek his approval. I was leaving my family and all their dramas behind for a new and better future.

IN MID-DECEMBER JOHN had to head back east to get ready for the Davis Cup finals. Neither of us felt ready to separate, so I went along, staying at his penthouse instead of the apartment I was renting. When it was time for him to leave for the finals, John told me that I couldn't come. It might be too disruptive for the Davis Cup team and, for him, too distracting.

I understood, but I still took the news hard. I was so much in love that I could hardly bear to have John out of my sight, and I didn't want to be alone for a week or ten days. Unfortunately, I knew also where I could find distraction from my loneliness: in John's safe.

There were drugs in it—some pills and at least an ounce of cocaine. Like many people in the 1980s, when coke was a staple at parties, John kept drugs around for hospitality, I guess, like having a wine cellar. For him, drug use was strictly recreational—take it or leave it—which I already knew wasn't true for me. I recognized that I did more coke for more extended periods than other people, but it was a whole new ball game to be left alone for days with a seemingly unlimited supply of coke.

I was miserable. I couldn't stay out of the safe. I loved John, and though I was worried sick about making him angry, I kept going back for just one more hit of coke. In between those, to slow myself down, I worked on the pills. All the while, I was whipping myself, tormentedly, obsessively asking, *What's wrong with me? Why can't I stop this?* and of course, *What am I going to tell John?*

Good question! By the time John got home, except for the pot, which I didn't like, the safe was empty.

John was horrified. "How could you do all those drugs?" he shouted. "Are you crazy, Tatum?"

I didn't have the language to answer him. I couldn't say "I'm an addict," because I didn't really know what was wrong with me. All I knew was that I hadn't been able to stop, which scared me to death, and that I hated myself for it and for making him unhappy.

To make matters worse, John's trip had been a disaster. Not only did the American team—and John personally—lose nearly every match, but the U.S. Tennis Association also censured them for their behavior, establishing a "code of conduct" that every player had to pledge to uphold. John was outraged and vowed not to sign the pledge, even if it kept him from playing the Davis Cup (which it did, for the next few years).

We were heading into the holidays and our new life together under some dark and heavy storm clouds.

Around Christmas, John told me that he loved me and wanted me to come live with him in New York. I said yes, of course—so happy—and we celebrated New Year's Eve together in Los Angeles. Shortly after midnight John went to bed because he had an early flight for a match in Las Vegas. I stayed up shooting pool and getting drunk with my half-brother Patrick, finally slipping into bed next to John at daybreak. Just an hour or two later, he nudged me to say that he had to leave.

"I'm coming with you!" I insisted.

He was shocked. Though he wanted me with him, he never dreamed that I'd make it after partying all night long. But this tournament was my very first chance to see him play live. John was suspended at the time we got together, and then he'd gone off by himself for the Davis Cup.

My hair, still bright red from playing Scarlet in *A Certain Fury,* stood out against the blue seats as I sat in the stands. I hoped that John could see it, so he'd know that I was rooting for him as he slammed away at Johan Kriek, a fast South African. Even when John lost his temper, stomping around the court, yelling at the umpire, I felt that I was where I belonged. He was my man, and I was so proud to cheer him on and, later, to share the incredible thrill when he won.

John seemed so happy to have me by his side that I was glad I'd trusted the instinct that urged me to get up early and go with him. I think that gesture helped ease any lingering doubts he may have had about me after the incident with the safe. It showed him how committed I was to him and to sharing his life, even if I did tend to overdo certain substances.

John actually had an idea about me and drugs that he was eager to test, as I would soon find out.

THIRTEEN

John's Cure

JOHN'S PLAN FOR ME was very simple: Get pregnant, get off drugs—and it worked.

It wasn't exactly a textbook cure for coke dependency in a twenty-one-year-old from an abusive, addicted family, but John knew me pretty well. He knew how determined and purposeful I could be and also how I thrived on giving and receiving love. In those days, John wasn't as warm as he would become. His parents were old-fashioned disciplinarians with a certain pride in their strict resistance to breast-feeding or spoiling crying babies with pacifiers. I was much more into affection—very big on hugging and cuddling—and John seemed to flourish at being nurtured.

So his plan resonated perfectly with me. I loved the idea of having a baby—John's baby—even if it did seem that we were moving awfully fast.

I'D MOVED INTO the penthouse apartment on Central Park West, which would be our primary home in the years that John and I were together. In the early months of our relationship, however, we were rarely there. I was traveling everywhere with John, staying clean, trying to get pregnant, and learning how to be a good tennis girlfriend, which was fun for a while but wound up being harder and lonelier than I expected.

On the road John adhered to a strict routine—sleeping certain hours, getting long massages, eating exactly three hours before matches, stretching, taping up, testing the tension on his racquet strings, and so on—which didn't leave much time for me. I understood that this was the nature of John's work, so I just hung out, trying to stay out of his way and help to keep him focused on winning.

Another challenge was John's notoriety. *A Certain Fury* was released in March 1985, and I didn't promote it, preferring to be with John (and paid the price, careerwise). John came with me to a screening, and we both agreed that the movie wasn't very good. Then, leaving the theater, we ran into a woman who asked, "Are you John McEnroe?"

When John said yes, she said, with an anger that shocked me, "I hope you lose!"

John didn't react, but that out-of-the-blue hostility from a stranger gave me a chilling sense of the isolation he lived with—and which I would soon grow accustomed to. Now I could see why John disliked being recognized. Once he even put on an Afro wig when he went to the deli to buy beer. He hailed a cab, and the driver, hearing his voice, asked, "Hey, are you John McEnroe?" The disguise didn't work.

I was proud that John wasn't a snooty "rich boy" tennis type, with country club manners, but his temper often made life harder for us. Sometimes he would joke about it. Not long after the screening, he blew up at Wojtek Fibak, a Polish player he thought was turning the crowd against him during a match.

Then he ran up to me in the stands and said, like a peace offering, "Do you think I'm lacking 'a certain fury,' Tatum?"

I laughed.

It was very endearing. There were also some very nice times, like at the French Open gala, when John publicly thanked me for being there and for "making my life better." We got to see a little of Paris together too, though everywhere we went, we were besieged by paparazzi. That drove us crazy.

I'd grown up under the constant scrutiny of the tabloids and the paparazzi. At nine years old, I was issuing little statements on which actors (whom I'd barely heard of) I considered my role models; I knew it was part of the job. John's relationship with the media was much more adversarial. He drew crowds because of his sheer brilliance on the courts, but it was his hotheaded reactions that propelled a stuffy "gentlemen's sport" into the headlines. So the press inflated every squabble into an out-and-out brawl, calling John names like "McBrat" and "King Sneer," and when he didn't give them enough fodder, tried their best to stir up controversy by baiting him.

Naturally, when John became involved with me, it set off an even more rabid feeding frenzy. He would complain that he was used to being in magazines like *People,* but that now he was fair game for the *National Enquirer.* He was so upset by the press in France that he asked me not to come with him to Wimbledon in July, where he was always the media's favorite whipping boy.

Yet the press war was just heating up. Later that year, two photographers in Australia went so far as to frame John, provoking him into a shoving match with one of them while the other snapped pictures.

It didn't help that John was losing. After his incredible victories in 1984, he was the man to beat—the guy every player was trying to knock off his pedestal. He'd lost the French Open to Mats Wilander and Wimbledon to seventeen-year-old Boris Becker. So the stress on John was intense as September, the time of the U.S. Open—which was played in Flushing Meadows, Queens, right near Douglaston, where he was raised—grew closer.

My father decided to fly out with Griffin to see the tournament. The two of them wound up practically sabotaging John's chances altogether. First, my father stayed only through the semis, which was like placing a curse on a superstitious athlete. Once again, my dad was totally unsupportive.

Then, when it came to the finals, we left for Queens from Oyster Bay, Long Island, where John and his family had summer houses, and were already running late when Griffin demanded that we turn back to get his contact lenses. John did it, which cost us precious time, then we lost even more getting stuck in the heavy tennis-fan traffic on the freeway. Because John arrived late, he had little time to stretch and get psyched up for the match. He wound up losing the 1985 U.S. Open to Ivan Lendl—and never again won a major tournament.

RIGHT AFTER THE OPEN, we left for Malibu. John had fallen in love with the Malibu beach and, six months before, bought a house there from Johnny Carson for a combination of cash and free tennis lessons. Johnny had proudly showed us how everything in the house was remote controlled—not just the TVs and the state-of-the-art sound system but also the curtains and even the beds, which automatically raised and lowered. I half expected them to push a button and make the deck move.

It was a gorgeous, modern house on Carbon Canyon beach, off the Pacific Coast Highway, on the stretch that would later become known as Mogul's Row. The inside was very luxurious, with white carpeting and a huge mirrored bathroom with a big Jacuzzi. John and I had brought in a pool table, since we loved to play, to make it feel like home. The house became a refuge we would enjoy on our rare breaks from the circuit.

It was there in Malibu, in September 1985, that I discovered that I was pregnant.

John reacted by throwing up, then spending four days in bed, sick as a dog. He blamed the illness on a casserole my mother served us, but I knew that the real reason was stress. Having lost three of the year's four Grand Slam competitions, John had plummeted from number one. He was becoming a father, which made him happy but also signaled major changes in his life. Both of these lightning bolts struck in a single week. No wonder he was a wreck.

And he was going to have to tell his parents—serious churchgoing Catholics—that his girlfriend had conceived a child out of wedlock, right on the heels of the disappointing U.S. Open. I was dreading that. I felt that they had been leery of me ever since John took time off when we first became a couple. His losing streak during our year together didn't make me any more appealing. I also believed that they didn't respect me because I was a Hollywood actress and, now that we were having a child together, would be upset that I wasn't a practicing Catholic.

John told me not to worry—that we were going to do things our way and that there was nothing his parents could say to us. But he put off telling them until *People* magazine forced his hand by getting wind of the pregnancy and calling John's mother for confirmation. Still, we tried to preserve our privacy by continuing to deny the rumor to the press. Then we were outed by, of all people, my father.

Earlier that year Farrah had had a baby, my half-brother Redmond O'Neal, and set off a firestorm of controversy by announcing that she and my dad had no intention of getting married. Now it was my dad's turn to blab to the press. In an appearance on the *CBS Morning News,* he told the world, "I'm going to have a son-in-law and going to be a grandfather."

I was furious at his disrespect for our privacy, especially since we hadn't quite worked out the "son-in-law" part. John had gotten down on one knee to propose to me, and I'd accepted his offer of marriage. He gave me a beautiful engagement ring, but the wedding date wasn't set.

Among other things, John warned me that his father was going to insist that I sign a prenuptial agreement. I was willing, but then months dragged on as I traveled with John. That brought out the cruelty in my father, who'd never cared about the wedding or offered to host it for me, like any traditional father of the bride, but now accused me of "trailing after John," who, he insisted, clearly didn't want to marry me. His words sparked the most serious fights John and I had ever had, until I came to my senses.

Then I realized that getting married—or not—was up to me. I was growing more heavily pregnant with each passing day. I didn't want to be a huge, seven-months-pregnant bride. I wanted to be beautiful for John in photos of a day we would cherish for the rest of our lives. I didn't need the aggravation of planning a wedding while John was still out on the tournament circuit. For his sake, my sake—even the baby's—I needed to be by his side. The wedding could wait.

NAUSEOUS, NAUSEOUS, NAUSEOUS, *nauseous, nauseous* . . . I filled an entire line in my diary. John's schedule was brutal, a hundred days of nonstop touring, and I was there with him in nearly every city. John would later say that this was his favorite time in our relationship, when I was totally focused on him and completely dependent.

I'd reunited with my mother soon after conceiving Kevin and invited her to come with us to a Loreto, Mexico, tennis camp. John had a "touring pro" contract there, which paid him tens of thousands of dollars for a few days of knocking balls around with well-heeled clients. I have a funny picture of the three of us standing under the camp banner, reading THE HOME OF JOHN MCENROE—though he spent at most two weeks a year there—in a desolate stretch of desert, surrounded by tumbleweeds.

Afterward we flew to Mexico City, where John, Guillermo Vilas, Hana Mandlikova, and some others played a charity tournament to benefit Mexican earthquake victims. Funnily enough, the celebrities on hand included Kristy McNichol, my costar from *Little Darlings*.

That trip was fun, and having my mother along helped ease my loneliness and boredom on the road. In years to come, I'd sometimes ask friends to accompany me as well. We were traveling at least thirty weeks a year, working the tennis circuit, so it was the only way to keep up connections. Even so, it was very hard to maintain any kind of consistent support network.

On tour I quickly grew really sick of the paparazzi, who were all fired up by my pregnancy. In Europe, especially, they drove John insane. I started keeping a list of press altercations in my diary: *Barcelona: I ended up kicking a guy who followed us into the lobby in the balls.*

The fans were just as bad. *Pushy, gross, sickly looking, smoking too many cigarettes—the plane was absolutely filled with smoke today. I felt ill. Grown people hunting after autographs and pictures like kids—they're crazy. I still haven't gotten used to the hysteria John causes wherever he goes . . . Sweden: Fifth country in eight days, and I'm starting to feel it.*

Back in the States, I took a break while John did the six-cities-in-six-days Tennis Over America exhibitions with Bjorn Borg. While on that tour, John later said, Borg encouraged him to fight his way back to number one. To do it, he'd have to play the Australian Open, which he had never won.

So we wound up in Melbourne at the end of November. It was a disaster. John lost to Slobodan Zivojinovic of Yugoslavia, who was the sixty-sixth-ranked player in the world. That hurt, and John screamed at him, "You're going to pay for this," drawing devastating boos and catcalls from the crowd.

On the way back John talked about taking a year off to get in shape and work on improving his game. *Boy, do I think that would be a good idea!* I told my diary. He was completely out of gas, physically and emotionally.

But John had to subject himself to one more test, playing the Grand Prix Masters at Madison Square Garden in January—and losing to Brad Gilbert. That's what finally convinced him that it was time to decompress, to retreat to Malibu, catch his breath, and become human again while awaiting the birth of our baby.

I was so relieved.

THOSE WERE SOME of the happiest days of our lives together. John grew a beard, played guitar, and smoked grass. In February I threw a lavish party for his twenty-seventh birthday. We set up a tent on the beach, where Bruce Springsteen and Stephen Stills played music, and got a huge turnout of stars from Hollywood and the record business. John was thrilled.

"I hope you stay in love with me forever," he told me later.

I'm madly in love with him, I wrote. *Devoted—and in love—the way he acts toward me—speaks to me—makes love to me—I LOVE HIM SO. I can't wait to have his baby. That will be the happiest day of my life.*

May twentieth was my due date. My blood pressure was up, and fearing toxemia, the doctor scheduled me for induced labor a few days later. The night before my delivery, John hung out in the back room, smoking pot and playing his guitar, resisting my pleas for him to come to bed.

"Fine," I said.

Then I locked the bedroom door. He was furious when he finally got ready to come to bed and couldn't get in. But I was mad too. I'd wanted so much to have him lie beside me on our last night as a couple, before everything changed and "we" became "three."

He was just too pigheaded, though. He had to cope with impending fatherhood on his own. He wouldn't even admit that he was nervous.

Then, the next day, after checking me into the birthing center at St. John's Hospital in Santa Monica, John forgot to put the car in park. It rolled down the ramp of the parking garage and crashed into one of the doctor's fancy cars. No one was hurt, luckily, and I had to laugh, thinking, *Hmmm . . . what would have happened if you were nervous, John?*

On May 23, 1986, after nine hours of all-natural, no-anesthetic, induced labor, our firstborn son wiggled his way into the world—all eight pounds and eleven ounces of him! We named him Kevin Jack McEnroe.

I had never felt such pride and joy.

FOURTEEN

The Wedding

I WASN'T GOING TO have a typical young-mother nesting period. On May 26, 1986—three days after Kevin was born—
Griffin was involved in a terrible accident. He'd cleaned up his
act a little at Habilitat, the therapeutic community in Hawaii.
But he soon began a downward slide, leading to an unimagin-
able tragedy.

Griffin had a role in the movie *Gardens of Stone,* a
Vietnam-era military-base drama being filmed near Washington, D.C., which was directed by Francis Ford Coppola and
starred James Caan. On one of his afternoons off, Griffin and
his friend Gian-Carlo, Coppola's son, rented a speedboat on
the South River near Annapolis, Maryland.

Griffin, who was driving, tried to cut between two slow
motorboats, not realizing that a towline was strung between
them. Seconds before hitting the line, my brother managed to
duck, but Gian-Carlo wasn't so lucky. The towline caught him
and flung him to the back of the boat, where his head shattered on the metal deck. He died instantly.

No one called me. I heard about the accident on the news
and for half a day believed that Griffin had died too. I didn't
even want to breast-feed newborn Kevin because I thought he

might pick up my shock and horror from my milk. I loved Roman Coppola, Gian-Carlo's brother, and knew the whole family well. I've never even been able to put into words the sorrow I feel for the Coppola family.

I felt too raw to discuss the accident with John. It was just too painful. Finally I heard from Griffin, who'd been charged with boat manslaughter, as well as recklessness and negligence. Devastated, he told me how much he wished he had been killed. He said that for an hour he'd sat with a shotgun barrel in his mouth but was too scared to pull the trigger.

So my bliss after the birth of sweet Kevin was clouded by terrible grief both for the Coppolas and for my poor brother Griffin, who seemed to have most of the cards in the deck of life stacked against him.

Just a few weeks later Griffin called me with more sad news—not about himself, thank God. This time it was about the dog I'd raised from a puppy, who had been staying with my half-brother Patrick at my father's beach house. The poor dog had run out onto the Pacific Coast Highway, where he was killed by a car and then buried by Griffin and my father.

What a month that was, late May through late June 1986—a seesaw between joy and sorrow, birth and death.

RIGHT AFTER KEVIN was born, both my parents, as well as John's, had shown up at the hospital and posed for photos. At twenty-two (me) and twenty-seven (John), we look like two teenagers, beaming as we hold our adorable son, who had the same green eyes as me and my mom. I began filling my diaries with pasted-up Polaroids chronicling sweet moments of

Kevin's babyhood, with captions: *What a bod!* (under the irresistible naked baby shots), *I'm going to get you, Tatiana!* (reaching for the cat), and *First diaper rash—a bad one!* (a sore red bottom—poor little guy).

I loved being a mommy!

The brief thaw in my relations with my family that followed Kevin's birth couldn't last. The break came a month or so later, when they all arrived for a two-week stay at the McEnroes' Oyster Bay, Long Island, compound. My father and Farrah brought baby Redmond, then about sixteen months old, as well as Griffin and my eighteen-year-old half-brother Patrick, who had befriended John in Malibu.

The compound was a five-acre former farm on Tennis Court Road, where John and his family spent summers. It had a big gazebo in the center, a multicar garage with caretakers' apartment above it, and a large main house, which was owned by John's parents, where the whole family often gathered for dinner. The garage and the main house were connected by a terra-cotta roof to the barn, which had been converted into a roomy house for John.

To the right of the barn, a walkway led to a cabana/guesthouse, which overlooked the swimming pool. There was a tennis court, of course, but it was as far from a slick, professional, country-club setup as you could get. It was endearingly funky, an old-fashioned clay court, a little uneven and run-down. I remember once seeing a wasps' nest in the net.

I put my father, Farrah, and Redmond in the cabana to give them privacy. I could only hope that there would be no dramas and that they'd be respectful guests, remembering that New York wasn't Malibu and that John's parents, who occupied the main house, were pretty straitlaced.

Sadly, I had no such luck. Pot smoke constantly seeped out of the cabana until it seemed that the entire compound reeked of it. I was so embarrassed.

Smoking grass never mellowed out my father, either. He was a tyrant on this trip, stomping out of the cabana and grabbing me to demand, "Who's supposed to be fixing Redmond's baby bottles? Why can't you?"

All I could think was, *I'm breast-feeding my six-week-old-son—and I'm the hostess, not your servant."*

Where my dad's craziness really erupted was on the tennis court. John was in the city, luckily, so we were able to avoid a repeat of the racquetball face-off. Instead, my dad and I and Griffin and Patrick played a few sets of doubles together, switching off partners. To me it seemed cool to be using the court of the best tennis player in the world.

It was Pat's turn to serve, but the ball glanced off his racket and hit my dad in the back. "Goddamn it," my father howled.

He threw his racket and ran at Pat, who jumped over the net, looking for an escape route. When he didn't see one, he just stood there, rocking on his heels as my dad came barreling after him, with his fists up, shouting obscenities.

He stopped just short of beating up Pat, maybe because it struck him that John's parents might be listening. Still, my dad had gone too far for me. Always protective of my brothers, I couldn't stand to see him terrorize them anymore—and certainly not on John's tennis court. He was a guest in our house—my new baby's home—which I wasn't about to let him violate with his rages. I was sick of feeling bullied and afraid.

I decided right then and there that I could no longer tolerate my father—that I was through with him, done! I was cutting him out of my life.

Yet what mattered more to him, because it was such a public snub, was that I cut him out of my wedding.

JUST BEFORE KEVIN was born, I had reopened the discussion of marriage with John. Over his objections, I'd started taking instruction from a Catholic priest so we could marry in the church, as he'd promised his parents. I actually enjoyed the study, since I'd always had a spiritual bent, even though I never reached the point of being baptized.

None of our children would be baptized either, because John and I both disagreed with many of the Catholic Church's policies. We did flirt briefly with the idea of godparents, but only Kevin ever got one: Vitas Gerulaitis.

The major obstruction to our marriage remained the prenuptial agreement. The document his father wanted me to sign was very restrictive, which was a little insulting. I wasn't some gold digger who'd latched onto John, but an actress, with my own money. Yet according to the terms of the agreement, we weren't supposed to commingle our funds—his would stay his, and mine would stay mine, as if we weren't even married.

I talked to a Hollywood lawyer who advised me not to sign the agreement because it was too unfair. It was also unrealistic. Though I had every intention of resuming my career, with a new baby and a man who wanted me touring with him 60 percent of the year, I wasn't likely to be able to work, or at least not soon.

The whole prenuptial issue depressed me, but it didn't

surprise me. John's parents had a certain hysteria about money. When John took time off from the tennis circuit before Kevin was born, his mother—whom I otherwise really liked and respected—warned me a few times that if he didn't get back to work soon, he was going to "run out of money." That became her mantra, though it upset me and John, and of course it was far from true. At the time, John was making about five million dollars a year.

When John started planning his return to competition, shortly after the baby came, his parents were relieved. "Now you can buy some diapers for Kevin," his mother told us.

You'd think we'd been living on the street. John didn't buy into their guilt trip. He asked his mother how much more money he'd have to make—five, ten, fifteen million dollars?—to convince her that we weren't teetering on the edge of poverty.

When it came to the prenuptial agreement, however, John wouldn't stand up to his parents. As my pregnancy progressed, he grew more entrenched, insisting that I had to sign the agreement or there would be "big problems" between us.

I wrote in my diary: *I'm trying not to let it affect me too much. There is too much to be happy about and to look forward to. . . . I want to stay with John for the rest of my life. That's what means the most to me.*

Once I had Kevin, the pressure to get married increased—especially from within me. Breast-feeding my tiny baby, I felt overwhelmed with love and the desire to nurture and protect him. I wanted to give him the security of a stable home, with a mother and father caring for him who were bound together for life—an image that was ultracompelling for me because of my own neglect in childhood. And I felt even closer to John, more strongly and lovingly bonded, when I looked at the beautiful little miracle of a boy we had created.

I wanted badly to become John's wife. Recognizing the depth of my longing, John grew even more adamant that I sign the prenuptial agreement. To turn up the heat, he resorted to psychological warfare—he stopped talking to me.

As usual, I had no one in my corner. I didn't have the sophistication to marshal lawyers who could beat the Goliath of John's team, headed up by his father. Even if I wasn't estranged from my family, they were too unreliable to advise me or back me up. On my own, I was too emotionally vulnerable, especially having just given birth, to resist John's arm-twisting tactics.

So I caved in and signed the agreement, with my fingers crossed and hoping for the best. *I love John more than any thing or person I have ever loved,* I told my diary. *I have to pull myself together and realize how good I've got it . . . I want to feel great about all the things I have to feel great about. Especially Kevin.*

JOHN AND I got married a couple of weeks later, on August 1, 1986, in Oyster Bay. He wore a dark suit with a red bow tie. I had on my grandma's antique wedding dress and, instead of a veil, a wreath of roses on my head. Kevin was utterly precious in a baby tux.

Weird as it may seem, no one in my family came to my wedding or was involved in any way. It was like a flashback to the night I won the Academy Award with no one but my grandparents at my side. My grandmother had sent me the wedding dress but was too ill to travel and so was my grandfather, who had Alzheimer's. Since my dad wasn't invited, it must have been too awkward for my half-brother Patrick, who was living with him then, to attend. I believe that Griffin was back in rehab, and I'd lost track of my mother, as I did from time to time when she hit patches of heavy drinking and drugging.

So John's mother took charge of the whole affair, whipping together a beautiful wedding and reception in record time. I have to give her a lot of credit—and thanks—for pulling it off. Certainly I had no clue what to do or even what to think about when it came to creating a wedding. Nevertheless, having the planning taken totally out of my hands, even if it passed into such competent ones, left me pretty alienated from the process of getting married. All I did at my own wedding was show up, as if I were a gate-crasher instead of the bride.

The ceremony was held at St. Dominic's Catholic Church, which had curtains draped over its old stone facade to foil the paparazzi. Press helicopters circled overhead, thumping and whining all during the service. Even our neighbors were out in force, packing the streets, behind police barricades, hoping to catch a glimpse of us. The attention felt a little smothering.

We only had about fifty guests, mostly John's relatives and some mutual friends. My maid of honor was my high school friend Andrea Feldstein, and John's brother Patrick walked me down the aisle. As I said my vows, I felt milk leak from my breasts, which seemed like an omen—but of what, I wasn't sure. After the ceremony, we threw the press a bone by smiling and kissing in front of the church for the snapping cameras.

Back at the house, there was dinner and a band. Mick Jones of Foreigner jumped up and started jamming and was joined by John and Vitas Gerulaitis. We all got blasted drunk. I had to pump and flush my milk down the toilet to avoid passing the booze on to Kevin.

Then I curled up next to my baby son and waited for John to come to bed. He had passed out somewhere in the house, so he never made it. It felt very odd to be spending our wedding night apart.

In retrospect, we should have eloped—just gone off somewhere and privately pledged our lives to each other—and thrown off the backbreaking weight of legal meddling and people's expectations. Including our own.

But I was determined to cultivate a great hopeful spirit when I awoke the next day as Mrs. John McEnroe.

FIFTEEN

Two for the Road

WE GOT MARRIED on a Friday and by Monday were on the road for Stratton Mountain, Vermont, with Kevin and Estella, our nanny, in tow—but not for our honeymoon. That should have been a sign . . .

Instead we were headed for the Volvo Open tournament, marking John's return from his six-month sabbatical. He'd originally planned to sit out tournament play for a year, both to recover from burnout and to step up his training, but he had changed his mind.

On the tennis court, John was an artist—fiercely passionate, intuitive, even magical—but he was now up against a new breed of players, some barely out of their teens, who were athletes, first and foremost; highly disciplined, with strength and speed on their side. Modeling themselves on the workout fanatic Ivan Lendl, who'd sadly knocked John out of his number one ranking in 1985, they were changing the way the game of tennis was played.

I wondered if John was truly ready. I remembered that when we first got together he was so burned out that he was almost phobic about competing. "Are you crazy?" he'd say when the subject came up, often because of remarks or unspoken pressure from his parents. "You want me to go back to that crazy rat race?"

During the six months of his 1986 sabbatical, he always seemed so relieved not to be playing. Certainly he'd made enough money—millions of dollars—to retire anytime he felt like it. Bjorn Borg had retired at age twenty-six, a year younger than John was now.

But I doubted that John could really spend the rest of his life just smoking grass and fooling with his guitar. As I told my diary: *I honestly feel that he's got to start practicing more and getting ready to get back on the circuit. The longer he takes off, the harder it will be. . . . He may be the best tennis player that ever lived. . . . After he feels that and still doesn't want to play, then it's up to him. Right now he doesn't feel that. He's depressed and down. He has to get up and excited. . . .*

He was on top of the world in tennis in '84. And he will be again, if I can help it.

John eventually did start training: doing yoga, weight lifting, practicing daily, and dieting so much that he lost thirteen pounds. Then, shortly before Kevin was born, he started to worry about his corporate contracts, which required that he play an annual minimum number of tournaments. Rather than forfeit those fees, halfway through his proposed year off, he decided to get back in the game.

John thought he could ease back in at Stratton Mountain, usually a fairly low-key competition. But instead he went into culture shock. There was a huge swarm of press—a hundred reporters and forty photographers, by one estimate—who were treating John's return as a major event. That jangled him terribly. Before the tournament even started, he got so mad at a photographer that he whacked tennis balls at him, hitting him in the leg.

John won the first round and made it to the semifinals, but he seemed to be unraveling emotionally. He spat at a judge and heaped verbal abuse on his opponent, Boris Becker. Then, after a very close call that John considered unfair, Becker beat him. John was devastated. He was convinced that the judges, other players, the press—all the people he'd ever offended by his shows of temper—were gunning for him, determined to see him fail. I felt so bad for my poor, discouraged husband.

THE NEXT FEW MONTHS weren't much better, however. John only made it to the third round of the Canadian Open, lost in the first round of the U.S. Open, and then got defaulted in the doubles for getting stuck in traffic and being late. From being the number one player in the world, he had plummeted, in just a little more than a year, to number twenty because of his losses and the tournaments he'd missed playing during his break.

John was miserable.

To qualify for the Masters, he'd have to play a grueling series of back-to-back tournaments. So we hit the road—Los Angeles, San Francisco, Scottsdale, Arizona—and John went on a roll, winning all three. That got my hopes up, though he was still really moody.

In Arizona I reported to my diary: *I have to get used to John's concentration before a match. He seems to be so down and unhappy, but he is just getting psyched up to play. . . . This is hard on me when it lasts for days at a time. . . . I wonder how long it's going to stay this tense, when John is going to relax. I feel his tension so much. I don't know how much more I can take. . . .*

This man is very sensitive, and I affect him very deeply. I have got to make an effort to be kind and helpful and un-self-serving. This career is not going to last forever, and I would like the next three years to be the best of his life.

But it wasn't easy. It didn't help that I was also breast-feeding tiny Kevin, who turned five months old at our next stop, Ixtapa, Mexico. From there we were off to Europe on the Concorde for the Paris Open, followed by tournaments in Antwerp, Belgium, and London. John's parents came along, adding another layer of pressure.

The strain built up when John started losing. He was racking up fines and pinning the blame on me—even claiming once that he'd deliberately blown a match to show me how badly I affected his play if I was cranky, disagreed with him, or failed to say "good luck."

When John finally lost to Pat Cash in London, I was devastated. Intellectually I knew that I couldn't have caused the defeat, but I was tormented by John's apparent belief that it was all my fault. After flying back to New York ahead of John, I holed up with Kevin at the Carlyle Hotel rather than return to our apartment. Guilty, defensive, and miserably depressed, I wrote John a letter, which ended, "Don't let my weakness ruin your tennis . . ."

I never sent it, and when John came to get me a few days later, we reconciled. Still, I found it hard to shake the irrational worry that John might be right—that maybe I was responsible for his losses; maybe even for toppling him, the man I loved, the best tennis player in the world, from his rightful place at number one. Just what spell I'd cast to make him fail, I couldn't guess, which made it worse. It was a very heavy load to carry.

FINALLY, AT CHRISTMASTIME, four months after we were married, John and I had our honeymoon in Sun Valley, Idaho. I have a hilarious picture of us on that trip, with me holding six-month-old Kevin and John staggering under the burden of eight heavy suitcases. I always traveled with too much luggage. I'd even brought along my cat, Tatiana, and wound up accidentally leaving her at the airport when all our bags were loaded into the car. It was a few hours before I discovered she was missing, but luckily, after driving back in a panic, I found her safe in the airport lost and found.

We stayed at the house John owned in Sun Valley, a rustic and charming three-bedroom cabin with beamed ceilings, wood-paneled walls, brick-colored carpeting, and a big stone fireplace. We had fun decorating a big Christmas tree, and I filled my diary with snapshots of Kevin in front of it (*Two teeth! More hair!*), sketching big, loopy hearts in the margin. I also devoted a page to my husband, pasting up a shot of him looking pensive, against a backdrop of snow-covered mountains, jokingly captioned *John in a good mood*.

For Christmas John gave me a beautiful ruby-and-diamond bracelet, which I loved. He had wonderful taste and, over the years, surprised me with many wonderful and generous gifts of jewelry.

On Christmas Eve, we went skiing, which was a blast because it was John's first time. Amazingly, just three days later, he was zipping past me down the mountains. I loved that. It brought back all the reasons I had originally fallen for him—his physical grace and quick intelligence, his bravado and drive. And he was so cute!

We were like our old selves again, enjoying our baby and each other, laughing together the way we had back in Malibu, when we used to race home like a couple of kids to play Space Invaders. It was a sweet, happy time—just the antidote we needed for the misery of the tour—and an affirmation of our marriage.

ON DECEMBER 4, I'd told my diary, *Started my period today—first time in sixteen months.*

Then—boom!—just two weeks later, in Sun Valley, on our honeymoon, I got pregnant.

When I found out and told John, he was stunned. He sat me down and demanded to know whether I was positive I wanted another baby. Not that either of us could have faced terminating a pregnancy, but that's how totally focused John was on tennis. He was desperate to redeem himself after the letdowns of 1986.

I was worried too because of the rockiness of our relationship. It crossed my mind that I was risking making John a bit jealous because, from the moment Kevin was born, it was clear that I cared more about motherhood than anything else. It had given me a new reason to live, a true purpose. Just hearing that I was pregnant had already sparked my feelings of love and welcome for the new child.

So I told him yes.

"There goes 1987," John said.

———

IT WAS A VERY stressful pregnancy. John went back out on the circuit in January and pressured me to come along, at a time when Kevin had some inevitable infant virus. Even with Estella's help, I couldn't imagine lugging an ailing baby from city to city while coping with my own early-pregnancy exhaustion and morning sickness. John and I fought, and I stayed home in New York.

I scolded myself in my diary for being irritable: *This is a problem I've got to fix, the spoiled brat side of me. The same thing I hate in my dad, I actually possess. . . . I've got to love and cherish John. That's what marriage and commitment mean. He needs me now but he doesn't feel that I'm behind him. I've got to change that, don't I?*

John kept losing matches, and now, for the first time, the fury he was famous for venting on the tennis court came spilling out at home. One night, after I wrote him a hurtful, fault-finding letter, he threw a wooden folding chair at me. Luckily, it missed—but not by much.

Around that time, I had a miscarriage scare. Believing I could lose the baby finally woke John up to accepting my pregnancy. It was a blessing when the bleeding stopped and I was back on course. Still, John never stopped complaining about how tough the pregnancy was on him and how it was affecting his playing. I felt he was grasping at straws.

Yet my heart went out to him as he scrambled to fix whatever it was that was throwing off his game. His back, hip, and shoulder ached from old injuries, so he kept trying out new masseurs and chiropractors. He took on new coaches and even spiritual advisers, some of whom seemed to have a guru-like influence that I resented. John was really struggling to get back on top.

I also fought to suppress my disapproval of his posse of male friends—fellow tennis players and assorted sycophants. It often upset me when John wanted to spend what little downtime he had with his pals, instead of with me and Kevin. Though I had friends of my own on both coasts, we were traveling so much that it was hard to keep up with them on a regular basis. I couldn't develop the kind of circle that John had. Now that I was pregnant, I wanted more than ever to be with him—and to have him be reassuring.

One of my strengths is the ability to find the funny side of difficult situations, so I tried to keep my sense of humor about the posse, even in my diary. *John says he's disappointed in me and that I'm not what he expected, so I'm going to tell him if he wants a disciple he should have married one of his tennis buddies.*

However, when John was on the road, he definitely wanted me with him. Then, in direct contradiction, I'd hear him in press conferences explaining that his game was off because it was so hard coping with a family.

Worse yet, he was growing increasingly punishing when he lost. During the 1987 French Open, when he was having a difficult time, he forced me into a chair, circling me while he raged, "You haven't supported me one day during this pregnancy. You need to look it up—the word *support.*"

It was as if he believed I knew some magic words that could fire him up or make him win. Of course, I didn't. I began to recognize that there was something pathetic—even pathological—in John's insistence on making me the scapegoat.

On one leg of that trip, John was going to fly to Düsseldorf with Kevin and Dimitria, another nanny, leaving me behind to drive from Rome to Florence and sightsee with my friend Vicky Morgan. He got to the airport only to find that I still had Kevin's passport. That was a major trauma because the private plane was stuck for hours on the runway while John sent someone to chase me down in Florence. I'd made an honest mistake, being pregnant and weary, but to John such slipups were acts of pure sabotage. He made me pay the rest of the trip with bouts of anger and what I hated even more—cold silence.

At least I had Vicky along, to serve as a reality check. Usually I was totally isolated on the tour. The other tennis wives shunned me, both because I was socially awkward—often too shy to cultivate strangers—and because of John. He was notorious for being a gloating winner and a bad, arrogant loser—at one point telling Diane Sawyer, "I have more talent in my little finger than Lendl has in his whole hand." He didn't have a lot of allies. So I would be alone and completely vulnerable, the captive victim of his moods.

WHEN I WASN'T TRAVELING with John, I spent much of that pregnancy in Malibu, perilously close to the toxic orbit of my family. I was only sporadically in touch with my mother, and Griffin still seemed to be in a kind of freefall. In December 1986, he stood trial for reckless and negligent operation of a boat and boat manslaughter in the death of Gian-Carlo Coppola. Fortunately, he was acquitted of the manslaughter charge, which could have sent him to prison for five years. Instead, he was placed on supervised probation for eighteen months, with drug testing, and required to perform four hundred hours of community service. Then, in May 1987, the Coppola family filed a civil suit against Griffin and seven other people for negligence leading to the accident.

I never heard the outcome of the civil suit, but I was all too aware of my father's reaction to Griffin's legal problems. "You fucking murderer," he screamed at my brother. "Look what you've done to us."

Even on probation, Griffin couldn't seem to stay out of trouble. He kept getting arrested for infractions like drunk driving, possession of drugs, and having a sawed-off shotgun in his car. He was sent back to—and escaped from—Habilitat and then was hauled off to a new psychiatric facility in a straitjacket. John and I helped out with some of his bills, to keep him from being totally under my father's thumb, but I was terrified for Griffin. He seemed to be on a collision course with suicide.

As for my father, I'd managed to resist contact ever since his abusive visit to Oyster Bay. But he'd taken to sending me long, bitter letters, enclosing news clips about himself, as if to prove that he deserved my attention. I wrote back urging him to get off drugs if he expected to recover a place in my life. Then I started spotting him jogging on the beach—he lived four miles away—always passing our house with his eyes fixed straight ahead. Softening, finally, I asked him in.

He was thrilled to see Kevin, who kissed him. He worked on my guilt about not having him at my wedding to the point that I fantasized about having a second, Los Angeles ceremony where my family could celebrate. Then he wangled an invitation to come back and bring Farrah, whom I didn't especially care to see, and baby Redmond, whom I didn't know at all.

That invitation sparked one of the worst fights John and I ever had. When I asked what he thought, he turned away coldly and, without a word, stalked out of the room. I trailed after him, confused and wanting his advice, but he refused to answer.

John's withdrawal opened the floodgates. I burst into tears, and all my months of frustration—of needing John throughout my pregnancy, of feeling overwhelmed by the problems of my brother and parents, of trying to be encouraging and strong but being rewarded with John's accusations or icy silence, of being blamed because John couldn't step up to the plate and take responsibility himself for losing—came streaming out. I'd been married for less than a year, and I felt disillusioned to the point of hopelessness.

"I'm leaving," I told him.

He didn't react right away. I went downstairs to sleep on the couch, sobbing until he came stomping angrily down the stairs. We launched into an incoherent war of words, screaming at each other until John snatched my arm and yanked it behind my back so hard I was afraid it would dislocate. With his hand gripping the back of my neck, he shoved me down onto the couch, smashing my face into the cushions. I had my glasses on, and they were cutting into my eye sockets as I gasped for breath.

I freaked out. After growing up with a violent father, noth-

ing terrified me as much as physical brutality. And I was pregnant. "Stop!" I cried. "The baby!"

"You fucking listen to me," John said. "If you try to leave
here, you are not taking Kevin or the baby. Do you hear me?
Answer the question! You know the kind of assholes who
raised you. You wouldn't have a leg to stand on. You'll never
get your kids—just try it, Tatum."

I was still shaken the next morning, when John launched
into a litany of my failings—what a drain my family was on
him, how selfish I was, how I didn't abide by his decisions.
"You need to follow the leader!" he insisted.

It struck me then how much John resembled his father,
who to my mind didn't treat his mother with the respect she
deserved. If his father was his role model, I had to wonder
what that meant for my own future.

As we battled on and off for the rest of the week, I tuned
in to the rhythm of despair in John's demands: "Can't you give
me some of the love you give to Kevin? He doesn't need it. We
can get nannies for him—but I'm your husband." And "Make
me happy! Why can't you make me happy?"

He's a wreck, I told my diary, *a frustrated emotional wreck
that can't bear the thought of losing or retiring. It's a nightmare . . . for a dream that he's already accomplished. Why more
suffering for something he doesn't enjoy?*

*In my heart of hearts, I believe that I'm doing good and try-
ing to love in an unloving situation. There is a ton of negativity
and sometimes it's hard to remain innocent and not bitter.*

Ironically, the catalyst for our terrible fight—a possible visit
from my dad—never came to pass. He called and made such
provocative, threatening remarks that I slammed down the

phone. Then I wrote him a letter thanking him for having the courage to try to reconcile but saying that I wasn't ready—that I still felt the scars of the past too acutely.

Besides, I already had my hands full with John, Kevin, and the new baby, who'd be coming before I knew it.

I'D HAD AN ULTRASOUND and knew I was having a boy. I could feel him moving vigorously all the time now, and though I was growing huge and lethargic, I was so excited at the thought of seeing him and holding him in my arms. I couldn't wait to introduce him to Kevin, who was so adorably playful that I knew he'd get a huge thrill out of his new brother, whom we were naming Sean.

Good night, Sean, I love you, I wrote. *I feel you kicking so maybe you heard me. Good night, dear Kevin, I love you too . . . And John—there's something you must lack, a hole that needs filling with constant reassurance. It's all right now. I love you the same—and I know that you will come out a good man.*

SIXTEEN

The Colony

ON SEPTEMBER 23, 1987, our son Sean Timothy McEnroe was born in New York City. I'd gotten a little spoiled by my experience with Kevin, who was born in a comfortable California birthing room. This time, I was induced in a conventional hospital, New York University Medical Center, and had nine hours of such intense pain that I feared something was terribly wrong. Still, I hung tough without anesthesia, and John was once again a wonderful birth coach. When it was all over I felt very brave and proud of myself and, of course, utterly delighted with Sean.

John immediately went back out on the circuit while I stayed in New York to settle in with my new baby, dividing my time between our Central Park West apartment and the Oyster Bay compound. I loved autumn in New York City and also seeing John's parents enjoy their grandsons in a more peaceful setting.

However, I did have words with my father-in-law on a few occasions over his sarcastic nicknames for John, such as "Mister Charm" or "His Royal Highness." I didn't want to hear my husband disparaged, but J.P. blew me off, saying, "He's my son, and he'll always be my son."

That gave me pause, making me wonder if he thought I had no right to object because I might not always be John's wife. It also gave me a new measure of insight into what made John tick and the ferocity of his drive to win, even at the price of his own—and his wife's and sons'—happiness.

Of course, such sticky moments were nothing compared to my own family's dramas. My father was still writing me angry letters, accusing me of disloyalty and demanding to see his grandchildren. When I didn't respond, he resorted to badgering me by phone, slurring his words as he claimed "I don't love you anymore" and insisted that he was a good father because he'd never "slept" with me. The sheer absurdity of his expecting credit for not being a pedophile convinced me that his drug and alcohol use was completely out of control. I felt profoundly relieved to be thousands of miles from La-la Land.

NOVEMBER 5, 1987, was my twenty-fourth birthday. I arranged a wonderful weeklong getaway for the five of us (me, John, our sons, and our nanny Dimi) at a villa on the beautiful Caribbean island of Mustique. While there, I made a list of self-improvement resolutions for the coming year, which I now see were mostly focused on John:

1. *To do my utmost to help John figure out what he wants to do with his life—to fight with all my might to give him what he needs for all of 1988.*

2. *To offer to rub John's feet, hands, and legs and help him stretch.*

3. *To avoid talking tennis with John unless he brings it up.*

4. *To try to get psyched about making love* (which had been hard because for most of our relationship I'd been pregnant or breast-feeding).

5. *To put up with John's friends and his father and speak of them only in the most positive terms.*

6. *To stop drinking to encourage John to stop smoking pot.* (This was the easiest resolution because all I ever had was an occasional glass of wine, and I hadn't touched drugs of any kind since early 1985, when I first started trying to get pregnant.)

7. *To stay cheery at all times—never complaining or getting depressed, even about my family.*

8. *To start doing something with my life so I won't be emotionally dependent on John or resentful and angry when he isn't around, and to give him room to breathe.*

Right after the New Year, when I could leave Sean for a few hours, I set to work on that last resolution—"to start doing something with my life"—by trying to get my GED. I'd never graduated from high school, and it really boosted my sense of accomplishment when I aced the verbal/reading part of the exam. The math section was something else again, so I enrolled in a refresher course.

I also tried auditing some acting classes with a great coach, Sandra Seacast, just to get a sense of how I felt about my career. I hadn't made a movie in three and a half years, and my confidence as an actress was shot. I knew John wasn't keen on my working again, and I wasn't sure I wanted to be away from my children just yet. Still, I was curious—and I found that I loved it.

At the time, though, the main thing I was "doing with my life"—apart from caring for my boys, of course—was renovating our New York apartment. I'd begun interviewing decorators while I was pregnant with Sean and eventually hired Robert Metzger, whom I'd seen in *Architectural Digest,* to begin what would be a two-year project. At one point, we'd even have to buy a second apartment, next to John's old bachelor pad on East End Avenue, to live in while the structural work was under way.

So I had a lot going on in New York after Sean was born— overseeing the penthouse apartment renovations and taking my GED and acting classes. Unfortunately, that was exactly the moment when John decided that he desperately needed to live in Malibu, so he could practice between matches. It was too tough, he thought, to keep up discipline in New York.

Just a couple of months before Sean's birth, we'd bought a beautiful three-story house in the Malibu Colony. We'd decided that the old Johnny Carson house, which was right on the Pacific Coast Highway, might be too dangerous for two young children. Our new place was in a gated community on the beach that was jokingly called "Star Central" because of its film-world residents. On one side of us was Jon Peters's home and, on the other, Larry Hagman's.

John pleaded with me to come to Malibu with him, and I knew I'd miss him terribly if I stayed in New York. Besides, the boys needed him. Kevin was talking enough to ask about John;

and though Sean was nearly four months old, John had barely had a chance to hold him, never mind bond with him.

So we all moved to Malibu in February 1987, just before John's twenty-ninth birthday. I immediately began to renovate that house too. It needed a new roof, and I chose green adobe tile, to be installed by, of all people, my mother's ex-husband Gary. Inside, I created a black-and-white master bedroom, a den for John with red leather sofas and a margarita machine, and a sitting room for me, full of flowery, pink country prints and flounces—superfeminine, I teased myself, to counteract the "little boy" in me.

WHILE IN MALIBU, I got to know Madonna and her husband Sean Penn, whom I befriended after bumping into them at the nightclub Helena's. We bonded when I asked Madonna if she was letting her hair grow, and she said, "Yes—and no more bleach!"

The four of us met for dinner at La Scala the very next evening. I loved hearing about the new David Mamet play, *Speed-the-Plow*, which Madonna was heading off to do at Lincoln Center in New York. She asked me all about my boys, confiding that she and Sean were hoping to get pregnant within a year. She told me that she never did drugs, apart from an occasional toke of grass, and never drank—and it showed. She had great skin and a terrific dancer's body. Having recently given birth to Sean, I was still plagued with a postpartum spare tire, and Madonna offered to set me up with her personal trainer, Rob Parr.

I found her tremendously inspiring. So I was shocked

when, a few days later, Madonna told me that Sean Penn was so violent that she sometimes feared for her life.

"You need to be happy," I told her. "You can't let a temperamental actor bring you down. Your spirit is too good to break."

The more I saw of her, however, the more I believed that Madonna could hold her own in any scuffle. When we had dinner again the following week, this time at Rebecca's, sparks flew when John and I began asking routine questions about their house in Carbon Canyon, whether they were using interior decorators—just making small talk. Madonna let loose a string of expletives about decorators, which seemed like overkill and made me wonder if she and Sean were feuding. I didn't mind her tough talk, but John got quite combative. He wasn't used to being around women who were as driven and hard-assed as he was.

If I ever had an idol, she's it, I told my diary. But as the months went on and Madonna kept calling me from New York, I saw more clearly how fierce she could be. When she talked about trying to make time to get pregnant, I recorded that I often told her, either frankly and indirectly, *Don't have a child unless you and Sean see eye to eye or it will rip you apart. . . . You need to be on the same wavelength. . . . And you need to become more patient with yourself and everyone around you. . . . You can't keep lashing out all the time when you have a child.*

But in various ways, Madonna was a huge help to me. First of all, she inspired me to get serious about working out—maybe too serious, for, as John would say in his book, moderation was never one of my strong points. I had grown up in L.A., where being thin and beautiful was all that mattered—to the point that my own mother developed a lifelong addiction to speed trying to achieve that standard. Everyone I knew, including my father and Farrah, was obsessed with weight loss. John had also been goading me, first hinting, then getting pushy about my need to drop the baby weight—slapping me on the butt when he saw me eating ice cream not long after Sean was born. At that point I resisted because I was still breast-feeding, but by the time I met Madonna, baby Sean was weaned and I was ready.

Now I went exercise-crazy—sprinting four miles, bike riding, and working out with Rob Parr for a couple of hours every day. It wasn't long before I lost my twenty pounds of pregnancy weight and then some, to the point that I was practically emaciated. I weighed 115 pounds, with nothing but lean muscle on my five-foot-seven frame.

My workout obsession would eventually take its toll. In years to come I'd wind up needing knee, back, and neck surgery, all because of overexercising.

ONCE I WAS THIN—again, with Madonna's inspiration—I started meeting with agents: John Burnham at ICM, Fred Westheimer at William Morris, and Jane Berliner at CAA. When I got callbacks saying they were interested, I hung up the phone and cried. I was so relieved that someone might actually believe in me and want me. But I was also scared to death.

By the time I met John, I was already feeling lost as an actor—my natural voice and self-esteem had been beaten down by my father's abuse, and being untrained, I didn't have the craft to compensate for my sense of emptiness. Being married to a man who saw me as an appendage—to the extent that he actually believed that I was responsible for his failures—hadn't helped me get a grip on who I was as a person, as Tatum. My chief source of identity was being the mother of Sean and Kevin.

So I was feeling pretty fuzzy and tentative when I went out on auditions. I'd sit in the car beforehand, fighting down nausea, from sheer nerves. When it came time to read, I prayed that my hands wouldn't shake, that I wouldn't break out in a sweat, or—my worst nightmare—completely choke. I was convinced that the directors judging me had huge expectations—that I'd be stunning, brilliant, etc., instead of merely good, because of my long Hollywood tenure. I was an Oscar winner, the youngest in film history! Certainly I had enormous and paralyzing expectations of myself.

Early on, I got excited when Dustin Hoffman suggested that I had a shot at playing Iris (Tom Cruise's girlfriend) in *Rain Man*—not only for the career break but also because working with "Dusty," my girlhood passion, would be fulfilling a lifelong dream. Ultimately, however, it didn't pan out. Other defeats followed, including *Lonesome Dove, Men Don't Leave,* and *Pretty Woman.* I was considered for a couple of plays—*Lulu* and, thanks to Madonna, *Hurly-Burly* by David Rabe—to no avail.

For a while my best prospect seemed to be *Miami Blues.* I memorized the audition scene and delivered my lines without one reference to my pages, and in such a good southern accent that the director, George Armitage, asked where I'd picked it up. "From my mother," I said proudly.

When I was done, Alec Baldwin, the male lead, started clapping and said, "Now, this is a real actress!"

George added, "And you and Alec have so much chemistry that we'll have to keep you apart."

"Not me!" I swore, laughing. "I'm a married woman."

So I felt hopeful, even though Ally Sheedy was reading after me. Later Alec told John that he couldn't understand why I was so nervous. As it turned out, neither Ally nor I got the part, which went to Jennifer Jason Leigh.

That was tough, but I knew reviving my career wouldn't be easy. I had to brace myself for rejection and fight succumbing to discouragement. In my diary I gave myself little pep talks: *The only way to make it work is to put real heart and energy into it!*

OF COURSE, I DID my best to protect John from my career anxieties. He was already ambivalent about my working and preoccupied with his own woes. I had vowed to tour as little as possible in 1988, since our travels the year before had been so disastrous to our marriage, with John blaming me for every match he lost. Besides, with Kevin getting older, I had to start getting him into preschool, and I was overseeing the renovations of our houses.

Still, all that spring, when he was on the circuit, John would phone, raging and blaming me for what he called his "downfall," insisting that my selfishness was ruining his career. "When I met you I was on top of Mount Everest," he told me, "and now I have to climb all the way up. I can't do it with you dragging me down."

When he wasn't ranting, John was coldly critical and snide, full of put-downs.

He's not even clear on what I've actually done, I complained to my diary. *He's so confused and hurt and angry—and it's all directed at me . . . I question how long I can withstand this without lashing out. . . . He has his mind set on making me the culprit.*

When John was home between tournaments, he was sullen and resentful if I didn't have a nanny constantly present so he could command my full attention. I warned him not to compete with the children—that it was a losing battle. And besides, they needed him. I threw Kevin a birthday party while John was off playing the French Open, and I have a tape of Kevin asking plaintively—missing him, loving him—"Where's my daddy?"

It was during this time that I first suspected John of being on steroids because his moods swung wildly and his behavior was so erratic. Sometimes he bullied me physically, jerking my arms up behind my back, squeezing my neck, or grabbing my nose between two of his knuckles and twisting so in a way that brought tears to my eyes. At the end of 2003, John would tell the press that for six years he'd been given "a form of steroid of the legal kind they used to give horses—before they decided it was too strong even for horses," without knowing what he was taking.

We tried counseling, but it only brought out John's killer instincts. He thought he was scoring points whenever the therapist took his side and started focusing less on the dialogue than on winning.

But as I wrote in my diary: *One of the things for me to remember is that I'm young and John's young, and we've gone*

through more in terms of life experience than most people. . . .
The kids know and love John, and I do too—that's all that
counts. I have to stick by him now because this is the hardest pe-
riod in his whole life.

WHEN JOHN LOST HIS second-round match at Wimbledon
that year to Wally Masur, he was devastated. I wasn't entirely
surprised because he'd been sick with some stomach bug the
day before. But he couldn't stop flogging himself about it, to
the point of being too ashamed even to describe the match
to me.

I was heartsick at hearing John so down and began to wonder whether it might actually be better for him, despite all his
complaints about how hard it was to focus, to have us with
him the road. Yes, he put me through a world of misery when
we traveled, but—let's face it—he could be just as nasty on
the phone. Clearly solitude wasn't agreeing with him.

He was on his way home, and we made a plan to go off together for a week, just the two of us. So at the end of June we
drove from Malibu to Big Sur, where we hiked and biked in
the mountains, ran races—I was now so strong and fast that I
easily beat John—and went skinny-dipping in a cold freshwa-
ter pond, which was exhilarating. I felt weird being away from
the kids for so long, but the trip was just the tonic we needed.
I'd been feeling so estranged from John—unjustly accused of
"ruining his career" and even victimized—and now I fell in
love with him all over again.

August 1, 1988: Today is the second anniversary of our mar-
riage. Hooray—we made it!

SEVENTEEN

R-e-s-p-e-c-t

LOOKING BACK ON my life, I can see it as a quest for just one thing. Not for money, though it was fun when I had it and could fully indulge my passion for stylish clothes. Definitely not for fame, which I achieved so young that I can hardly remember unfamous. Not for love, which I've luckily been blessed with, though not yet the happily-ever-after kind. Not even for emotional security, which I experienced too little growing up—or even later on—to know if I was missing anything.

The one thing I've struggled my whole life to get is respect—simply, to be treated with a little dignity. *Dignity* isn't a word usually associated with Hollywood, and aspiring actors certainly get a lot more rejection than respect. That's how things were playing out for me in the late 1980s and early 1990s. I continued to audition, even while wondering just how I'd juggle two young boys and a constantly touring husband if I did get a role. But I saw kickstarting my career both as a means of personal fulfillment and as a strategy to shore up my marriage. If I could accomplish something on my own, I believed I'd feel stronger and better about myself and more equipped to resist being sucked into the quicksand of John's deepening furies and depressions.

I was auditioning so badly, though. I read for *My Blue Heaven, Dogfight, Mortal Thoughts* (losing out to Demi Moore) and even got as far as screen-testing for the female lead as a tough-gal cop in *Lethal Weapon III.* That role went to Rene Russo. Though John was leery of my aspirations, he did make a good suggestion: that I try to build up slowly, doing a few independent films before going all-out for the big studio movies.

I did land a part in *Little Noises,* an independent comedy featuring Crispin Glover (at that point best known for playing the father of Michael J. Fox in the *Back to the Future* movies) as a young man who courts fame by stealing a friend's poems. But the film was widely panned, for as Vincent Canby of the *New York Times* noted, "Its only distinguishing feature is that a mature Tatum O'Neal appears in it." I also made a TV movie, *Fifteen and Getting Straight,* set in a drug-rehab unit for teenagers. Later that would seem ironic, as if I'd been back to my own future.

Determined to beat discouragement, I kept trying to develop my skills. Back in New York, I enrolled in Sandra Seacast's topflight acting workshop, which met three days a week. My fellow students included Don Johnson, Lynda Carter, Jessica Lange, and Isabella Rossellini.

I was assigned to do a scene from Chekhov's *Three Sisters,* with Don playing my lover. He was grossly flirtatious. I was mortified at the way he kept grabbing and hugging and kissing me in front of the class and calling me at home.

Then we were paired up for a sensory awareness exercise, exploring each other's faces with our fingertips for many long minutes. It made him tremble, he told me. He kept tilting his face in close to my neck, so he could deeply inhale my perfume.

The whole encounter made me queasy. Even when I was single, I never went in for that playing-with-fire kind of dallying—not that I was a prude. But Don, like me, was a spouse and a parent—and his wife, of all people, was my old pal Melanie Griffith, whom he'd married and divorced in his youth and recently re-wed.

It was all so incestuous.

Having grown up in that incestuous Hollywood family, I knew all the other siblings, as well as the parents, aunts, uncles, and cousins. I confronted my own history every time I turned around. I was auditioning for directors and competing against stars—some of whom I'd known since childhood—I saw at parties. That made it downright weird when John started insisting that a surefire way for me to get movie roles was to cash in on his celebrity by changing my name to Tatum McEnroe.

It hurt too. It made me feel that my life achievements—including some well-acknowledged classic movies—didn't count at all with John. I'd expected to find that attitude in the unforgiving, what-have-you-done-for-me-lately climate of Hollywood, but not from my husband.

I had dropped out when I was nineteen, the middle ground between youthful and adult roles. I now had to reinvent myself as a grown-up actress against an ever-expanding field of new leading ladies like Jodie Foster, who'd achieved admirable success as an adult, ironically, after playing Addie in the unsuccessful TV series spun off *Paper Moon*.

Yes, I was having trouble finding my feet, but so was John,

trying to hold his own against the new breed of Lendls, Beckers, and Agassis. We were both hitting the same wall.

JOHN AND I DID manage to find enjoyment in a realm outside our own bruising worlds of tennis and filmmaking—the New York art scene. We fell in with the downtown crowd John first encountered in the early 1980s, when Richard Weisman and Vitas Gerulaitis took him gallery-hopping in Soho.

We spent some lovely weekends at the Amagansett home of the art dealer Larry Gagosian, hanging out with the painters Eric Fischl, April Gornik, and David Salle. That led to dinners with other leading artists of the day, Julian Schnabel and Francesco Clemente. We went to openings for Chuck Close, Bryan Hunt, Richard Serra, and the photographer Jean Pigozzi, among others; as well as dinner parties given by Ross Blechner, Jann and Jane Wenner, and Yoko Ono. It was a lot of fun.

Movie stars never awed me, of course, but artists were something else. At first I felt self-conscious about my lack of formal schooling. But I quickly learned that people in the art world, unlike those in the film business, tended to be down-to-earth, patient, and eager to explain their work. And they were fun, besides. I got the chance to advance Francesco Clemente's cultural education by presenting him with CDs by some emerging rap artists, including Queen Latifah and the Geto Boys.

I really felt that I was blossoming in the vibrant culture of New York in the early 1990s. The art world was exploding with exciting new ideas, so it was tremendously stimulating to be involved. And it was a huge relief to have something besides tennis as a focus, especially since my career seemed to be getting off to a slow start.

STILL, I NEVER for a second regretted having taken time off to have children. Kevin and Sean were the lights of my life, and I wouldn't have missed hearing them say their first words or watching them take their first steps for the greatest movie role of the century. I loved my boys and was completely devoted to them. My highest ambition—what I most wanted to achieve in life—was to be a great mom.

John too was a loving parent to our kids. But at times I wondered if he didn't resent my commitment to them, which he thought deprived him of the attention he needed. We had a lot of arguments in which I had to point out that our children couldn't live without me but John certainly could.

Especially when the boys were babies, I hated to have them out of earshot. We spent one of John's winter breaks in Sun Valley, not in our own place—which, like all the rest of our homes, was being renovated—but in a big modern, multi-story house we rented from Barbra Streisand.

Since Sean had been fussy, I wanted to put his crib in our room, but John said no—that Sean should stay with Kevin and our nanny Estella three flights below our top-floor master bedroom. Reluctantly, after much protest, I gave in.

A few nights later, Estella came knocking on our bedroom door to tell us that Sean was sick. "He'll be fine," John said and buried his head in the pillow, worn out from a night on the town with his friends. Estella had Sean in her arms, with his little head slumped to one side, his breath coming in rasps, and his skin burning with fever. He'd been having convulsions.

"Oh my God," I said, taking Sean from her. Cradling him, I snatched up the phone and called a Sun Valley acquaintance whose wife was a nurse.

"It's twenty degrees outside," she told me. "Take Sean out there to cool him down and then you better take him to the hospital."

I was terrified. I ran out into the snowy night with Sean, holding him till his temperature dropped a few points. Then I went back inside and shook John, who woke up grumbling, "What the hell is wrong?"

"Come on, we have to take Sean to the hospital," I told him. I was crying.

"Fucking calm down," he shouted. "Fucking pull yourself together."

The whole way to the hospital, he berated me for being hysterical. I'm sure I was, being a young mother in a strange place in the middle of my first big childhood-illness crisis. It was very scary—and it certainly didn't improve my state of my mind to hear my husband howling, "Why can't you shut the fuck up? Stop fucking panicking!"

Sean was admitted to the hospital with a bad case of croup, a respiratory virus. I spent the night on a cot in his room, shaken both by his illness and by John's vicious scolding. I hated him for not respecting my justifiable fears, for screaming at me with a sick baby in arms. All I'd needed was some reassurance and comfort from a man who constantly harped on his own need for "support."

What am I doing in this marriage? I asked myself.

———

THEN IN THE MIDDLE of 1990, I started noticing babies again—baby girls, to be specific. When I was pregnant with Sean, I'd told my diary: *I think it's just as thrilling to have another boy. I'm not sure I'm ready to have a girl anyway. I think they're tough to deal with when they get to be fifteen or sixteen years old. But I would like a girl one day.*

John wasn't thrilled with the idea, but I was in the grip of baby lust and also thought having a child might help my marriage. Finally John agreed to go along. That summer I got pregnant.

Once again I wanted to have my mother in my life. She had been counseling me on my troubles with John, urging me to stick it out. Unfortunately, when she spent time with us, she often wound up wreaking havoc. Her antics were becoming legendary.

I'd invited her out to Oyster Bay in 1989, where she came upon some painkillers John was taking for his back. She nabbed the bottle then vanished into Manhattan on a three-day bender, claiming that she was kidnapped by a limousine driver.

It was a hell of a story, delivered with my mother's usual flair. She was, after all, the best actor in the family: "Honey, I don't know what happened. He took my purse, and he drove me someplace far away. I tried to open the door and jump out of the car, but I couldn't—he was going too fast. And then he wouldn't drive me back. So there I was, lost in New York, without my purse—not even change for the phone—and, honey, I didn't know what to do . . ."

. What really happened? To this day, I have no clue.

Another time, she came to get me and the kids at the L.A. airport when I was returning to Malibu from Germany, where John had played an exhibition. She was in a strange mood, cranky and argumentative, and picked a fight with me in the car. When we reached the house, I brought the kids inside, along with a couple of pieces of luggage, leaving my carry-on bag, containing my jewelry and John's earnings—around $8,000, paid in cash—on the front seat.

When I came out of the house, she was gone. I called around frantically, trying to find her, with no luck. Finally I had to hire a private detective. A week passed before he managed to track her down.

The minute he called, I drove out to the spot where she'd been sighted. I found her walking down the street, blind drunk, pushing a bicycle—God only knows where she got it—trailed by a dog I didn't recognize. At least she still had her wig on.

I checked her into the hospital. Then, with the help of the detective, I recovered the car. It was parked haphazardly, with the doors open, and there on the front seat was my carry-on bag. It had been rifled and its contents strewn all over the car. Luckily, the jewelry was still there, but the money was long gone.

John didn't usually comment on such incidents. But now and then, casting himself in the role of victim, he'd say, "If only I'd known that I was marrying into such a crazy family . . ." or "I wish I'd known ahead of time how insane your parents are."

Weren't you listening? was all I could think.

About five months into my third pregnancy, I got an emergency call from Griffin. He was supposed to babysit for my half-brother Redmond, then six or seven years old, but couldn't make it, for some reason. Since I was nearby in Mal-

ibu, he asked me to go over and pick up Redmond at my father's house.

At that point, I hadn't spoken to my dad in ages, and our
last encounter had been heated. He and Farrah co-owned and
were costarring in a television series called *Good Sports*, playing rival anchors on an all-sports network. Real-life athletes including George Foreman and Kareem Abdul-Jabbar had
appeared on the show, and my father had badly wanted John
to do an episode. When John said no, my father was angry.
He'd made no secret of the fact that he hoped the show, which
was struggling, would help revive his career.

For all I knew, my dad was still fuming about the rejection.
Knowing how violent he could be, I was afraid to go over there
alone. So I asked John to come with me.

"No," he said. "I've got to practice."

"Please," I pleaded, "I'm afraid something bad is going to
happen."

John shrugged, not understanding my fears, and again
said no.

Practically shaking, I drove over to my father's house, with
my sons in the car, thinking the sight of them might appease
him. As soon as the three of us walked in the door, my father
came thundering out of his room. "What the fuck are you doing here?" he demanded.

"I'm here to get Redmond," I told him.

"The fuck you are."

He started manhandling and pushing me, trying to shove
me out the door. Suddenly I felt a wave of contractions in my
womb. I backed out of the house, horrified, sure that I was losing the baby.

My sons were crying hysterically, frightened by my father's shouting. Then, as soon as I'd gotten them back in the car, Sean remembered the little painted sword he'd brought along to show his grandfather. He had left it in the house.

The last thing I wanted to do was go back in there, but Sean was inconsolable. So I had to face my dad's fury one more time.

When he saw I was back, my father started howling, "John should have done *Good Sports*! Doesn't he know who I am? Doesn't he read *Vanity Fair?*"

My father and Farrah, as well as the show, had recently been profiled in the magazine by Jesse Kornbluth.

As I searched frantically for the sword, my father came at me again, yelling, "Get your brats out of here!"

I eased back out of the house and got myself home and to the doctor. Fortunately the baby was okay. For days, though, I couldn't stop crying, both because of my father's attack and because of John's indifference. How could he have let me go alone? I just couldn't understand it, never mind accept it, and the pain of that abandonment ate away at me. I was so unhappy.

I STAYED BEHIND with the kids in Malibu at one point when John made a trip to the Far East. Flipping through a tabloid paper, I came across photos of John and Billy Joel in Hong Kong, apparently out drinking with some U.S. Marines. In one shot a big hand was grabbing at a lens, and in another John was snatching a camera away from a photographer to rip out his film. There was also a woman in the picture.

I called John right away to see what was up but was determined not to make a mountain out of a molehill.

"What's going on over there?" I asked.

"Oh, Tatum, nothing," he told me. He knew just what I was talking about, though. Was that a sign of guilt?

"You, of all people, know how the press is always setting me up."

"And that woman . . . ," I said, as casually as I could.

John began to sputter defensively, acting offended by my implication and insisting that he had done nothing wrong.

It wasn't impossible to believe. Sure, there were groupies on the tennis circuit and lots of other women eager to throw themselves at any kind of celebrity. John had his faults, but skirt chasing wasn't really one of them—and certainly not the Olympic-caliber womanizing I'd witnessed in Hollywood. John was more earnest—as I was—and more moral.

Still, this time I smelled smoke, and where there's smoke, there's usually fire. I felt pretty sure that he'd had an affair—but I chose to take him at his word.

AROUND THIS TIME we took a family vacation to Hawaii to visit John's friend Kenny Margerum, who used to play pro football with the San Francisco 49ers. There was only one direct flight a day to Kona, which left at 9 A.M. from San Francisco. To make it, we had to get up at the crack of dawn and catch a seven o'clock plane from Malibu—not an easy task with two small boys.

After we landed in San Francisco, Kevin asked to stop in

the bathroom. I took him, while John, Estella, and Sean went ahead to find the gate for the Kona flight.

Little did I know that the gate was in a far-off wing of the terminal. I was pregnant and tired, and four-year-old Kevin was on Toddler Time. After the bathroom, he wanted to stop and smell the flowers in the planters. I let him. Then he made a beeline for the gift shop, with me clutching his hand. He started patting the fuzzy Elmo dolls, playing with some miniature cars, and picking up shiny souvenirs. We were just being silly, fooling around, until I thought we'd better mosey on to the gate.

We got on one "moving sidewalk," but by the end of it, we hadn't even reached the right concourse. We took another "people mover"—and then a third.

I remember what happened next like it was yesterday.

We were coming off the final walkway with something like fifteen minutes to spare when I spotted little Sean in the distance, lying on the floor. John was standing over him, screaming his head off. I nearly panicked, thinking Sean had gotten hurt.

Grabbing Kevin by the hand, I started running as fast as we could for the gate. As I got closer, I could see that John was tugging at a gate attendant's arm. Then he caught sight of me and threw his hands in the air, bellowing, "Where's the fucking tickets, Tatum?"

"They're in the diaper bag." He had it slung over his shoulder. "I told you where I put them."

"No, they're not, Stupid!"

"John, they're here," I said, pulling them out of one of the diaper bag pockets.

Meanwhile, a gate attendant was calling the police for backup, while others began closing the door to the boarding ramp.

"Great, Tatum, perfect. Take the kids and go sit down," John snarled.

Fighting to keep the door open, he started pushing and shoving the attendants, ranting all the while, "I've never missed a fucking flight in sixteen years. . . . Here are the god-damn tickets. . . . Let us on that plane . . ."

The boys were clutching at me, wide-eyed, murmuring "Mommy, Mommy" as the attendant announced, "Mr. McEn-roe, we're putting you under citizen's arrest. You can do this to other people but not to us."

Then the police arrived and handcuffed John.

There was talk of formally booking John for disorderly con-duct and harassment. Ultimately, the airline decided not to press charges. After holding us for an hour at the airport police station, they put us on another flight, this one with a lengthy stopover.

As we started boarding, John shook me roughly, saying, "Now are you happy with yourself?"—as if I were the one who'd made us miss the once-a-day direct flight by getting bombastic and then arrested.

That disgusted me. A woman who'd witnessed the fight at the gate had asked, "How can you stand being married to him?"

I thought: *I don't know if I can.*

EIGHTEEN

Coming Undone

THE ROCKINESS OF MY marriage eased up briefly after our sweet daughter, Emily Katherine, was born on May 10, 1991. A baby can bring two people together, though not for long.

Like Kevin, she came into the world at St. John's Hospital in Santa Monica. It was my third induced birth, anesthesia free. Somehow, it was important to me not to dilute the fullness of the experience.

Emily was such a joy. The boys were, naturally, alternately loving and jealous, especially Sean, who was old enough at three and a half to recognize that he'd lost his billing as baby-of-the-family. Being a Libra, he was more fiery in temperament, anyway, than Kevin, my Gemini, who, even at five, was taking on my own, all-too-familiar role as the earnest and responsible "oldest child."

I told my diary: *Last night, when I wasn't looking, Kevin carried Emily around the room. When I realized what was happening, I didn't yell because he was together and unafraid. It was a sight, I must say!*

My boys are the greatest! . . . But I always have to make sure Sean doesn't feel left out—and if I forget it, he reminds me, with

*loud outbursts. I love Sean so much. I have to keep telling him! . . .
The boys asked to kiss Emily "sixty times" today.*

Not surprisingly, having three children under the age of
five made my life supremely chaotic. *I get so stressed when I'm
nursing and they both pounce on me, wanting to kiss Emily's
face,* I wrote. *I've got to say, "This is Emily's quiet time, and you
need quiet time too."*

But quiet time was at a premium. Sometimes I had to confess that I was totally overwhelmed: *No time, three kids, so much
work . . . I'm tired . . . I'm reading Dr. Spock and trying to get an
organized file of what I'm doing. Man, I have nothing to draw
from! . . . The kids are always doing something: pulling, running,
jumping, hitting, throwing, biting, spitting, pulling hair. Etc.*

John used marijuana and transcendental meditation to
cope. He complained about my nursing Emily, which I believe
made him jealous. But there were times when he handled the
kids with more firmness and patience than I could muster, and
that's when I felt most partnered with him.

We could still have fun too. We celebrated Emily's first
Halloween in New York, dressing her up as a puppy Dalmatian
to go trick-or-treating in our building. Kevin went as a prince,
Sean was Batman, and John decked himself out in a Ninja
Turtle shell.

IF DEALING WITH THREE kids at home was tough, it was going to be even crazier on the road. I'd promised myself to travel
more with John, both because he seemed so miserable without us—even if he blamed us for making him lose when we

were along—and also because, once Kevin and Sean started school, which they would soon, we could no longer join him as a family on the circuit.

I took pride in having done the tough job of getting both Kevin and Sean into private schools. The top echelon of Manhattan elementary schools and even preschools were as wildly competitive as Ivy League colleges, and the applications were almost as daunting, especially for me, a high school dropout. It was tempting to laugh at questions about the "strengths" and "interests" of four- and five-year-olds. "Uh, strengths? Like playing in the sandbox?" I wanted to say. "Interests? Like firetrucks? Cookies? Popsicles?"

For driven, overachieving Manhattan parents, getting into a prestigious school, even at the kindergarten level, was like a matter of life and death—something that would supposedly benefit or haunt the child for years, possibly even into adulthood. Having always seen school as a straitjacket myself, I didn't buy into that obsession. Still, I would be as thrilled as any parent when all three of my kids in turn got accepted by our first-choice school, and I sent them off, one by one, all dressed up in their little suits.

WHILE WE COULD, though, I was determined to hit the circuit. From the time I got pregnant with Emily—which made it tough to look for movie work—I always had a set of bags by the front door, packed and ready to go. When my children were young, I did two tours of Australia with John and even went to Finland. Cities became a blur: Venice, Florence, Verona, Paris, Lyon, Düsseldorf, Munich, and more, all with

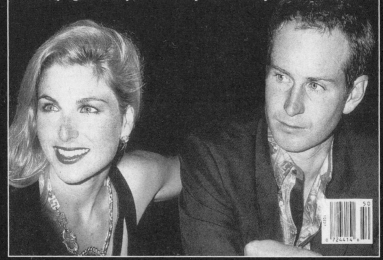

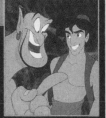
People *magazine cover, December 14, 1992.*

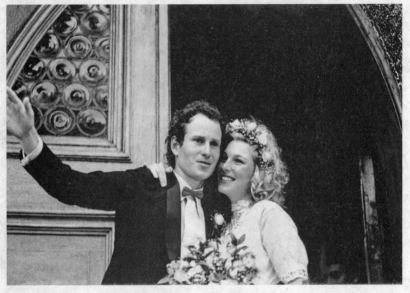

True love. The Oyster Bay Catholic Church in New York. August 1, 1985.

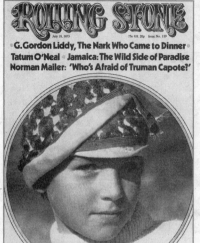

Rolling Stone *in 1973.*

COURTESY OF ROLLING STONE/WENNER MEDIA, COVER PHOTOGRAPH BY STEPHEN JAFFE

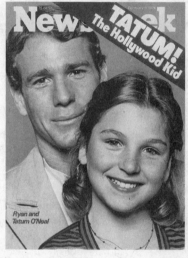

Newsweek *in 1976.*

COURTESY OF *NEWSWEEK*

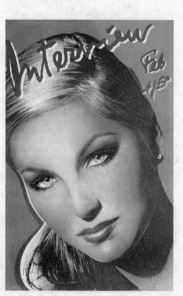

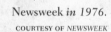

Interview *magazine in 1980.*

INTERVIEW MAGAZINE, FEBRUARY 1980, COURTESY BRANT PUBLICATIONS, INC.

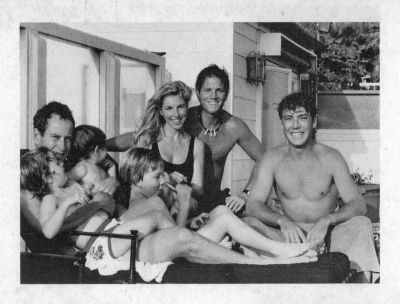

My two sons, Kevin and Sean, in a rare photo with their uncle Redmond "Red" O'Neal (far right) at the children's table at the house my dad shared with Farrah Fawcett on Antelo Road, in Bel Air, California. Circa 1988.

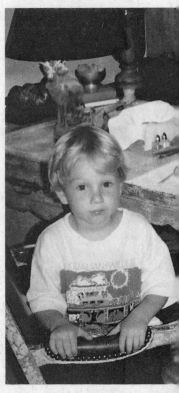

My family photo (the way we were back in Malibu in 1992 just before the split). (Left to right) Sean Timothy McEnroe, John McEnroe, Emily Katherine McEnroe, Kevin Jack McEnroe, me, Patrick Young O'Neal, Griffin Patrick O'Neal.

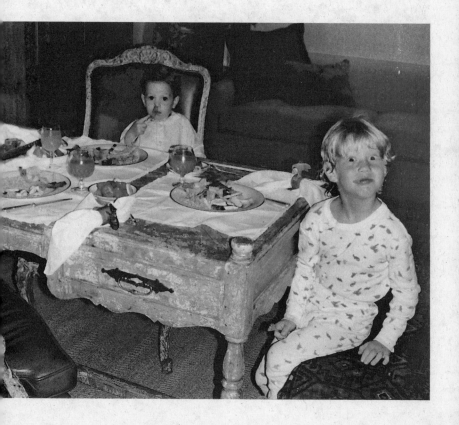

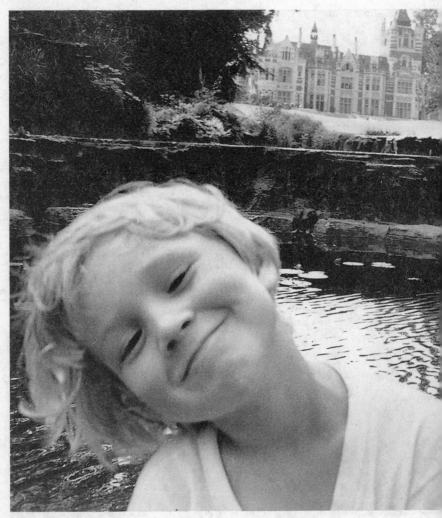

Smiling Kevin McEnroe in front of George Harrison's mansion in England. Boy, we had fun.

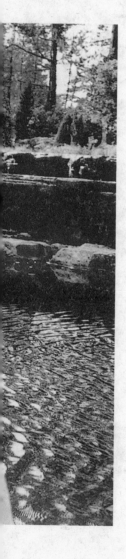

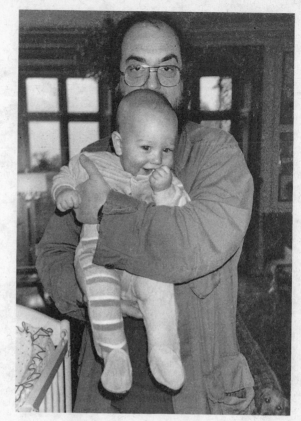

*One of my favorite photos. My son Kevin with the great
Stanley Kubrick at his house in England.*

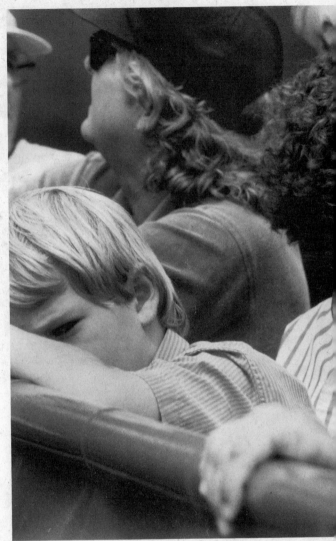

The loyal tennis wife. And who's that little guy on the left? (Our tired Kevin McEnroe.)

© AP/WIDE WORLD PHOTOS

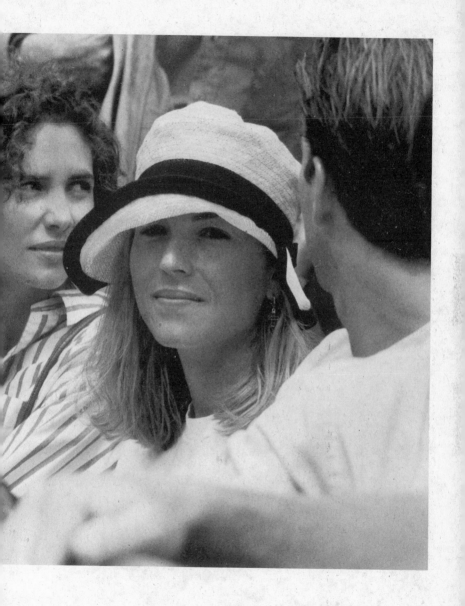

A photo of me with dark hair
(age twenty-four) with my sons
Sean and Kevin on the front porch
of the old Johnny Carson house.

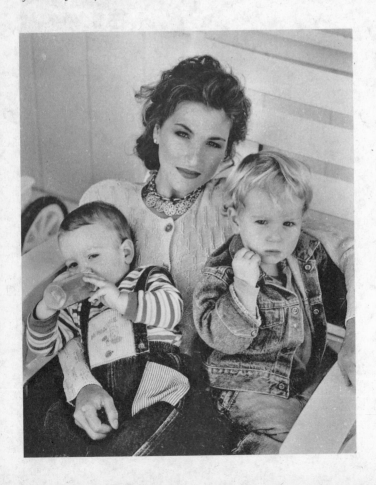

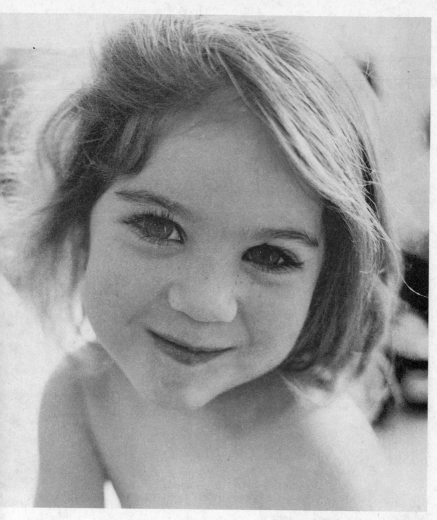

Sean and Kevin's favorite picture of their sister, Emily. Circa 1994, New York City, East End Avenue.

PHOTOGRAPH BY DEWEY NICKS

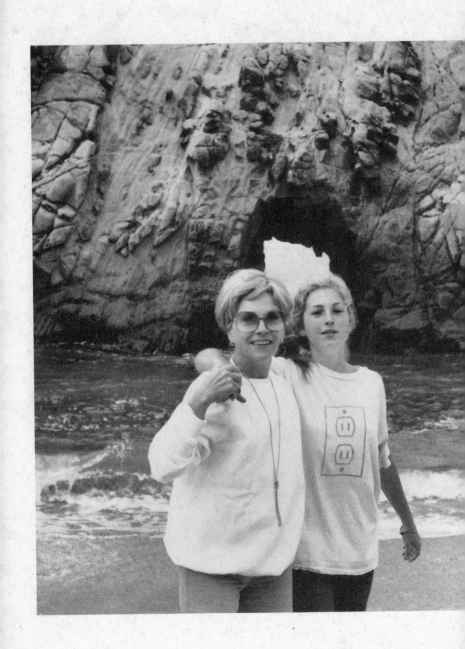

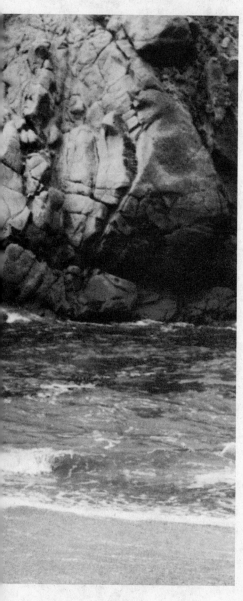

*Reconnecting with my sober mom.
We're enjoying the fresh air of Big Sur.
Circa 1980.*

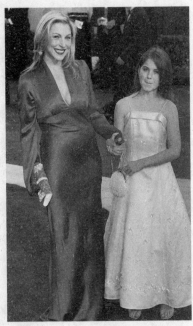

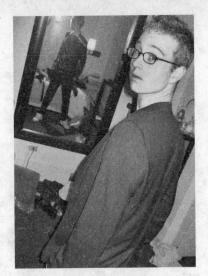

My eldest son, Kevin. So tall, smart, and handsome. He's headed for college this fall.

Like mother like daughter. Me and my best Academy Award date ever: Miss Emily McEnroe. Here we are on the red carpet at the Oscars in 2002. It was wonderful sharing this experience together.

WIREIMAGE.COM

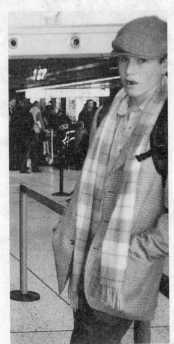

My handsome son Sean in the Dublin airport during our Christmas vacation last year.

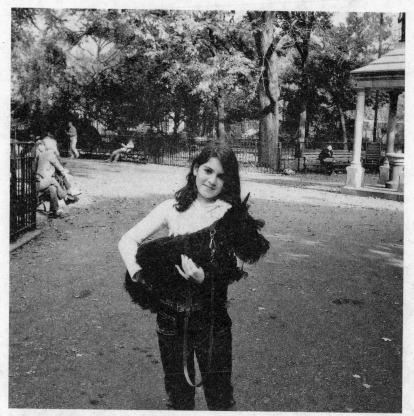

Emily and our Scottish Terrier, Lena, in Tompkins Square Park, New York City, last summer.

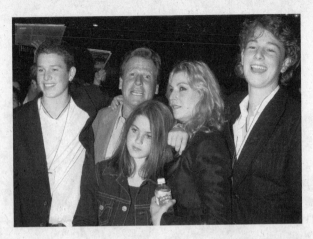

Last year in Hollywood at the thirtieth anniversary of Paper Moon and the launching of the DVD. It was a poignant moment where my father and I and my three kids were in a rare photo opportunity together. My father and I look so uncomfortable, which makes me so sad. But that picture below of just me and my children brings me pure, total joy.

WIREIMAGE.COM

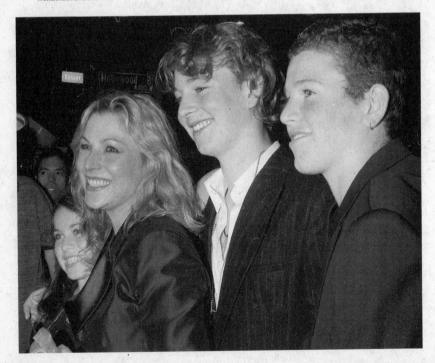

the kids, nanny, diaper bags, juice bottles, toys, and carry-ons in tow. I remember getting lost with the kids in Toronto and Montreal, as well as in Wisconsin and Cincinnati—the tournament grounds were all so huge and confusing.

At least traveling with the kids gave me more common ground with the other tennis wives. Even if they never became true friends, it helped to have women to commiserate with when the men were preoccupied—practicing, having massages, or after the matches, decompressing by getting high and watching sports. I told my diary: *I think every tennis wife has traveling down to a science.*

A month after Emily was born, I drove from New York to Newport, Rhode Island, to watch John play for the Davis Cup. He won two matches, which seemed to bode well for our tour. From there we headed to England for Wimbledon, where I pumped my milk to get Emily through the long matches, so I wouldn't have to breast-feed in the stands, under the surveillance of photographers with zoom lenses.

That trip to London gave me a chance to introduce my children to some old friends. I brought Emily to a lovely restaurant lunch with Eric Clapton, who later invited me and John to his Chelsea flat. In the heat of discussion—and after a fair amount of wine—I blurted out an impetuous remark and had to apologize to Eric. Bigmouthed Tatum!

Mick Jagger had stolen his girlfriend but then called to ask Eric to join him in a live concert. Eric thought it over and decided to accept. But in the meantime Mick had decided to invite Tina Turner instead, without so much as calling to inform Eric.

"You're a sucker," I told him.

"No," he replied, "I'm not a sucker. I'm a gentleman."

And he was—is—then, now, and always.

Another friend I reconnected with was Vivian Kubrick, whom I still loved and idolized. John referred to her as my guru.

She's amazing, so full of life and learning, I told my diary. *So honest, always trying to make herself better and those around her.* While coveting her close relationship with her father, I noted, *She's twenty-nine now. I hope she moves on in some way so that she doesn't have to be financially dependent on him for too much longer.* She was so gifted and talented that I hoped she would find some fulfilling means of self-expression. *She's a little too fearful still, which she inherited from Stanley.*

One of the highlights of our time in England—maybe even of my whole life—was a visit to the Henley estate of George Harrison. To me George was a hero, part of my own history and a great artist, but also a genuinely kind, gentle, and charmingly eccentric man. It amused me when he told me how much he hated opening letters and always hoped there was no mail for him.

The house at Henley was a centuries-old castle, surrounded by a moat. Inside George had a special room devoted to his musical instruments, the wonderfully ornate sitars he had collected in his travels as well as his guitars. The grounds around the castle were beautiful, with a man-made lake. I have a photo of Kevin in a canoe on that lake, with his little blond head highlighted against the rough-hewn ancient walls.

John gave Dhani, George's son, a tennis lesson on the estate's clay court, and we were all treated to "follies"—traditional skits, with music, that made us feel as if we'd stepped back into the eighteenth century. George and Olivia could not have been more gracious and welcoming. It was a lovely and memorable day.

From England, we flew to Washington, D.C., our next stop on the tennis circuit, where I hauled the kids around in sweltering, hundred-degree heat. While we were there, I ran into Peter Guber, then head of Sony/Columbia studios, in an elevator. *I feel regretful that I don't have a career,* I wrote that night. *It's just, how can I work when John is traveling the whole year? My work takes me out of state . . . I can't see how I could leave or uproot the boys, not to mention Emily, that little angel. I love my kids, though they're major work—harder than I can bear sometimes. But I feel so fulfilled being a mom . . . I can't figure it out.*

JOHN HARDLY SEEMED TO appreciate the effort I was making. He kept carping at me about losing the baby weight, being too outspoken, not wanting to have sex whenever he felt like it, picking at my face—I was always so nervous, and my complexion seemed to go haywire after my pregnancies—nursing, not keeping the children quiet enough, not doing enough to cultivate this or that tennis wife. With all the laws John was laying down, I came to feel like just another member of Team McEnroe—John's personal cadre of trainers and masseurs—instead of his wife. It was a little like being in the military.

The worst was when John would belittle me in front of his friends or even my children. We all have peculiar tics, and John would cruelly taunt me about mine, telling the kids, "Ha, ha, ha, listen to your mom making that sound [or doing what-ever]. She should be on David Letterman, she's so funny . . ."

It was childish, painful, and, of course, all too reminiscent of my father.

John was so hypercritical that I grew even more watchful and self-conscious. To be fair, I was often on his case too, for spending so much time in front of the television, watching sports, instead of being with his family, and also for smoking so much pot. When he wasn't playing, he was sometimes in a pot fog. We did a lot of fighting.

I did my best to keep things in perspective, writing during that year's U.S. Open: *Now I know why John was being such a jerk. He was so nervous he couldn't see straight.*

But within a few months, I was recording the details of a fight in which I told him, *If you really feel these things about me, why don't we separate? Why don't you leave?*

I was feeling terribly stuck, living with a man who was so completely self-involved. But fed up as I was, I promised my diary: *I will keep trying to make this marriage better—and I hope it will be.*

THE AUSTRALIAN OPEN in January 1992 seemed just too far away and too challenging to attempt with three children. John went alone, and two weeks later, I was to take three flights from New York to hook up with him in Kona, Hawaii, for the first round of the Davis Cup. But on the second leg of our flight, Kevin grew gravely ill. By the time we arrived, he couldn't walk. Needless to say, I was terrified.

We weren't in a major city but on the island of Kona, so I

took Kevin to see the team doctor. Since he had intestinal cramps and was vomiting, the initial diagnosis was food poisoning, but it soon became clear that something more serious was going on. My poor son was in terrible pain. There was blood in his urine. The doctor was stumped.

John seemed to view Kevin's condition as an annoying distraction from tennis. He expected me to buck up and deal with it on my own. He didn't really believe in illness—to him, it was all a question of mind over matter, of just toughing it out, even for a child.

John hardly reacted even when Kevin's whole body started swelling, though I was beside myself. Alone and sick with worry, I took Kevin to the hospital three times over the next ten days. All the doctors could do was keep running tests that came back inconclusive.

Three nights in a row, I sat up with Kevin, rocking him, trying to comfort him as he cried and writhed in misery.

"I want to take Kevin back to New York," I told John.

"Kevin's fine," he insisted. "Don't be ridiculous."

Then he started to pressure me about his own needs—for companionship, for support, and, of course, sex. "Don't you understand what I'm going through?" I said. "This is our son. Don't you even care?"

"You're overreacting," John kept saying. "It's just a virus. You're getting hysterical."

Finally Kevin started developing bruises all over his body. He was visibly losing weight. Now I was in a panic. By the time we left Hawaii, Kevin was so black and blue and swollen that we had to take him onto the plane in a wheelchair.

I took it as a powerful statement of John's disaffection that he wouldn't even push the wheelchair. It seemed to offend his macho pride—as if John believed Kevin's illness was just some drama I'd manufactured, which made him look weak.

That turned my stomach. It was at that moment when I realized I had begun to despise my husband for his profound, unfeeling selfishness; for being such a narcissist that he was unmoved even by the obvious pain of his own five-year-old son.

That was the beginning of the end of my marriage.

When we reached New York, John and the nanny brought Sean and Emily home while I took Kevin straight from the airport to the doctor. His verdict was scary, if optimistic: a 1 percent chance that Kevin had leukemia but a 99 percent chance that he had a rare childhood blood disorder, Henoch-Schönlein purpura. It wasn't life-threatening like leukemia, thank God, though it could lead to kidney disease. He arranged for us to see a hematologist the next day.

All that night, I cried out of fear for Kevin—hoping, praying that he didn't have leukemia—and also out of despair over what my own life had become. I had three small children who needed a father, but that father was fast asleep in the next room. He wasn't sharing my fears—which were legitimate, by anybody's reckoning—but punishing me for having them, as well as for needing him.

I'd loved John with every cell of my body—so much that, for years, I could hardly bear to have him out of my sight. I had truly believed he was my soul mate and that we'd been put on earth to complete each other. But his black hole of an ego, his surly coldness, and his cruelty had slowly leached my love away. All that was left in me that night was a terrible grief.

I cried so much that, by the next morning, I'd blown an infection into my ears and had to be put on antibiotics. I pulled myself together for Kevin's hematology appointment, and John rather begrudgingly came along. The doctor had to draw a large quantity of blood, which terrified my son. I wanted to soothe and hold him during the procedure, but John kept yelling at him and me, "Kevin, just sit down. Tatum, leave him alone."

His angry bluster only fueled my loathing. I had to choke back tears and compose my face so I wouldn't frighten Kevin as they strapped him, wailing, to a gurney. It seemed to me an extra—totally gratuitous—trauma to inflict on a child.

Mercifully, the blood tests showed that Kevin didn't have leukemia. He was treated with steroids for Henoch-Schönlein purpura, kept out of kindergarten for six weeks, and monitored to be sure that his kidneys hadn't been compromised.

That, to John's mind, was the end of the crisis. But for me, it had just begun. When he had to go back on the circuit, leaving me behind to care for Kevin—and to process my rage and confusion—I was so relieved.

WHEN I LOOK BACK on that time—especially the months after Kevin got sick—I can see that I was like a swimmer stranded far from shore. Though I hadn't consciously decided to leave John, I was flailing frantically for something to cling to that could pull me from my marriage before I drowned.

For the first time, I began to make new friends of my own in Manhattan, including several from my acting classes, and to get involved in community activities, like the New York City Ballet, Art Against AIDS, anti-gay-discrimination groups, and the Democratic Party. I kept on top of the art world, at one point making the rounds of openings with Matt Dillon, my young costar from *Little Darlings*.

I kept on looking for work, interviewing agents and reading for movies, but that was still a disappointing slog.

As usual, I also reached out to my family. Griffin had been doing better, and when he was sober, no one could be funnier or more loving. Then he'd started to experiment with crack cocaine and twice that year was arrested for assaulting his girlfriend—once for firing a gun into her car. He described it comically, talking about "killing her car," but it was clearly a sign that he was unraveling. He was sentenced to a year in drug rehab.

Around that time, my mother had an accident in her Jeep on the Pacific Coast Highway, which cost her three fingers on her left hand. Her dog was thrown from the car and killed. When I called her at the hospital, I could hear her screaming in the background, "Tatum, I was sober! I wasn't drinking, I swear!"

Maybe she wasn't, but again, to this day the true circumstances of the accident remain unknown.

Later she sent me pictures of her mangled hand. *I have never felt such revulsion and grief in my life,* I told my diary. *It was a horrific sight. What was worse is that you could see that she wasn't dealing with it at all. In one picture, she was laughing hysterically. It was surreal.*

So, no help there! It's probably lucky that I was still estranged from my father, considering the unhappy state of the rest of my family.

Then, I began an affair.

I still have a lot of shame about it. I didn't see it as a way out of my marriage. It was more that I was just so sad, yearning for gentleness and kindness, needing to feel beautiful and desired, rather than required to serve a man. When I met John, I was only twenty years old, and all the romance in our relationship had expired. I no longer knew what was normal or even possible between two loving adults.

I suppose I also felt very alone in the world, with a totally unreliable family, three small children, and no real anchor. I wondered if I could ever attract another man. So when I felt an electric zing from an acquaintance who seemed to radiate the sensuality, tenderness, and kindness I was longing for, I didn't fight it very hard.

He was also married, which made it feel oddly safer, like more of a toe in the water than a plunge off the high board. But, never being one to do anything halfway, I started to grow obsessional about my secret lover. That forced me to admit that what I was doing was wrong.

I knew I owed it both to myself and John to sound out where our marriage was headed without the emotional racket of some ultimately fruitless fantasy. So, after a few months, I broke it off.

Still, the affair taught me some hard-won lessons about love and loss and sensuality and what I had to offer as a woman. It continued to reverberate in my life, for better or worse, long after it was over.

NINETEEN

The Last Party

JOHN AND I had what amounted to a last hurrah—though I didn't recognize it then—in the middle of 1992. It started with a romantic week we stole together, just the two of us, at the Ritz in Paris.

We truly love each other, I reported to my diary, *but I also see how I've changed and needed to, rightly—meeting new friends, getting involved in the art scene and a more sophisticated social group. All that was essential for a full and happy life. John hasn't had that yet, but when he settles down, he will find the time.*

. The kids and I then accompanied John to Wimbledon, where he played so well that it made me proud. Bono from U2 called to offer congratulations, and the whole band sent John a bottle of champagne. Joanne Woodward, Ron Wood of the Rolling Stones, and George and Olivia Harrison all showered him with praise. That thrilled John so much—and when he was happy, a brilliant sun rose over my world.

But by autumn, I was telling my diary, *I am beginning to hate John. I hate being so needed in such a negative way. . . . He acts so self-centered and can't verbalize anything, and then when he gets frustrated, he lashes out at me! His forehead crinkles and his body starts twitching and he starts his barrage of insults and innuendoes and my shoulders start burning and my stomach starts aching and I want to scream!*

The death knell of my marriage was already tolling.

LATE IN OCTOBER, I was asked to host a benefit screening in New York for *The Last Party,* a documentary about the Democratic convention made by my friend Donovan Leitch, the son of the singer-songwriter. It featured Robert Downey Jr. as sort of a Michael Moore character, interviewing both ordinary and famous people, ranging from Jerry Falwell to Spike Lee, about the political process. The film was barbed and funny, and I was delighted to get involved, never suspecting the reaction I would get from John.

He seemed jealous, not only because I was doing something on my own, with new friends whom he didn't know, but also because he hadn't been asked to be a cosponsor. Wasn't he, after all, the bigger celebrity in the family?

Since he'd just come in off the tour the week before, I doubted that he'd even want to come to the screening. But he clearly did, so I invited him.

We had a tolerable time, though a bit tense, and came home early. I was in my bathroom at the penthouse getting undressed when John came barging through the door. I always hated that, and he knew it. When he was in a bullying mood, he made a point of violating my privacy.

"Can you please knock?" I asked.

"Excuse me? Knock?" he said. "No, I can't. This is my fucking house. If you don't like it, you can get the hell out."

"What?"

"Get your fucking shit and get the fuck out of my house."

Grabbing my arm, John yanked me out of the bathroom. As I tried to pull my clothes together, he flung my purse at me.

The apartment was very large, four floors overlooking Central Park. Slapping at me, he shoved me toward the stairs.

"What the hell are you doing?" I protested.

He started pushing at me, kicking me, until I stumbled backward and started slipping down the staircase. All I could think of was Kevin sleeping in the next room. If he opened his door, he'd see his mother tumbling down the stairs and hear his father railing, "You fucking bitch! Who do you think you are?"

"John . . . ," I pleaded.

I scrambled to my feet and backed down the stairs as John came raging after me. "Remember what you were when you met me? You were nothing! And look at you now! Look what I've done for you! You should respect me."

He was ringing changes on the same old tune I'd always heard from my father: "I made you. You were—are—nothing without me."

I wasn't going to hear it anymore. He grabbed at me but I pulled out of his grasp.

I'd reached the front door and had my hand on the knob.

"Where the fuck are you going?" John demanded.

"I'm out of here, John. I've leaving you."

"You wouldn't dare."

I didn't answer. I was gone!

OUT ON THE STREET, I had no idea where I was heading. I knew that a friend was staying at Mick Jagger's town house, so

I grabbed a cab, and luckily, he was there. He let me crash in one of the rooms upstairs.

The next morning I went back to get the children. John agreed to move out for the few days remaining before he left for the Paris Open. Though we decided not to announce it yet, we were officially separated.

I feel sick through my whole soul, I wrote. *This situation is ripping me apart. John has cried both times I talked to him. . . . He is so sad. He kept saying, "Tell the kids I love them," and he got off the phone saying, "I love you, baby." The only thing I know is that I need this time apart more than anything. . . . I've been so unhappy in my marriage. But to hear him so upset breaks me up so hard . . . I'm so depressed I can hardly write.*

Of course, the hardest thing was talking to the kids about it. Kevin started wondering where his father was, and I had to explain that John and I were going to live apart for a while, adding that their daddy missed them very much. *Kevin asked me if we were getting a divorce and I said NO!* I recorded. *Sean just kept saying, "Turn on the TV. Turn on the TV."*

It was all so horrible.

Right away I started seeing the effects in both of the boys. Sean insisted on sleeping in my bed night after night, and Kevin grew increasingly sensitive, complaining that, since John left, "No one loves me in this house."

Of course, I covered him with kisses, assuring him that I— and Daddy and Sean and Emily—all adored him. I reminded him that, earlier in the day, when he'd pinched his finger in the kitchen cabinet, Emily had kissed him and rubbed his back.

That seemed to cheer Kevin up, but it made me feel even more depressed—and so terribly guilty for having fallen in hate with John.

If my marriage had been purgatory—a place of punishment and torment—the next phase in my life was going to be hell.

I MOVED INTO JOHN'S old apartment at 200 East End Avenue, for which he charged me $6,000 a month in rent. I paid him with the money I'd saved from my movie work.

As soon as the word got out, everyone in my life started weighing in with opinions. My mother was horrified at the thought of my leaving John. Her own life had been such a struggle that she urged me to stay married, if only for the money. "For God's sake," I said, "I'm not a high-class whore, Mom."

Behind my back, she'd telephone John, which drove me crazy—she was such a conniver that I couldn't even guess what game she was up to—and warned me that he'd put a "tail," a private detective, on me. Whether that was true or not—and I came to believe that it was—her meddling was very destructive.

I knew it was inevitable, but I hated the thought of losing contact with John's mother, for whom I had genuine affection and respect. I soon started catching a whiff of attitude from some of his other family members and friends, to the effect that: "Tatum's nothing but a spoiled movie star—not even a practicing Catholic—so what do you expect?"

That hurt me deeply because it was so unfair. Anyone could see that John was a difficult husband. He had even made a career, as one of my lawyers later put it, out of being "the most notorious hothead in the land."

I just couldn't take all that rage and drama anymore.

Whether I was an unbaptized Hollywood actress or a Buddhist housewife living in Des Moines, I had a right—or so I thought—to try to change my life, to escape an abusive man, and to grasp at happiness.

QUITE SOON, HOWEVER, I began grasping at happiness with some unlikely individuals. It's practically a cliché that recently separated people are desperate to test their appeal on the dating scene. John did it, with a range of women including one of my friends. I did it too, with such dead-end crushes that my shrink once asked whether I was trying to convince myself to return to my marriage.

That's when some advice from my "guru," Vivian Kubrick, got me into trouble. Vivian was on a mission to bring truth into all relationships. Her mantra was "risk getting real." I was talking to her several times a day and, within weeks of my separation, brought her to New York for a lengthy visit. *Her knowledge is boundless, and I suck it up like a sponge,* I told my diary.

Perhaps common sense should have dictated that both I and my situation were too unstable for me to "risk getting real." I was caught in the crazy whirlwind of contradictory emotions that inevitably spin off the unraveling of a marriage: despising/missing and loving John, wanting validation/vindication/forgiveness, feeling anguished/panicked/empowered/embittered/enraged/ elated/liberated/lonely/inconsolably miserable and sad—the whole gamut. "Real" for me at that point was a moving target. What I most needed to get was a grip.

Instead I got "real" to the point that I alienated friends, at a time when I should have been circling the wagons around me. And I got "real," unfortunately, with John, confessing my one-shot affair, explaining what I'd gained from it, and even naming the man.

I pointed out that John himself once had an affair—or at least once that I knew about—that time in Hong Kong with Billy Joel.

This time he didn't deny it. "But it's not the same at all, Tatum. That was just sex. You had feelings for the guy."

"That's the difference between men and women," I tried to tell him. "Is it better—less of an infidelity—if it's 'just sex'?"

Angry and hurt, he seemed to think so.

I honestly—and foolishly—believed that my confession would clear the air, make John see the error of his ways and realize how unhappy I'd been in our marriage, help establish a new dialogue between us, etc.—all the benefits that Vivian, who was equally naive, attributed to "getting real."

That's not what happened, of course. Instead, John immediately cut off all my bank accounts and credit cards. Barely a month after we separated, we were careening toward divorce court. The high-powered McEnroe machine—a huge legal juggernaut—was speeding straight at me. I didn't even have a lawyer. I had "risked getting real" and now I risked getting splattered.

What a mess! To make matters worse, my mother tipped off the press, which had a field day with headlines like "The Final Set," "Game Over," and "End of the Love Match."

THE DIVORCE HEADLINES, of course, drew the attention of my father. Against my better judgment, I accepted his invitation to bring my kids and join him, Farrah, and Redmond on a vacation in Hawaii at the end of the year. As a buffer I brought along my old friend Esme Gray, hooking up with her in San Francisco so we could all fly together to Kona.

In my bag I had a script for a TV miniseries, *Woman on the Run*, based on the true story of a wrongfully accused killer, Lawrencia "Bambi" Bembenek. For all the uproar in my personal life, I had continued to audition. Days before we left for Hawaii, I got the job.

I was ecstatic. I'd been reading and screen-testing so much (in the short stretches when I wasn't pregnant or banishing baby weight) with such little payoff that I was beginning to lose faith. I had a great many near misses, which didn't encourage me but made it worse because I got so psyched and hopeful when directors were flattering or asked for callbacks. I'd even been mulling a possible film that required me to do a nude scene. I wasn't sure I was ready, and John hit the ceiling. But I'd consider almost anything if it gave me the chance to get back in the saddle and working again.

I was so pleased with *Woman on the Run* that I made the mistake of discussing it with my father. Even though we'd been estranged and were supposedly trying to bury the hatchet—and even though I was trying to reorient myself in the midst of a painful, public separation—he played on my vulnerability.

"Tatum, there's no way you can carry a whole miniseries," he told me. "I'm going to get involved and help you out."

It was just like the old days, when my father would show up on a set and start bossing me around, contradicting the director, because he couldn't stand my working independently. He had already seized total control of Farrah's career. He'd gone so far as to buy an editing machine so they could cut their own versions of episodes of *Good Sports,* the TV series they'd done together.

"Dad, no," I protested. "This role means a lot to me, and I need to work it out on my own."

He couldn't resist going for the jugular. "But, Tatum—you suck! You're a terrible actress!"

I hated him!

Things didn't improve during the rest of our time together. After druggy nights, my father would sleep past noon and be ultravolatile during his waking hours. One day we were tossing around a Frisbee on the beach, and little Kevin threw it into the water. My father went wild. He started chasing after Kevin, and I had to snatch both my sons out of his reach.

"Don't you dare lay a hand on one of my kids," I told him. "If you ever touch one of them, I'll kill you."

"Oh yeah?" he said. He backhanded me across the face. "Who's gonna kill who?"

It made me sick to hear him screaming at my half-brother Redmond. *Poor Redmond!* I wrote. *What a screwed-up existence—exactly the life I led but without a Farrah in it. . . .*

When my dad had invited me to Hawaii, I'd allowed myself the fantasy—which I desperately wanted to believe—that maybe now my family would "circle the wagons" around me, love, support, and help me through the breakup with John. Instead I felt blindsided, kicked while I was down. I vowed, yet again, never to speak to my father.

TWENTY

Woman on the Run

JOHN HAD THREE BIG BOXES of my belongings sent over to East End Avenue. Opening them, I discovered that a precious box Lucy Saroyan, the daughter of Carol and Walter Matthau, had made for me when I was eight years old was completely smashed. I cried and cried—that was such a potent symbol of loss, of shattered dreams.

Even so, I felt lucky to be out of my marriage, telling my diary, *I have been a prisoner inside a terribly unhappy relationship for so long.*

John had phoned me a few times in Hawaii, raging and calling me names. But it was still both traumatic and frightening when, on January 8, 1993, he filed for divorce. It was the point of no return, when I had to acknowledge that my life with John, the father of my children, in whom I'd invested such great hope and profound, all-consuming love, was finally over. I felt like I was on the verge of a nervous breakdown.

WORK WAS A VERY welcome distraction. The following week, I met for the first time with "Bambi" Bembenek, the woman I was portraying in the miniseries. An ex-model, she had become a cop in Milwaukee and married a fellow police-man, Fred Schultz, who was divorced.

Then Fred's former wife, Christine, was found bound with clothesline, gagged with a blue bandanna, and shot to death with what the prosecutors claimed was Fred's gun. Laurie (as she preferred to be called) was convicted of the murder and sentenced to life in prison.

She insisted that she was innocent and, possibly, the victim of a conspiracy by her own husband and his allies on the police force to suppress evidence that would exonerate her. She man-aged to escape after eight years behind bars, including seven months in solitary confinement. After hiding out in Canada, she was recaptured after being featured on *America's Most Wanted*. By then, enough new evidence had accumulated to allow her to cut a deal—if she would plead guilty to a lesser charge, she could be resentenced only to parole and time already served.

To stay out of prison, she took the deal, but to this day, she continues to fight to clear her name.

I felt a certain resonance with the story of a tough, deter-mined female underdog. After our first meeting I recorded my impressions of Laurie in my diary: *Tall, stoic, thin, long beauti-ful nails . . . intelligent, sad—often on the verge of tears—but rehearsed, closed off.*

I came up with my own list of interview questions to try to get inside her head: Did she like to sing and dance? Where did she learn to play pool? It was a whole new challenge to play a living person—not at all the same as creating a fictional char-acter, which you could make your own. It was a lot of work.

Then I was off to Toronto for the shoot. I wanted to bring the kids, but the boys were in school, so they stayed behind in

New York with John and the nanny. It was twenty below zero with the windchill factor in Toronto, but my emotional state was harder to weather than the cold. Being on the road, separated from my children, in the process of a divorce, I felt completely unanchored, adrift as a human being. Yet because I was newly single, I felt utterly desperate for this miniseries to work, to jump-start my stalled career. Sometimes I felt that I was reeling under the pressure.

I think my anxiety showed in my work, and I wasn't at all happy with the first thirty minutes of the final cut. When John finally let Emily come to visit me on the set—after prolonged negotiations—I felt better, less insecure and more grounded, both in myself and in my acting. As my confidence improved, so did my performance.

Woman on the Run was number one in the rankings when it aired in May 1993 during "sweeps" week. One of the reviews noted: "Tatum O'Neal's performance in the title role steadily conveyed the impression of a virtuous woman undone by diabolical men."

It was like getting a fortune cookie that was all too apt! I certainly hoped that wasn't about to happen to me in real life.

DIVORCE DEFINITELY BRINGS out the worst in people, not only the dissolving couple but also everyone else in their orbit. That summer and the next, when I rented houses in the Hamptons, I watched in dismay as all our art-world friends chose sides. Since John was the wealthy partner in our marriage, most of them aligned with him. That made me feel like the "odd girl out"—as ostracized and sad as I'd been back at

Ojai Valley School. I also think John played the pity card, casting himself in the role of the abandoned husband, while I didn't really try to court sympathy from anyone.

Even my household staff began to defect, following the money. At least I could hire new nannies and cleaning ladies. I couldn't replace people like my half-brother Patrick, who had become part of John's posse and, after writing me a scathing letter, actually moved into the house John and I had shared in the Malibu Colony. That hurt—not only to be abandoned by my own flesh and blood but also to have Patrick living, surrounded by my possessions, in a place I'd personally renovated from scratch yet stood some chance of never seeing again.

I felt that I had a better support system in California—though my family was there, with all the troubles they posed, I also had old friends like Esme Gray, who might be more inclined to stay loyal. With so many allies jumping ship, I worried that staying in New York would compound my growing isolation. Los Angeles was my birthplace, my original home, a place I'd introduced to John. I didn't expect him to claim it as his own.

Cher, among others, urged me to fight for the Malibu house. She also counseled, "Don't let him take your jewelry."

"Oh, he wouldn't do that," I said.

I was so trusting, at the beginning of our wrangling, that the prospect never even occurred to me. I was the mother of John's children. We had fallen deeply in love, probably too young, and even though that love had soured over time, I fully believed that John would honor our history. It wasn't just me who had failed as a spouse. The truth was that neither of us knew how to build a loving marriage.

John would never terrorize me—or would he?

John had an image of himself as an iconic great man, and even then I believed he was. I'd learned a lot from him about consistency and morality—qualities never much in evidence when I was growing up. I had absolute faith in his sense of righteousness and fair play.

But, of course, that's not how divorce works. Too often it comes down to "I'm the victim—so you're the perpetrator."

That's what happened to us. And that's when the aspect of John's psyche that I'd failed to consider, being so focused on his moral sense, came into play. He was a champion, a win- ner—the number one tennis player in the world. He was about to unleash all the power and fury he had wreaked on Vi- las and Connors and Lendl and all the other adversaries he vanquished over the years in one last epic match, Tatum ver- sus McEnroe.

I thought, *You cannot be serious!*

FEELING MUCH IN NEED of mothering, I invited my mom to fly out and keep me company in the Hamptons in the sum- mer. There was one condition, however—she wasn't allowed to drink. She agreed to the terms, which I repeated when I picked her up at the airport. "Please," I said, "I'm having a hard time right now and doing my best to manage myself and three small kids."

"Oh, honey, don't worry," she told me, with a flourish of her ever-present lit cigarette.

I so needed to believe it.

Her smoking hand now was the one she'd damaged in the car crash, and she had her cigarette lodged between her two remaining fingers. She'd written a short story, which she'd sent me, about a woman interacting with a grandchild who kept staring at "Nana's little hand."

In Hollywood there were a lot fewer grandmas—the word was too old-lady-sounding—than there were nanas.

The visit went well until the night my mother, who was a very good cook, decided to make bouillabaisse. She was singing as she added each new ingredient to the pot with such exuberance that I began to suspect something was up. We'd reached the tipping point, I knew, when she picked a fight with me.

For my whole life, that had been her "checking out" signal. She would get so provocative that whoever she was with would kick her out, and then she'd be free to go to a bar and drown her sorrows. So I went to her room to investigate, smelling booze as soon as I opened the door.

Everywhere—under the mattress, in the closet, in the clothes hamper, in her suitcase—she had stashed little bottles of vodka. She had been blasted every day when I believed she was staying sober.

So she had to leave. I was sobbing, heartbroken, as I drove her to the airport.

"Mom, you promised—how could you do this?" I asked.

She tearily denied that she'd done anything wrong and begged me not to send her away.

Typically, because my mother was such an alcoholic, in such denial, I capitulated.

I knew from long experience that I couldn't really count on my mother, but nevertheless I was devastated. My father was out of the picture, and I had nowhere else to turn. She was my last ally.

Now she too had jumped ship and was submerged in the

sea of addiction. Heading into my divorce, I felt utterly lost, alone, and abandoned—again.

ONE MAJOR NIGHTMARE was the prenuptial agreement, which I'd signed under duress right after Kevin was born. Under its provisions, I had no right to any property—not the New York apartments, not the house in Sun Valley, and not the house in the Malibu Colony. When I tried to reason with John about making some deal that would allow me to reoccupy the house in California—if only to give the kids some continuity—he blew me off. "Don't blame me if you and your lawyer were stupid enough to sign the prenuptial agreement," he said, before slamming down the phone.

Nor, apparently, was I entitled to keep any of the jewelry he'd given me or any of our cars—we had five—including my own. All I was permitted to take out of a six-year marriage was the money I came in with—unless, of course, John felt like being generous. He really wasn't in the mood.

A cannier, more manipulative woman would have mapped out her exit strategy before taking a stand against unhappiness. A woman like Madonna, for example, who called when she heard the news of my divorce to inquire, "So, what did you get?"

But I wasn't that kind of woman. I'd hired a lawyer who had represented lots of famous people, who thought my case was a lost cause, so I replaced him with William Beslow, whom I had met while making *Woman on the Run*. He seemed to think we could put up a fight. The truth was, ultimately, that I didn't care about the property and money as much as I wanted to be treated equitably and with respect.

However, there was one thing I cared about deeply—really the only thing that gave my life meaning, as John well knew—and that was my kids.

He demanded joint custody—two weeks with him, two weeks with me. At that point, I had never been separated from my children for more than a week, during the rare "marriage renewal" vacations John and I had taken. If my experience on location for *Woman on the Run* had taught me anything, it was that I couldn't stand to be away from them.

John knew that I couldn't bear to be alone. I hadn't yet confronted most of my demons—all the abuse and neglect and the buried addictions of my childhood—and the kids were nothing less than my bedrock. They were like part of my own body, especially Emily, who was only two years old. Motherhood—and being good at it—was the foundation of my identity.

Besides, even on the face of it, John's plan was unworkable. He was still traveling most of the year, and the boys were in school. He'd either have to uproot them and drag them along or leave them at home with nannies and no parents, just to ensure that he got his full turn.

That's when I began to think that—much as John valued fatherhood, and he did, greatly—the joint custody demand was less about seeing the kids than it was about depriving me.

It was my punishment, for not being the wife he'd wanted me to be—and for daring to leave him.

I couldn't accept it. At that point the kids were staying with me, and I wasn't about to give them up—not for any amount of money. Then John whacked me with a hundred-mile-an-hour volley—he refused to see the children at all until I agreed to his proposal for two weeks on, two weeks off.

Eventually, seeing how much the kids were hurting—missing him, unable to understand—I agreed to meet John for a walk in Central Park, just the two of us, without lawyers. It was a bad idea, considering that I was up against the world's best gladiator, to take him on unarmed and alone. However, all I could see was that my children's happiness—their need for their father—was at stake. I had to try to break the impasse, and of course, I got thrown to the lions.

That day I made an agreement with John to receive a financial settlement, keep my jewelry, and grant him joint custody on the terms he wanted—two weeks on, two weeks off.

I didn't understand then that, for joint custody to work, the separation has to be amicable. Joint custody means constant contact with the other parent and, if that parent is full of rage, constant opportunities for conflict—for suffering and inflicting pain.

It was like a pact with the devil. Our arrangement meant that, for the next nine years, John and I would be in and out of court, as *Anonymous* v. *Anonymous,* scratching and biting to challenge every aspect of the other's parenting skills and child care provisions—you name it. I got plenty of licks in, and I'm not proud of them. All told, over the years I would spend a million dollars on the legal expenses connected with my joint custody agreement.

That was a mighty costly walk in the park!

As someone once said to me, "John doesn't have to win, he has to destroy you—to obliterate his opponent."

I came very close to destruction, partly because of John's infinitely superior legal firepower, but also, I must confess, because of my own actions.

TWENTY-ONE

The Rabbit Hole

ONCE I WAS ON MY own and dating again, I found myself drawn to men who were the polar opposite of John. Fire in the belly, the will to win, roughhousing, bravado—even loud, blaring sports on TV—were total turnoffs for me. I felt too badly burned by that whole combative, macho sensibility.

What I wanted now was sensitivity, romance, gentleness, an aesthetic bent. I was yearning for culture, to immerse myself in all the emerging art, literature, and theater that were making New York such a stimulating place. I wanted to be part of a bohemian scene—to experience, I suppose, the youth I'd missed out on as a lonely, abandoned teenager in L.A. and as a wife and mother in my early twenties.

A poet would be good, I thought.

Early on, the men I got involved with were often European and younger than me—among them, a handsome French actor named Daniel, from a talented and sophisticated family, and a tall German guy with long, blond hair whom I visited in Munich. The one who finally captured my heart was a soulful, young art-world apprentice. I'll call him "Sal."

When we first met, I assumed he was gay, the lover of a mutual friend. But there was something about him that intrigued me. He was thin, finely made, with beautiful hair and eyes. *I wish I wasn't so curious,* I told my diary. *But I am.*

He asked me to lunch at a bistro in SoHo, showing up in baggy green painter's pants, splotched work boots, and two big shirts, one on top of the other—very eccentric and endearing. He assured me that he was not only straight but that he also found me attractive. I was so nervous that I broke a glass.

We hung out all day, then, not yet ready to part, impetuously decided to take the bus to Atlantic City. It had been years since I'd had such a spontaneous, carefree adventure. Since Sal was underage, I had to sneak him into the casinos. I felt less like a mother of three than a kid myself as we plugged fifty-cent chips into the slot machines—I won forty dollars—strolled along the boardwalk hand in hand, and sat smoking pot, under the stars, on a bench overlooking the ocean.

How romantic!

Over the next few days, our relationship rapidly progressed. Sal sent me a favorite poem by fax, and we exchanged tapes of our favorite songs—by Bob Dylan, the Pixies, Fugazi, Hüsker Dü, Polly Jean Harvey, and Liz Phair. Sal told me of his favorite authors, Allen Ginsberg and William Burroughs—pretty heady talk for a high school dropout, who'd been subsisting on a diet of televised sports. I was already crazy about Sal when he finally blurted out, "Tatum, as much as I know how to, I love you."

It was scary, though. We hadn't yet made love, but the emotions for both of us were so intense. In our hours of sharing confidences, Sal had also confessed that he was a junkie.

He told me all about his introduction to smack and about running away from rehab at age eighteen. He'd slipped up since then but, for the past two months, had been clean.

Of course, I plied him with questions. I was certainly no stranger to drugs or, for that matter, to rehab. Half the people I knew, including my mother and brother, had been through the spin cycle of using and detoxing. More than in New York, rehab was seen as ordinary—even, practically, as an accepted rite of passage—in the Los Angeles film and music communities.

Yet most of those people were kicking pills or coke, which had been viewed as fun-enhancing, available at every party, in the 1980s. Nobody quite grasped that coke was addictive until people started getting hooked left and right. Heroin was different, a street drug, hard-core and dangerous. I never really knew anyone who had done it. Users didn't get talkative and lively—they nodded out. They used needles, which were scary even apart from the fact that they spread diseases, including AIDS. Junkies could OD and die.

It was this dark mystique that seemed to make heroin so appealing to many in the art world—and even considered chic—in New York in the 1990s. It also roused all my nurturing, protective instincts toward Sal. I wrote: *He showed me a cigarette burn on his stomach from nodding out. I want to take care of him, to hold him.*

At that point, I was just getting reacquainted with drugs myself. John's cure had actually worked. When I'd met him, I'd had an undeniable coke dependency, but I'd cleaned up completely when we started trying to conceive Kevin.

I spent most of the next six years either pregnant or breastfeeding, and I would never have done anything to endanger my babies. Having a few margaritas or glasses of wine meant that I'd have to pump my milk and throw it away, which was a pain. As a result, I didn't even drink much, especially when I was trying to encourage John to cut down on his pot smoking.

Now and then, I'd dabble with grass, which I never much liked, but for the most part, I'd stayed entirely off drugs—not because my addiction had faded but because it had shifted.

In the beginning it shifted to John, making me long to be with him just as desperately as I had ever wanted cocaine. After each of my babies was born, it shifted to working out, as I got obsessional about taking the weight off and staying thin. For a long time—perhaps the most productive use of that powerful energy—it shifted to my children, boosting my natural mothering drive. That might have created problems when they got older, but when they were babies and toddlers, completely dependent on me, my near-total absorption with them and their needs seemed perfectly appropriate.

Now that John was keeping my children for long stretches—two weeks at a time—there was a vacuum in my life that I was desperate to fill. Maybe there are people who get hooked on drugs—painkillers, for instance—purely by accident. In my case, however, there were reasons: no doubt some kind of family predisposition but, even more, a profound self-loathing and sense of worthlessness instilled over many years of abuse and neglect. Losing myself in John or the children was just treating the symptoms, without addressing the underlying illness. And for me, the illness—the belief that I didn't deserve to be on earth—would prove life-threatening.

———

TATUM IS SO SAD! I wrote, giving myself a lecture in my diary. *Sad all the time . . . This boy loves you. Aren't you happy? Why don't you try to be a little happy?*

Okay—I will— I replied, breaking off the entry in midthought. Even now, my handwriting looks a little tentative.

I could see that Sal was seriously into grass. Whenever we were together, he pulled out a joint or a hash pipe, which I started sharing, so we'd be on the same wavelength. But one day when we'd spent hours together at my apartment without smoking, I noticed that he was slurring his words and acting woozy. "What's wrong?" I asked him. "You seem strange."

"Oh, I just copped a couple Dalmanes."

They were heavy-duty sleeping pills. It shocked me a little that Sal needed to get high that badly and made me wonder if he was starting to relapse. *His desire to go back uptown and cop drugs—that could hurt me terribly,* I wrote. *It scares me.* Remembering my bad old days—like the time I was left alone with John's safe—I could understand the impulse all too well.

Still, I was wild about Sal. *We are going to soar, he and I,* I reported. *I feel a powerful love—so strong that I am in a state of bliss.*

He sent me a copy of a Leonard Cohen song, "I'm Your Man," which thrilled me so much that I passed it on to my mother and all my friends.

By now John had gotten wind of our relationship, and it seemed to upset him. We fought about it on the phone, and Sal overheard my side of the conversation. When I hung up, he grabbed the phone from my hand and called John back. "If you're going to talk about me, do it to my face," he said.

That shut John up, I told my diary.

I felt so protected.

My joy wasn't unalloyed, however. Sal had the living habits of a young bachelor, and I was a neatness freak. He never helped cook or clean up after himself, which sparked some bitter fights. After one of them, I sat down and wrote a poem of my own, deploring my temper and my resemblance to my father. It ended:

> *I blame like you*
> *I hate like you*
> *I love like you*
> *I hurt like you . . .*
> *I'm alone like you.*

I had also begun to criticize Sal's drug use. It shook me terribly when the young actor River Phoenix died of an overdose outside the Viper Room in L.A. Sal kept running through pot as fast as I could buy it and showed up one night high on Percodan. He started telling me stories about friends of his who were shooting heroin.

Then, one morning, he woke up unable to stay clean anymore. He said that he was going downtown to see Herbert Huncke, whom he'd told me was a writer and an addict featured in *Junky,* the famous book by William Burroughs. Sal wanted to do a speedball, which was a combination of heroin and coke.

I was horrified at first, but also curious. The more we talked, the more I convinced myself that I needed to try it too. It was the beginning of the end—of trying to die again. I have certain regrets in my life, and this is one of them.

"Downtown" meant a broken-down building in the East Village. Herbert opened the door. He was, I later recorded, *the vision of a pure junkie—missing teeth, back hunched, dark circles under his eyes—hard making eye contact.*

I waited uneasily as Herbert and his boyfriend, the photographer Louis Cartwright, went out to score the drugs for us. But nervous as I was, I was also growing excited. I'd always been a little too brave for my own good, always up for an adventure—and this was a headlong plunge into the unknown.

When they got back, I watched Sal mix the drugs with water and shoot a little into a vein. Then it was my turn. No needles for me—I snorted a line and felt an immediate rush of warmth and relief. It was as if all the anxiety and sadness I'd carried in my mind and body for so long was simply dissolving and melting out of me.

I took a little more and broke out in a sweat, suddenly gripped by an uncontrollable wave of nausea. I began to retch violently. Luckily my stomach was empty. This exhilarating toxin was so powerful that my body couldn't handle it.

"That happens," one of the guys reassured me, "especially the first time. Just take it slow."

It was hours before we got home. By then I was wrung out, but Sal kept going, alternating between heroin, to get mellow, and coke to fire up again. He was like a jack-in-the-box. He finally nodded out around nine-thirty, eyes rolling every time he picked up his head.

That freaked me out, even after I saw that he was okay. It left me feeling too solitary. Going through what I knew would be a life-changing experiment, I couldn't stand being so alone.

In the middle of the night we both woke up sick, with blinding headaches. I spent most of the next two days throwing up. I couldn't eat at all. My brain felt parched and like it was rattling around in my head.

It was internal, external, metaphysical—full-body—sickness, I told my diary. *A much-needed experience, I might add.*

What I meant by "much needed" was that I hadn't even realized the depth of my grief and depression until that brief shining moment when the drugs took it away. It was like a breakthrough, a brilliant starburst of freedom from the rage and self-hate that still smoldered from my childhood, as well as the pain of my failed marriage and the vicious, ongoing struggles with John. I had turned all that fury and pain in on myself, like a death ray.

The next day, there was still a little coke left and, sick as I was, I wanted to do it. My old addictions were flaring up again. I badly wanted to recover that sense of relief, of freedom, of escape. But Sal smacked the coke out of my hand, sending it flying into the air.

"What the hell are you doing?" I demanded.

I knew the answer. Having struggled with his own addictions, Sal could see what he'd awakened in me—though it was too late. Pandora's box was open, and there was no slamming it shut again.

SAL AND I were together for more than a year. He even asked me to marry him. That spring, however, while John had the children, we went on vacation with some artist friends. It was then that I noticed fresh needle marks on Sal's arms.

Drugs had quickly become an important element of our relationship. As often as not, I was the one who suggested that Sal score some coke or smack on his way over to visit. Doing drugs together was one thing, and since I only snorted them, I convinced myself that we were just social, recreational users. Shooting up alone was hard-core-junkie behavior. Now Sal was not only shooting up behind my back but also, judging by his tracks, doing it fairly often.

I must somehow come to grips with the fact that he is an addict, I wrote. *I realize he has a disease and I will be pulled into its very complicated web if I'm not careful. . . . No way can I manage a heroin-addicted person in my life right now.*

I confronted Sal about the tracks, insisting that he consider going to rehab. We split up, a few times. Soon, however, I had to admit that there was another heroin-addicted person in my life, whom I definitely couldn't manage—and it was me.

I had no idea how ravaging—physically, mentally, and emotionally—the drug could be. I had started craving it psychologically, longing to sink into oblivion. Then, without it, I began to experience frighteningly dark depressions, with fierce anger as their flip side. I knew I was in real trouble when my body kicked in too, with the classic symptoms—the hyper restlessness, aching bones, vomiting, and goose bumps—of withdrawal.

Finally, I had to take action. I broke up with Sal, for good. Then I checked myself into Beth Israel Hospital to detox. I was put on antidepressants, which seemed to help, but in the therapy aspect of treatment, I wasn't yet able to reach out to people.

It was as if I was enclosed in a bell jar of fury, trapped in rage and pain over the misery of my childhood and the cruelty of my divorce. Had I been able to smash through those imprisoning walls of anger, to ask for and receive help from others, I might have gotten well then and been spared the years of self-destruction to come. As it was, I emerged from my first rehab quite lonely and fragile, but clean—for a while.

TWENTY-TWO

Getting Straight

DURING MY TIME WITH SAL, I'd continued to look for work. That got complicated for a while when my manager, Irwin Stoff, dropped me because I refused to grant an interview about my divorce to *Vanity Fair*. He just couldn't stand seeing such a hot publicity break go up in smoke. But my day-to-day dealings with John, as we shuttled the kids back and forth, were hard enough without the press stirring the pot.

Through my new managers, I got the chance to audition for a George Lucas film. *I sucked,* I confided to my diary. *I suffered so much—the head auditioning sometimes brings out in me is so scary . . . I tried my hardest and that's all I can do. I have to respect my bravery.*

I did better at the tryout for a TV miniseries based on the Ken Follett novel *Lie Down with Lions,* starring Omar Sharif and Timothy Dalton. But when that didn't come through either, I was a little relieved. I would have had to go on location in France and Luxembourg for two months, just when Sean and Kevin were starting school. *Horrible timing,* I wrote. *I have been doing so much work with the boys, it just wouldn't be a good idea if I left right now. It just wouldn't.*

It would have been even harder to do *The Quest* with Jean-Claude Van Damme, which was to be shot in Thailand and required a four-month commitment. My agent advised against it, thinking it was a bad career move for me to make a martial-arts action movie. Still, I badly wanted some kind of film role, if only for the money, and Jean-Claude strung me along for months, assuring me that I was his first choice.

At the end of 1994, he asked me to meet him at the bar of the Peninsula Hotel in L.A. He was in the process of divorcing his wife and was sitting with a woman who I assumed was his date. Then, when I asked him if we could step outside to talk business, he began flirting with me wildly, telling me how expressive my eyes were but that I looked too pale—he wanted me to spend a month walking in the mountains before we starting shooting the movie together, to build up my strength. He was a charmer, all right.

I wound up having a brief fling with him. He told me that he loved me and would never hurt me, that he needed to take care of me and even wanted to go on a ski trip with me so our kids could play together. He promised to call me the following week, when he would be in New York.

But he didn't. Instead, four days later, he left a message with my agent, claiming that he was no longer sure he wanted me for the movie.

What a relief! *What was I thinking?* I asked my diary. It was having the carrot—the hope of working—dangled in front of me for so long that had held my interest, not the role itself, which would have been a professional disaster. As for our personal connection, I'm not sure that I could really have found happiness with the man who spoke of himself, using his initials, as the "third biggest star in the world": "The first is Tom

[Cruise], the second is Arnold [Schwarzenegger], and the third is me, JCVD!"

A few months later, I was honored with a Best Actress award for *Woman on the Run* at the Monaco film festival. That led to a curious brush with royalty. Prince Albert wined and dined me, inviting me to meet him not at the palace but at his "ladies' flat," the special apartment he maintained for his mistresses. When I walked in, I was shocked to see an autographed photo of Farrah hanging on the wall. It was not an aphrodisiac.

He got as far as removing my dress, then vanished into the bathroom. As I lay on his bed, I could hear him brushing his teeth, coughing, and spitting in the sink. That did it for me. I jumped up, yanking my clothes back on, and called out some lame excuse about having forgotten my contact lenses. Then I fled into the night, running all the way back to my hotel, as if the palace guards were hot on my heels.

That was my almost-dalliance with a real prince!

THE MOST SATISFYING WORK I did during that time was just a cameo in a movie that was close to my heart because it was set in the art world and directed by my friend Julian Schnabel. *Basquiat* was the story of a brilliant young black artist who was living in a cardboard box on the Lower East Side when his bold, original, and colorful graffiti brought him to the attention of Andy Warhol. Though he was only in his twenties, he quickly became a worldwide sensation.

But he was also a junkie. At the height of his fame, Jean-Michel Basquiat died of an overdose at age twenty-eight.

The story was so compelling that the independent, labor-of-love film attracted an all-star cast: Christopher Walken, Benicio del Toro, Dennis Hopper, Willem Dafoe, and Gary Oldman, with David Bowie playing Andy Warhol. I played a rich art collector and was gratified to see my performance, brief as it was, described in print as "scene stealing."

That meant a lot, at a time when it seemed that I couldn't get arrested in Hollywood.

OF COURSE, THE MOVIE also hit close to home because of my own involvement with drugs. My first stint in rehab never really "took"—I hadn't yet gained the tools to cope with my crushing rejections on the career front and, even more challenging, the sheer pain of living. Totally estranged now from my family and unable to be alone in my desolation, I tried to lose myself in obsessional relationships with men. That never worked for me before, and now all it did was increase my self-loathing.

My relationship with John was more of a struggle than ever because he'd just settled down with a new woman, the rock singer Patty Smyth. She and her daughter were living with John—and during his "two weeks on," my kids—and now she was pregnant. Patty had a temperament that was very similar to John's—intense, driven, and determined to win, which, of course, made me, John's ex-wife, the loser. It was not an attitude likely to help resolve the frequent impasses between me and John that kept us running to our lawyers, to improve our still-bitter, accusing communication, or to make our split any easier on our children.

So I started slipping again. During the half of each month when John had the kids and I was alone, filled with despair, I started calling contacts downtown, who would deliver drugs to my house. Nothing seemed to ease my terrible emptiness and pain as well as snorting heroin.

Yet I never embraced drugs as a way of life and kept on trying to get clean. John celebrated the new year, 1996, with the birth of a new daughter, who'd come seven weeks early. I spent the holidays in rehab, alone, having checked myself in at Hazelden in Minnesota.

I hated it—being locked up for three months with a bunch of women all bellyaching about their need to drink or to use drugs. My roommate had a vanilla extract addiction and actually went into delirium tremens right in front of me. She was only twenty-five. Still, I stuck it out to keep John from suing me for full custody of the children, to whom I wrote letters every few days. They were the only thing that was keeping me alive.

As if I needed a reminder of why I was an addict, my father called me on Christmas Day—not to offer seasons greetings but to tell me, yet again, "I just don't like you, Tatum."

Cher—who I still love—cheered me on from the sidelines, telling *Entertainment Weekly,* "Anybody can hit a bump. It doesn't mean they can't straighten up and fly right. I know Tatum will."

I would—but it would take a while.

When I got out, John made me submit to a regimen of constant drug tests, to prove that I was staying clean. That felt like an incredible violation—to give my ex-husband such control over me that he even had the right to monitor my bodily fluids. Still, I did it for the kids—determined not to lose custody—and for a year and a half managed to fend off my lethal urges.

I'd decided that it would help to make a totally fresh start. With my settlement money, I bought an apartment on Central Park West that had belonged to Michael J. Fox. It was closer to the children's schools, as well as to John's apartment, which I hoped would ease their transitions between households. I immediately set about renovating it, staying in the Sutton Hotel while the work was going on. I felt good about putting East End Avenue, with all its unhappy associations, behind me.

I even hooked up with a boyfriend who was relatively sane, a New York firefighter.

Then, toward the end of 1997, my house of cards came crashing down. There was a terrible crisis, involving my mother.

I HAD BEEN SUPPORTING her since I was in my teens. In the mid-1990s, I was giving her $2,000 a month just for living expenses, as well as paying her bills. However, when I realized that she was not only drinking but also back on amphetamines, I told her that I was not willing to bankroll her drug habit. I felt justified in my decision when she had five arrests for "driving under the influence" in quick succession.

Then, not long after I cut her off, she was diagnosed with lung cancer. Her entire life, she had smoked with the same huge enthusiasm she devoted to everything else—laughing, cooking, singing, entertaining, and, of course, boozing. Now it was killing her. I didn't even know until the day she called me in New York and said, "Tatum, I have two months to live."

I felt responsible, as if my withdrawal of support had sent

her spiraling downward. Of course, I was also devastated by the prospect of losing her. Though she could never come across with the kind of mothering I'd wanted—the protection, affection, and closeness I had tried to provide for my own children—she was my confidante, my inspiration because of her urgent lust for life, and the sole pillar of support (however flawed) in my family. Whatever else she may have been, she was my mother, the giver of life—and the bond between us was primal and unshakable.

I flew out to see her a few times during my "two weeks off," when John had the kids. She was fading fast. Shortly after my thirty-fourth birthday, I rented a house in Indian Wells so I could take her out of the hospital, to be cared for by hospice nurses.

She is so sick, I told my diary. *My heart aches for her, this shrinking woman—she has lost so much weight . . . I will miss her essence, her presence, her perfume, jewelry, and wig; her makeup, her accent, her aura; the way she would bring me coffee in the morning—the way she would love life.*

I sat beside her, holding her hand, weeping with remorse over every time I'd scolded her, telling her over and over how much I loved her, though I wasn't sure she could hear me. Now and then, a friend of hers would drop by, but most of the time it was just the two of us. Griffin wasn't around because he was using heavily and couldn't cope with the tragedy. Once my father called, in tears, and I put the phone next to my mother's ear so he could say good-bye. That broke my heart.

I called John when my mom seemed close to the end, and it is a measure of how ugly things had gotten between us that he was unmoved. He said, "When does the statute of limitations run out on my feeling sorry for you?"

"John, she's dying!" I insisted. "I just want you to tell the kids."

"Bullshit," he said. "I can hear her laughing."

She was wheezing, desperate for breath. That night, while I was asleep in her room, she called out to me, afraid. I crawled into bed beside her, just as I had done when I was little, and lay there to give her comfort.

The next day, November 23, 1997, I cried alone as she died in my arms. I still have not come to grips with that.

Even then, instead of sitting the kids down and explaining her death, as I'd asked, John took them swimming at Reebok, his health club, and told them in the pool. That made me furious. Unlike my father, whom they'd rarely met, my children knew and loved my mother. They needed comfort—more than I could offer in those first, miserable hours after losing her—and a chance to grieve. And her passing deserved to be acknowledged with respect, no matter what John thought of her—or me.

Once again, I took complete responsibility. I made arrangements for the funeral at a church that had a nice outdoor space. Afterward, Griffin and I took my mother's ashes back to Americus, Georgia, where she was born. I'd never seen it, never met her relatives. I stayed on the farm of the one living cousin whom she'd loved.

It was a powerful journey, showing me a side of my mother that I knew nothing of during her life. She was so secretive about her past. Seeing her roots, understanding just how far she'd come, made me feel much closer to her and reaffirmed my love and respect.

Did she have a full life? I asked my diary, and answered, *YES!*

———

LOSING MY MOTHER threw me into more of a tailspin than I ever anticipated. John wanted to take the kids to Malibu for Christmas, so I decided to go too and stay in a hotel, so I'd have the chance to see them. I was yearning for a sense of family and even thought it might be possible to reconcile with my father. He'd seemed kinder when my mother was dying and more vulnerable too, because he had split up with Farrah—this time for good—after seventeen years of mutual torment.

But when it came to my family, nothing was ever as it seemed. It started out fun: *The kids are getting a dose of O'Neals that they have never gotten before,* I wrote. *They are having a blast!*

It wasn't long, however, before I recognized that Griffin was badly strung out, that my father was still very heavily into pot, and so was my half-brother Redmond—only thirteen years old. My father was bullying Griffin and Redmond and started in on me just a few days after Christmas.

At that point I'd been clean for a year and a half. In the few weeks since my mother's death, I'd taken a breather from my twelve-step meetings, so I was very vulnerable. *Yikes,* I told my diary. *Relapses . . . It's all a part of grieving and being here in this trigger house*—my father's place in Malibu.

I started out drinking and soon progressed, for the first time, to shooting heroin and coke. Clearly I wasn't coping too well with the loss of my mother. Griffin, who used speed and coke, smoked crack, and drank, thoughtfully introduced me to a product that allegedly made your urine test clean for any drug. Still, I was way too scared to rely on it. The idea of failing a drug test just freaked me out too much.

As 1998 dawned, I examined my condition in my diary.

What is my New Year's resolution?

No more drugs, ever—I hate them!

However, a few months passed before I was truly ready to stop and get myself back into rehab.

BEFORE I DID, the unthinkable happened—an incident that still fills me with profound shame. I did my best to hide it, but I'd now grown too deeply addicted to just stop shooting drugs during my "two weeks on" when I had my children. Not that they were ever neglected or endangered—I always had nannies around; and I loved them too much not to want quality time with them. All three of them loved to crawl into my bed at night to snuggle—that was so nice. My diaries from that time are filled with drawings we did together, as well as pasted-in snapshots. I titled the diary chronicling my mother's death *Infinity of Love*, and below it wrote *Emily, Sean, Kevin— Gods—Children.*

My need for the kids was visceral. I ached when they left to return to their father's, and Emily, especially, often balked at going. *She screamed and cried and held on to me,* I recorded on more than one occasion. *It breaks my heart in two. She misses me so much. . . . The truth is that it kills me too.*

It was seven-year-old Emily, my baby, who came toddling into my bedroom one night and found something I never wanted her to see: a syringe.

When that got back to John, he pounced on it. Now, along

with the drug tests, I had to endure the indignity of supervised visits, with John controlling the schedule.

I can't say that I wouldn't have reacted the same way if I thought for an instant that my children were imperiled. However, I believed—naively—that John knew me and recognized my absolute commitment to motherhood. He knew that, whatever had happened, my children loved me and wanted to be with me—and that I needed them. I thought that even the courts would acknowledge that and give me a little credit for being a good mother and for fighting so hard to get clean.

But drug use was demonized in New York, more so than in California. Nobody gave me credit—especially not judges. Especially not judges settling custody issues between a local hero with a powerful legal machine and a vulnerable woman.

I was David up against Goliath, but without a slingshot. I didn't stand a chance.

TWENTY-THREE

Free Fall

BEFORE I WAS FINALLY through with drugs, I would make the rounds of several major rehabs: Hazelden in Minnesota and New York, Silver Hill in Connecticut (twice), and the Caron Foundation in Pennsylvania. But the stint I did in 1998 stuck with me for a couple of years.

Part of the reason was that I finally had the support of an insightful psychiatrist, Dr. Richard Rosenthal, who believed in me at a time when other doctors suggested that I could never get clean. Another part of the reason was that I'd found temporary solace for my loneliness with a man I had decided to marry.

In 1999 I met Steven Hutensky, a beautiful, charming, and funny young executive at Miramax. I ran into him at the wedding of Jessica Bellafotto, my yoga instructor. *He is perfect,* I exclaimed to my diary. *Gentle, hardworking, smart, elegant, going places, concerned and loving. Spiritual. I can tell he'd be great with the children.*

I was right—my kids loved him—and so did I. We did sweet things, like get stickers made from a photo of me kissing him, which I pasted in my diary, ringed with a big heart. When we'd been together a year, he proposed to me during a carriage ride in Central Park, which was so romantic. I said yes.

The truth was, however, that I wasn't yet healthy enough to marry anyone. I had too much unresolved emotional pain, which I didn't know what to do with, now that I wasn't drowning it with drugs. It took me a while to recognize that, and I'm afraid Steven caught the fallout.

Then, knowing that I couldn't face another divorce, I decided to return Steven's ring. I believe that I broke his heart, and I still have a lot of guilt and regret about that. But considering what lay ahead for me—"hitting bottom," as they say in AA—he probably dodged a bullet.

I STILL HADN'T FULLY accepted that I was powerless when it came to drugs. My undoing was my weight. I'd gained fifteen pounds during that period of clean living—a major obstacle for a woman who wanted to act. In the culture of Hollywood, thinness was everything. So I went to a diet doctor, without telling him my history of addiction, and got a prescription.

Of course, for me, the recommended dose—one pill every four hours—quickly became four pills every one hour. But I managed to keep myself together, at least in the beginning. I lost the weight—and I landed a role in a movie.

The Scoundrel's Wife was set in a small Louisiana bayou town during World War II. There were German submarines off the Gulf Coast, and local fisherman were suspected of trading with the enemy. Glen Pitre, the director—whom Roger Ebert called "legendary . . . arguably the world's only Cajunlanguage filmmaker"—had grown up in the area and based the story on rumors he had heard in his childhood.

I played the widow of a shrimp boat captain whose neighbors thought he was a smuggler and murderer. Already an outcast, I become suspected of sabotage and collaboration with the Germans. Tim Curry played a priest who was a probable spy, and Julian Sands was the German refugee doctor, possibly Jewish, who becomes my love interest.

The movie, which had a lot of heart, aired at film festivals all over America and even as far away as Moscow. It won the Best Feature Award at the San Diego Film Festival but never got picked up for general release. Still, I welcomed the reviews, praising my "quiet dignity" in the widow's role. I felt I was coming back.

IN MAY 2001, my father started having stomach pains. He went in for tests, which showed that his white cell count was sky-high. He was diagnosed with chronic myelogenous leukemia.

The press couldn't resist jumping on the irony that in *Love Story,* my father's most famous movie, he played the husband of a young woman who was dying of leukemia. His costar, Ali McGraw, even called to cheer him up, saying, "I hope you didn't catch it from me."

My father laughed and milked those stories, but they were lost on me. I found the news horrifying on so many levels. I was still grieving for my mother, who'd come to mean "family" in all those years of estrangement from my father. I already felt rootless, and now all my childhood abandonment terrors came rushing back. My father was all I had, whether or not I could cope with his volatility or could even imagine a relationship with him. Without him I felt that I would fly off the planet.

Of course, I genuinely loved him—deeply—and I always had, even when I hated him. Blood is the thickest substance on earth; connection to a parent is the fundamental human relationship.

Even beyond that, I still cherished the image of my father as my white knight—the beautiful Irishman, full of warm humor, who rode motorcycles and teased me and raced me in front of the Pierre; who rescued me from squalor and made me his companion; who showed me the world and brought me into show business. He'd been throwing the fact that he "made me" in my face for years, which I of course loathed, but I was grateful. I knew I owed him.

My heart went out to him, for all the fear and panic he must be feeling confronting a fatal disease. And I knew how alone he was, because he had driven everyone out of his life through his violence, drug use, and womanizing. He had no friends and had even hurt his career by being, as Norman Mailer, who directed him in *Tough Guys Don't Dance*, put it, "meaner than cat piss."

The flip side of my love and sympathy was a definite caution. Even apart from his treatment of me and Griffin, I'd witnessed my father's brutality to Redmond, who'd wound up in his first rehab at age fourteen. Now, at sixteen, he'd been hospitalized for shooting "glass," a mixture of coke and speed, after my father kicked him out of the house. Farrah had just gone public about a letter my father had written her banishing Redmond from his life.

So I knew what I'd face if I went out to Los Angeles—an all-too-familiar horrendous mess. I'd been to that well for water so many times and found it not only dry but also with a big fist coming up out of the depths to drag me down.

I wasn't sure that I could fight it. I was in the middle of a relapse, not yet fully engaged but again flirting dangerously with drugs.

Still, my father was ill. He was living alone. There was no one who could give me a straight answer about what was going on. So I went.

What happened was all too predictable. After I'd told my father I loved him, needed him—that he was the love of my life—that I wanted to take care of him, we almost got into a fistfight.

We were shooting pool at his Malibu beach house, and I was winning, which always made him cranky. The subject came up of his new girlfriend, who was even younger than me. I found that a little weird, and when I said so, in my usual earnest way, my father flipped out and came charging after me.

His illness hadn't softened him at all. It had made him even crazier and more angry, if anything, which was just too incredibly sad.

It was like a one-two punch—first the illness and fear of loss and then, after I'd made a normal, human, loving response, the knockdown. I already had one foot on the slippery slope of relapse, and that rejection was a shove, which sent me tumbling down into the darkest night of drug use I'd ever had.

THE SPECIFIC CATALYST FOR my last bad slide was September 11. I was home in New York. The kids were over at John's, and I called them in a panic, desperate to hear their voices and make sure they were all okay. Once I knew they were safe, I fell apart. Alone in my apartment, I watched that ghastly, paralyzing loop of the planes hitting the towers, the fireball, and the smoke billowing out, over and over. It was like the world was coming to an end, and the horror sent me spinning out of control.

By now, I was in my third or fourth year of the urine-testing nightmare. I must have suspected what was coming—that I wasn't going to stay clean. John and I had continued to battle in court over the issue of visitation rights. I'd taken to recording his abusive phone calls for my lawyers, and after my complaints about his blowups with the kids, he'd been mandated to anger-management therapy. Having long since taken the gloves off, we were now pummeling each other with brass knuckles.

I wasn't going to do it anymore. I might win a battle or two, but if I didn't get off the field, I was going to lose my life in the war.

So I told John, "You win. I'm defaulting. If you're that determined to get custody of the kids, you can have it."

I MOVED TO L.A., ostensibly to look for work but more to cast around for a way to live—or not. I was in free fall yet again. I had spent my whole life trying to fix the outside of myself—through exercise, bulimia, diet pills, and cocaine, not to mention the heroin—without managing to fix the inside, despite plenty of therapy and rehab. I would have to peel away a lot more layers of the onion—nearly destroying my physical body—before I could fix my heart and soul.

By then I was convinced that I was a failure as a human being—a bad mother, an incurable addict, worthless, and unlovable. I wanted to take my own life, but believing it would irreparably scar my children, I instead chose the slower death of drugs. I soon hooked up with a drug dealer boyfriend and started doing drugs 24/7.

I couldn't stop. I drifted from apartment to apartment, from hotel to hotel, scoring coke to hype up, pills to cool down. I was like a ghost of my former self, down to a skeletal ninety pounds, and so strung out that I was "reptilian," as my psychiatrist would later say. All my emotions had been seared away by the drugs.

Even my face had changed, growing so gaunt that no one recognized me. My arms were bumpy and discolored by cellulitis from infected tracks. The veins in my forearms collapsed, and I wound up in the hospital more than once. But as soon as I got stabilized, I was back on the streets, looking to score.

I spent the night at my father's during that time. He looked at my hands, which by then were scarred and wasted, rattling bones, and said, "Eww, you are so disgusting. You'll never get work with hands like that. You need to eat something!"

The next morning he made me breakfast—one sausage and just half of a frozen hash-browns patty. It was such a clear, begrudging symbol of rejection that Griffin said, "Dad, Tatum needs more food than that!"

"No, that's plenty. She'll be fine," my father insisted.

At least I was healthy enough not to stay there long.

At one point, I returned to New York, wanting to see my children. John reiterated what my father had said: "God, you need help. You look worse than I've ever seen you."

He didn't sound any too kindly or concerned—it was more judgmental. Still, he let me see the kids. I ran into Kevin in the lobby of John's building on his way to go work out. "You're so big," I told him, laughing.

"I know!" he laughed back.

He'd had a growth spurt, shooting from my height to over six feet tall. In my absence, he was becoming a man.

"Mom, hurry up and come back to New York," he urged me.

It was then that I realized how much my children missed me—that, far from hating me, as I'd feared, they were unhappy that I wasn't around. I knew that John was enraged with me, but his anger hadn't turned them against me. If anything, it had roused their sympathy.

"I'll come back soon," I promised.

My emotions were so conflicted. On the one hand, I'd surrendered my place in my children's lives, and I was consumed with shame. On the other hand, I was thrilled to see them all visibly thriving. They were all growing up so fast.

If I didn't get it together, I was going to miss out on their whole childhood. I resolved to clean up my act, but it wasn't long before I got sucked back down again.

I came close to death.

Then my life was saved by my brother Griffin.

TWENTY-FOUR

The Comeback

GRIFFIN WAS FINALLY sober. By 2002, he'd developed a huge support network in the Los Angeles twelve-step community. I didn't want to stop using, but he grabbed me and started dragging me with him to meetings. So did my great friend Louis, the tour manager for a prominent rock band. I'd be sitting alone, and he would pull up in his car, saying, "Hey, Tate, it's meeting time," and haul me out of the house.

The twelve-step community took me in, embraced me, and as the AA saying goes, loved me until I could love myself.

A lot of those twelve-step slogans are true. Miracles can happen.

The greatest miracle was a call from my eleven-year-old daughter, Emily. She said, "Mommy, I want you to come home."

I didn't believe her. I couldn't even conceive that I deserved her love, and I wasn't sure what John had told her about me. So I made a lame excuse: "Well, baby, you know, I may be getting some work out here . . ."

Emily said, "Just tell them that you have a family."

I thought, *That's right*—and burst into tears. It blew me away that this little kid of mine still loved me—that she still had an image of all the times I'd gotten up with her in the middle of the night, nursed her, bathed her, dressed her up, delighted in all her little drawings and expressions. I had lost my grip on who I was, on my identity as a mother, but Emily hadn't lost sight of it. She was fighting for me, reaching out to claim me.

I thought of my own mother. Orphaned so young, she never had an example or a template for mothering. Yet, despite all her betrayals and addictions, I had never stopped seeing her as my mother and loving her, incapable as she often was of rising to the job.

It wasn't going to be that way for my daughter, I vowed. And I got on a plane.

I WASN'T CURED. That's not really a concept that applies to addiction. Getting clean is more of a constant slog, just keeping your head down and putting one foot in front of the other, one day at a time.

There would be a number of false starts and backslides before I finally made my way back to New York to live. During one big slipup, my talent management pushed me right to the edge of the cliff, to take a huge leap: to out myself.

John had recently published his autobiography, *You Cannot Be Serious,* and the media had been calling to see if I would comment. In mid-2002, at the urging of my managers, I talked to *People* magazine and went on Barbara Walters to proclaim what I'd been saying—anonymously—in countless twelve-step meetings over the years: *I am an addict.*

It was a frightening confession for me. I'd rarely granted

other people admission to my life. I used drugs alone, suffered alone, never wanted to let anyone get too close to my pain. Now I was showing it to the world—and on national television, no less.

That was very scary, but liberating too. It was a huge first step toward overcoming the shame and self-loathing that were keeping me tied to drugs. From there I needed to move toward forgiving myself, and toward asking for forgiveness.

Talking about my experience also made me look more closely at the DNA of my addiction. It's astonishing how deeply my entire family—my morphine- and Percodan-dependent grandmothers; my father with his pot and pills; my alcoholic, chain-smoking, speed-freak mother; Griffin; me; and now Redmond—has gotten mired in drugs. It was as if I'd fulfilled some dark destiny by growing addicted.

It's not that I totally blame heredity, but clearly, I had something extra to overcome. When I realized that, I came to see that the way I'd navigated my life was, as Vivian Kubrick once put it, "like walking through a minefield blindfolded." It's a legacy that I want my children to understand so they'll have some hope of escaping the O'Neal family curse.

OF COURSE, MY TALKING to *People* and to Barbara Walters was bound to infuriate John. By then we had been battling, both in and out of court, for the better part of a decade. Though I'd held my own, to some extent, during our marriage, after the divorce I'd fought mainly through lawyers. It was too daunting and scary for me—alone—to try to take on John and his armory of attorneys, siblings, and parents.

Through it all, I'd never, ever bashed John publicly until the autobiography. It wasn't that the book was so bad. It was simply the straw that broke the camel's back, after so many years of verbal and legal assaults. I felt that he was kicking me when I was down.

Now I kicked back. In my interviews, for the first time, I offered the press a glimpse of the reality of my marriage. Though that outraged John, fighting back proved to be the turning point in my recovery.

I'd felt victimized because of my guilt over using drugs, the same guilt that gave him control over what I cherished most—my kids. Feeling bullied and powerless was a huge factor in my addiction, because drugs both eased the pain and let me inflict punishment on myself, instead of on my victimizer.

I remembered an insight John once offered about Ivan Lendl. "If I hadn't made Lendl fight me," he said, "he never would have reached number one. I got him so infuriated that he decided, 'I'll never lose to McEnroe again.'"

I felt the same way as Lendl—I was so mad that I was determined never again to lose to John. Once I started fighting back—slugging at my ex-husband by telling the truth—I started getting well.

So I owe John a debt of gratitude for beating the war drums all those years. Though it nearly destroyed me, it awakened my inner strength and the tough, fighting spirit that I'd all but lost.

I am grateful to him too for the care he gave our children during the times when my life slipped out of my grasp. That must not have been easy—being both mother and father to our kids—and he has reaped the payoff of their love and re-

spect. He and I often don't see eye to eye on child rearing—
his brand of parenting is more demanding and conditional
than mine—but our kids are stunning human beings. He—
we, each in our own way—did a good job.

So, thank you, John, from the bottom of my heart! I hope
that someday we'll be able to sit down together and bask in enjoying and appreciating our three children, our crowning
glory—a much more cherished, enduring achievement than
any movie role or tennis ranking.

I KNEW THAT, with my kids, it was going to be a long, hard
trudge before I could fully recover their trust. We'd had a
minireunion at Christmas in 2002, when I was still living in
L.A. Though we'd been in constant touch by mail and phone,
I hadn't laid eyes on the kids in a few months, which was unbearable. I called Kevin, in tears, to say, "I miss you all so
badly. I really need to see you."

They were planning to spend the holidays at the Malibu
Colony house. When Kevin told John how much he, Sean, and
Emily missed me, my ex-husband agreed to let me take the
kids out for a day. I picked them up at the Colony gate, since I
wasn't welcome in my own former home, and we just hung
out—driving around, doing a little shopping, stopping off for
hamburgers and shakes at lunch, then winding up back at my
place in West Hollywood to watch movies. We laughed so
much, and now and then, one of us would start crying, just
from the joy of being together.

John let the kids spend part of Christmas Eve and Christmas Day with me too. We exchanged gifts—the boys gave me

videos, and Emily got me a candle. I loved my kids so much. Just touching them—smoothing their hair—made me ecstatic. Whatever it was going to take, I had to live with them again. I just had to figure out how.

MARCH 2003 WAS the seventy-fifth anniversary of the Academy Awards. Every living Oscar recipient was attending, so of course, as the youngest-ever winner, I had to be there. I was thrilled when Emily called to ask me if she could come along.

She flew to California, and I helped her pick out a sweet, light blue taffeta gown to wear to the ceremony. I'd decided on a red satin dress for myself. We had such a fun, girly time trying on the jewelry we were going to borrow from Harry Winston for the big night, then getting our hair and makeup done together. Emily was almost twelve, in that adorable stage between being a little girl and becoming a young woman. I was so proud of her.

On Oscar night, a big stretch limousine came to bring us to the ceremony. The war in Iraq had just started, so the red carpet parade outside the Kodak Theater was fairly subdued. To Emily, though, it was very glamorous; and while I usually found big Hollywood events painfully overwhelming, I enjoyed seeing this one through her eyes.

When we got inside, I took Emily backstage, where a lot of stars were milling around. She was so excited (and so was I) to see Bono of U2. Joel Grey and Karl Malden promised to look after her when I had to take my place onstage with the other winners. A truly dazzling array of stars had turned out, all the greats, seated alphabetically. I was in a row with Jack Nicholson,

Maureen O'Hara, and Jack Palance. It was like a living history of Hollywood—of the art form of cinema—and I felt so honored to be part of it.

That night I also felt that I was sharing some essential truth about myself with my daughter. She was just two years older than I was on the night I won the Oscar for *Paper Moon*. Having her there, seeing with her own eyes what it must have been like for me to be a little girl onstage, showed her more about who I was than I could ever convey in words. The experience would bring us closer, let us know each other more fully and deeply. I wanted the same connection with the boys, before they were grown and gone. That would be impossible to achieve long-distance. I knew then that I had to return to New York.

FINALLY, IN THE FALL of 2003, I completed the arrangements that would let me move back for good. By then my transformation was so apparent that John didn't even make me undergo drug tests in order to see the kids. I was shocked and, of course, relieved. That's when I really felt that I was putting the nightmare behind me.

The kids were still worried about me, though. One night when I stayed out late with friends, Kevin called me three times. When I finally got home at two in the morning, I heard his voice coming through the machine: "Mommers, where are you?"

I snatched up the phone to reassure him, "Hey, babe, here I am. And I'm all right."

His concern was so touching—and saddening too.

I gave myself credit for one thing. When my mother was strung out, she always tried to pass on the blame to boyfriends, cabdrivers, or me and Griffin. From the very beginning, I told my kids, "I have a terrible problem. It's entirely my problem, and it has nothing to do with you. I'm trying my best to fix it.

"I can understand it if you're angry at me. You can be furious, you can feel disgust. But please don't punish me. I've already punished myself more than anyone else in the world possibly could."

They responded with more kindhearted, loving sympathy than I could have ever imagined. "People make mistakes," Sean told me. "You just made some of the wrong ones."

Did I ever.

I WISH I COULD report that I'd won the forgiveness trifetca. But the third finisher—my father—remains stalled at the gate. He has bounced back with the help of the antileukemia drug Gleevec, gone on to appear in the movies *Malibu's Most Wanted* and *People I Know,* and made a short-lived TV series, *Mismatch,* with Alicia Silverstone (whom he told the media was the "daughter I should have had").

Over and over again in twelve-step meetings I've been told that injecting myself with needles was just reenacting the beatings I've received at my dad's big hands. Every time I've let down my guard and been lulled into a relationship with him, I've come out the battered victim of his anger and manipulation. What I've learned is that love definitely *doesn't* mean "never having to say you're sorry." So I decided that I would just have to let it go.

———

LITTLE BY LITTLE, as I got stronger through sobriety, I started working again. It wasn't easy—there aren't all that many second acts in Hollywood. I made an independent movie, *The Technical Writer*, which premiered at the Sundance Film Festival in 2003. Last year I did some television work, including guest roles on *Sex and the City, Eight Simple Rules for Dating My Daughter,* and *Law & Order: SVU.* Recently, I've been running a workshop at the School of Visual Arts in New York to help young directors learn to work with actors.

One of my most rewarding projects is my new home, a loft in a historic building in downtown Manhattan, a much more vibrant, youthful place than my stuffy old co-op apartment on the Upper West Side. It's filled with paintings by my artist friends and pictures of my kids—and better yet, half of each week, my three kids themselves.

I spend the weekends with my kids exploring my new neighborhood—all the little shops and galleries—which they love. It's so much fun to rediscover the city through their eyes. I may not be able to provide the same glamorous trappings as their father—not these days, anyway—but I can offer them the pleasures of an ordinary life. Of course, the greatest pleasure of all is just being together.

Having an ordinary life is completely new to me. Since I was seven years old, I've been a celebrity, living in the glare of publicity—as the youngest Oscar winner ever, as Ryan's daughter, as the wife of John McEnroe, the number one tennis player in the world. All rather oppressive identities.

Today I'm sometimes stopped on the street by an autograph seeker, but for the most part celebrity is what I make of it. It's less a straitjacket than a cute topcoat. When I want it, I can lint-brush it, shake out the wrinkles, and put it on, for protection or fun.

These days I'm so happy just being Tatum—a work in progress, but growing more complete and vivid with each passing day.

EPILOGUE

Tatum's Time

FORTY IS AN AWKWARD AGE for a woman in this youth- and beauty-obsessed culture, and even more so for an actress. Growing up in Hollywood, I've spent my whole life surrounded by the world's most spectacular-looking people, especially women, wondering if I could possibly measure up. I no longer judge myself by that yardstick, and at forty, I don't feel oppressed by age.

Instead, my dominant emotion, here at the midpoint of my life, is excitement.

It may sound funny, considering that I became a movie star when I was eight, but I am a late bloomer. It's taken me this long to start waking up every morning full of eagerness and joy.

The past decade of my life has been like a white-light experience, a passage through death and a rebirth. I wouldn't wish the experience on anyone, but maybe it was necessary, on some level, for me to nearly destroy myself in order to etch off the ugly scars—physical and psychic—of deprivation and abuse.

For years I could hardly look people in the eye; I was so internal and cautious and untrusting, even victimized and bitter. Now that I've burned away the painful debris of my life, I feel courageous and open, less a celluloid image of a woman than purely, authentically Tatum.

It's left me a better mother. I've always wholeheartedly loved my children, but now I have even more to offer them— new lessons on tapping the bedrock of strength that lies within each of us. They in turn continue to teach me plenty about acceptance and the healing power of empathy. Of course, I'll always wish I could unring the bell and make their life growing up perfect; that I had been the ideal mother I wanted to be.

It's astonishing to think that Kevin is in college, and Sean isn't far behind—and that my beautiful daughter, Emily, is almost a teenager. My kids are my joy, and the greatest excitement in my life is the renewal of our relationship.

My rebirth has left me more creative—for the first time ever, comfortable in my own skin and confident in my own voice. Emotional pain, anxiety, and rage suck up all your vitality. Now I feel that I have an exciting new wellspring of energy to bring to my work as an actress. It would be nice to end this book with a major career triumph, like a starring role in some brilliant epic film. Who knows? Maybe I'll have that someday.

It's left me more open to love, which I'm finding all around me, in the warmth and support of friends, as well as romantic possibilities. As for marriage, I think I understand it better now and believe more than ever that the old cliché is true— that in order to make it work, you first have to love yourself. I'm working on that.

And, above all, it has confirmed my faith in the Higher Power that I first glimpsed in the hospital after being thrown from the Jeep on the freeway when I was in my teens. I felt then that I'd been spared for a reason, and after losing sight of that benevolent light for the past long, dark decade, I've been saved again. Clearly there's something more I'm intended to accomplish on this earth. I'm excited to see what it will be.

I often think of the theme song from *Paper Moon* and the line that goes, "It won't be make-believe if you believe in me."

What I've learned is that no one else—not fathers, not mothers, not husbands, not even adored and loving children—can define who I am and my reasons to love life. I have to believe in me, and I'm starting to now, which is exciting. It's taken me forty years, and it's time.